Investments:

Theory, Behavioral Aspects and Applications

SECOND EDITION

Walter J. Reinhart, Ph.D.
Loyola University – Maryland

Investments: Theory, Behavioral Aspects and Applications

ISBN-13: 978-1491246542
ISBN-10: 1491246545

Cover design: Diversiform.info, Kyle J. Reinhart
Cover photo: © Reinhart and Associates

To my family

Aaron, Ashley and Anna
Kyle and Daisy
Richard, Sarah, Henry and Warren

And in memory of
Sadie, Mokie and Pumpkin

This page is left blank intentionally

Why ice fishing?

Investments: Theory, Behavioral Aspects and Applications

Table of Contents

Contents

SECTION II: VALUATION AND RISK 34

SECTION III: STRATEGIES AND APPLICATIONS   89

Chapter 8
Equity Investment: Styles and Strategies

Chapter 9
Global Investing

Chapter 10
Yield Curve and Bond Strategies

SECTION IV: DERIVATIVES 160

Section V: MODERN PORTFOLIO THEORY AND EVALUATION 194

PREFACE

Investments: Theory, Behavioral Aspects and Application covers behavioral aspects of investing, investment strategies including buy and sell disciplines, technical analysis, plus the more standard textbook topics of security valuation and risk analysis, asset class management, investment applications, derivative valuation, portfolio construction and investment evaluation. The behavioral topics range from psychological factors to "deadly sins" of financial decision making. As part of the behavioral aspects, a brief overview of technical analysis is presented.

The first two chapters set the stage for investing by presenting various elements of investment management and behavioral aspects. These chapters help lay out the environment in which investors and others operate. The next three chapters present basic valuation and risk characteristics of bonds and stocks. Bonds and stocks are two main asset classes that are large, global, part of "everyone's portfolio," and are the basis for many derivative instruments. Next we turn our attention to strategies and applications. Disciplined stock selection and tactics are presented in Chapter 6, while the most important decisions relating to investing, namely asset allocation, is discussed in Chapter 7. Styles and strategies, and global investing are then presented in the next two chapters respectively. Chapter 10 presents the term structure of interest rates and bond strategies. Our attention then turns to derivative securities in Chapters 11 and 12. The book concludes with a brief introduction to modern portfolio theory and investment performance evaluation.

The main body of the book is divided into five sections and the chapters present the material in an outline form with essays to expand on the material. For the more advanced reader the outline provides a synopsis and allows the reader to decide if they need to refresh their knowledge or if they need to expand their knowledge by reading the essay portions. For the less advanced reader the outline provides a summary of the material and the essay portions fill in the details for a fuller understanding of the topics presented. Each section has a brief overview of the material contained in the section. For each chapter thought questions are provided for student learning. Additionally, the student should expand their learning experience and explore the Internet. In fact the student is strongly encouraged to explore the Internet and other sources to further enhance the chapter material and their learning experience. For example the derivative chapters should be expanded by visits to the Chicago Options Exchange and the Chicago Board of Trade websites.

Our goal in this book is to blend the theory of investments and asset pricing with the behavioral side of investing and introducing "pragmatic applications." This is not a book that only prescribes what investors should do nor does it present detailed examples. Instead it recognizes that the savings and investment process is dependent on individual choice and the decisions regarding the appropriate investments should be based on risk tolerance. The models presented in the text and detailed examples are readily available on the web. Various Internet sites are prese Questions nted in Appendix A to assist the exploration and learning process. Moreover, data for the models can be gained from various websites such as yahoo.finance.com, sec.gov/edgar/searchedgar/companysearch.html, google.com/finance,

Morningstar.com, ValueLine.com, and freeedgar.com (see Appendix A). The data from many of these websites can be downloaded into an Excel spreadsheet and because Excel already has many of the models the data can then used in the models. As we delve into the chapters, you will develop an appreciation of challenges faced by the individual investor, investment advisors, and portfolio managers.

This book benefits from my experiences as a Fulbright Scholar, Universität Passau, Germany, Summer 2003 and Summer 2004, as a visiting professor at Bond University, Australia, Summer 2005 and 2007, and from teaching at the Universidad Jesuita Alberto Hurtado, Chile, Summer 2001.

The knowledge contained in this book can help you become a better investor. However, it is not the golden grail or the yellow brick road that leads to riches. Instead it presents investment theory, behavioral aspects and applications. The keys to success are forecasting ability along with buy and sell disciplines. Of course, having a fortunate dose of luck is always helpful. The American Association of Individual Investors (AAII) is an excellent source of information for investors. AAII assists individual investors with knowledge, means and advice/suggestions to build wealth. Their model portfolio has done quite well over the years compared to the S&P 500. For full disclosure it should be noted the author is a life member of AAII.

Before presenting the text information, a "philosophic overview" of financial models, the CFA certification, and ethical behavior is presented.

It is important for the reader to recognize the importance of theory, including financial models, and the implications of applying theory and models in the pragmatic world. Theory is developed with the use of assumptions so a model can be developed. Assumptions are needed because it is "impossible" to model the pragmatic world with all its vagaries, characteristics and minute differences. Theory thus becomes the standard upon which pragmatic applications and settings are judged against. Having a model on which to compare allows for comparison of actual situations that occur. Without a base to judge from, comparing a series of different events and/or outcomes is extremely difficult if not impossible.

Theoretical models, while not exactly portraying pragmatic settings, allow the investor to gather accurate, comparable and useable information. One needs to be careful to avoid the trap of thinking that financial models provide "answers." Instead, we must keep in mind that models only provide information for the portfolio manager, the financial manager, the financial analyst, and/or the investor. This information in turn allows the user to make better, more informed decisions. Moving from theory to practice is what the Chartered Financial Analyst [CFA] Program and exams are about. The CFA Institute assembled a body of knowledge that forms the basis of the CFA study and examination program.

Standards of practice and ethical behavior are fundamental issues for any profession. Practicing professionals, at a minimum, must have knowledge of the applicable laws and regulations that affect their profession. Professional standards and ethical behavioral should go beyond a strict adherence to the letter of the law. In the investment/portfolio management profession, these values involve responsibilities to the public, clients, employers, and fellow investment professionals. From what my students, who have taken the CFA exams, tell me, ethical and professional standards are becoming more and more important.

Ethics and honorable conduct are typical for the field of finance. This is true whether we are discussing Investments/Portfolio Management, Banking or Financial Institutions, Capital Markets, or Corporate Finance. A major battle we fight in the field of finance is that a small minority of practitioners who lack honor and behave in unethical ways are the ones that make the headlines in the media, and give a less than favorable impression about ethical behavior in finance. This is further compounded by the fact that there is an opinion among too many people that profits are "bad." It should be noted that in academics there is a set of literature and field of study that deals with ethical behavior known as Agency Theory. Succinctly put, Agency Theory deals with the potential conflict of interest in a principal-agent relationship. For example: (1) Who does management work for – themselves or the share/stakeholders of the company? and (2) Who does the financial advisor work for – themselves or the investor? As we well know, it only takes one rotten apple to spoil the barrel. Hence, in the field of finance, especially in the pragmatic world, it is a constant battle to overcome the negativism that the media projects about finance and business in general. We should highlight the fact that the finance profession is by and large ethical!!

The CFA Institute has established a code for ethics and set of professional standards for its members, and others who are trying to become members. Simply put the Code of Ethics is a set of principles that defines the professional conduct expected from members and Chartered Financial Analyst (CFA) candidates. In turn the Code works in tandem with the Standards of Professional Conduct. The Standards of Professional Conduct sets "clear" guidelines for members as to what constitutes fair and ethical business practices. The code and standards are not presented here; instead, it is highly recommended that you go to the CFA Institute website [https://www.cfainstitute.org] and download them. While you are at the website, explore the rest of the site and see what you can learn. Having a CFA certificate should help you in your career and/or your investing.

To conclude this brief discussion on ethics the definitions of ethics and moral from the *Oxford Advanced Learner's Dictionary* are presented:
- Ethics: a system of moral principals or rules of behavior; a) moral principals that govern a person's behavior, b) the branch of philosophy that deals with moral principals.
- Moral: 1) concerned with principals or right and wrong behavior; ethical; 2) based on one's sense of what is right and just, not on legal rights and obligations; 3) following right and accepted standards of behavior, good in character; 4) able to understand the differences between right and wrong; and 5) teaching or illustrating right behavior.

The text assumes the reader has successfully completed basic finance, accounting and economic courses; and is familiar with basic finance terminology, equity and debt instruments, security analysis, time value of money, and financial markets. As such detailed mathematical models and examples are not presented in the book. If the user feels a need for examples they should explore the Internet. Moreover, students with strong backgrounds should not have difficulty reading the text.

As in any learning environment, from classroom experience to projects and homework, the responsibility of learning lies with the student, not with the teacher/professor! The responsibility of the professor is to present the opportunity for learning to the student, and to "press" the students to higher levels of achievements. Note the plural since all students will not achieve the same level nor the same achievement. As in the sport of swimming, each student should strive to do and be better each time. Furthermore in a classroom setting I am also a 'student' and fully expect to learn from the students over the course of the semester.

Comments from colleagues, and former students have made many helpful suggestions for improving this text book and they are gratefully acknowledged.

While attempts have been made to eliminate ambiguities and mistakes from this book, some undoubtedly remain. If you find any, it will be appreciated if you would let me know what they are. Additionally, any suggestions for improvement will be greatly appreciated.

To stop being a student is to stop living!

Walter J. Reinhart, Ph.D.
Professor of Finance
e-mail: Reinhart@loyola.edu

As you learn about investing
reflect on your lessons learned
and relate to ice fishing ☺

This page left blank intentionally

Investments:
Theory, Behavioral Aspects and Applications

Section I: Investing and Behavioral Considerations

Investing is primarily about risk and how to maximize return for the risk undertaken. One of the major tasks of investing is to determine how the current market price compares to the value of the investment. If the price is less than or equal to value the security/asset is a possible candidate for investment. Whether or not you would invest in the security would depend on your risk profile and portfolio implications. If the price were greater than value the security/asset would not be a candidate for investment unless it was a candidate for a short sale. Again, your actions would depend on risk and portfolio considerations. The goal of this book is to provide some insight and guidance on how to value securities and make investment decisions.

Behavioral aspects and changing financial markets (from bubbles to bursts, and from changing regulations to a readily available global market) make investing and portfolio management a challenging and fun opportunity. The opportunities are not without hazards and rewards. As we explore and learn about investing an overriding thesis should be responsible and ethical investing, especially of funds entrusted to financial advisors and managers. In the first section of the text investing (from players and forces of change to asset classes and market efficiency) and behavioral considerations are presented, respectively, in two chapters. Investing and portfolio management is about risk and diversification while the behavioral portion presents human aspects of investing. Financial markets are a key element in investing and they are constantly changing. Markets range from domestic to global and with modern technology capital flows easily between all of them. Additionally, what matters is the future and not the past. In the investment world a well known saying goes something like this: "past performance is no guarantee of future performance." As the world becomes "smaller" with all the technological advances and data availability it is important to develop systematic buy and sell disciplines based on the objective and goals of the investor. The objective and goals should be based on the risk tolerance that is appropriate for the investor.

As you read the text keep in mind the changing investment environment, and that capital markets are at best complex. Financial markets are moving from a "real asset" based environment to more of a "financial asset" environment. Additionally, the world is becoming a smaller place where the Internet and global investing is becoming common. We are in more of a financial asset environment than real asset environment because risk is being transferred from financial institutions to individual investors. For example, mortgages are rarely kept at the financial institution that originated the loan instead they are securitized, sliced and diced and eventually sold to investors and portfolio managers. This trend will continue as retirement plans continue to move from defined benefit to defined contributions and individuals become educated and manage their own funds. Part of the challenge with this risk transfer move is that many investors are not aware of the risk they are undertaking in their investments, nor do many of the participants understand the structure of the financial instruments. Are we facing disaster, or will investors diversify enough so that a failure in one area will not overly adversely impact the portfolio? The subprime mortgage "crisis" of 2007 – 2008 and the resulting lack of liquidity in the financial market place is a prime example. Diversification is essential, and is the main emphasis behind portfolio theory, and we will constantly reference it in our discussion of investing. One does not only invest in one security, rather one should invest across asset classes to reduce overall risk and enhance return.

Generally in academics we assume or create situations where returns are annual, or annualized. However, the Securities and Exchange Commission [SEC] form N-1A indicates that total returns for a period less than a full fiscal year should state the total return for the period and disclose that the return is NOT annualized. The benefit of annualized returns is that they are comparable, while period returns of unequal length are not comparable. Hence, it is advisable to have the returns in both ways, period and annualized. For ease of presentation, the discussions and models presented in this book assume returns are annual.

Demographics are fact, and they do influence financial decisions and capital markets. One challenge that the markets, investors, and portfolio managers face is the baby boomer bubble that is moving towards expected retirement with lots of benefits promised by government and others, and yet the vast majority of the boomers are under-funded for their retirement. Even those that appear funded may be in for a surprise because they have not adequately considered longevity risk. With rapid advances in medicine and drugs, the average life span is increasing and will continue to do so in the foreseeable future. The rate of growth in life expectancy in the West has accelerated. In the mid 1800s people lived on average to around 40, today the average is expected to hit 80 and some forecast that for people born today the average age could be 120 or higher. The *Wall Street Journal* reported in early 2008 that 8,000 Americans are turning 60 years old each day. Based on demographics of today the growth of the portion of the U.S. population aged 65 and over will see a huge surge from around 2012 to 2030, moving from approximately 12% to 21% of the population. Estimates of average life span for people who are currently 65 years old is 19 to 20 years. The rest of the developed world will see similar increases in the over 65 populations. Tremendous challenges exist for society, and investment opportunities need to be explored that address these challenges. For example as the population ages their attitudes towards risk, behavioral patterns, and reactions change. Additionally, an aging population needs "retirement/old age services," from health care to housing. Last but certainly not least: Who is going to pay for all the expenses of an aging population, and the benefits promised by governments? What are the implications of your answer?

In Chapter 1 the two basic underlying features of risk-return trade-off and market efficiency are discussed and related to investing and portfolio management. Behavioral considerations are introduced in the second chapter. Psychological factors and "deadly sins" of financial decision making are presented along with a short discussion of technical analysis. These two chapters help set the foundation for the book. So let us now turn our attention to investing and behavioral aspects.

Chapter 1: Investment Management and Environment

CHAPTER OVERVIEW

The first and foremost fact to recognize is that investing is about managing risk, and maximizing return for the risk undertaken. Chapter 1 describes how the growing availability of financial and economic data, quantitative tools, and underlying financial theory have facilitated the task of developing strategies and investment techniques for addressing investor needs. We also briefly introduce portfolio management because investing needs to be beyond just investing in an individual security/investment. When investing one needs to be aware of financial markets and also the other participants in the marketplace. Two underlying critical features of financial markets – the trade-off between risk and return, and the concept of market efficiency – are presented and related to investing to conclude the chapter.

Introduction
- Investments/investing – **manage risk, not returns!!!**
- Investors needs are defined in terms of risk and cash requirements
- Investors should maximize expected return for the risk undertaken
- Portfolio management consists of three major activities
  1. asset allocation
  2. weighting shifts across major asset classes
  3. security selection within asset classes
- Critical underlying features of financial markets
  - trade-off between risk and return
  - concept of market efficiency
- The future is what counts!

As an investor one should keep in mind that returns follow the risk undertaken. Hence, one manages risk not returns. Investment strategies should recognize the risk inherent in the objective, and the objective should be based on the risk tolerance of the investor. Cash requirements are also a critical determination in investing or the construction of the portfolio. If more cash is required in the immediate or near future, the investment should be liquid, have less volatility, and, based on needs, perhaps have a cash flow (e.g., dividend stream or interest payments). If the investment is a publically traded portfolio (i.e., mutual fund or exchange traded fund) the objectives need to be in "plain English" and clearly state the risk so investors know the level of risk including the expectations of cash flows.

The three major activities of portfolio management [asset allocation, weighting shifts across major asset classes, and security selection within asset classes] are not only theoretical concepts, but they are an essential part of everyday management of investments. Asset allocation is based on the risk of the investor and therefore is the main driving force for selecting securities/assets and the resulting returns on the portfolio.

3

The trade-off between risk and return must be understood and believed. There is no such thing as a "free lunch," nor is there an investment that is safe yet yields high returns (especially not *ex ante*). Forecasting is key to successful investing, and one must recognize that past performance is not necessarily indicative of future performance. Forecasting ability determines the level of investment activity and influences the strategies undertaken.

****

Risk and Return Relationship Including Behavioral Aspects

The question to ask is how do risk and return relate to each other? Normally we assume there is a positive relationship between the two – the higher the estimated risk the higher the expected return. Furthermore a linear relationship is generally assumed since, at a minimum, it makes the math less complicated and it is easier for people to follow and understand.

Risk is defined as the probability (or likelihood) of loss, or in financial terms, receiving less than expected. On the other hand return (r), in a simplistic manner, can be defined as future flows less initial investment divided by initial investment, or $r = [(P_1 - P_0 \pm C)/P_0]$. While expected return is based on risk the previous definition does not provide guidance regarding risk. Therefore it seems reasonable to look at return from a "required return" point of view, or return as a function of perceived risk. Mathematically this can be expressed as:

$$r = f(\text{perceived risk})$$

then expanding

$$r = f(R_F + R_P + R_\Psi)$$

where

R_F =	*real rate of return plus inflation risk*	
R_P =	*business risk based on items such as: type of business, liquidity, profitability, size, exchange rate (country) risk, et cetera*	
R_Ψ =	*psychological factors*	

This required return relates to total risk and allows one to focus on maximizing expected return for the level of risk undertaken. Moreover, it allows for the recognition that psychological factors (e.g., fear and greed) exist. Even though these psychological factors are not easily translated into dollars the relationship implies efficient markets, at least in the macro and/or pragmatic sense. In the past academics and to a large extent practitioners have ignored behavioral aspects (i.e., the psychological factor) in the market place, at least in an ex ante sense. However, behavioral finance is becoming more accepted as academics explore psychological factors and other aspects of the financial decision making process.

The risk return relationship presented above raises several questions regarding the financial environment and investing. How does one relate these concepts to the current market place, and is

4

it relevant to do so? What is the role of technical analysis, and fundamental analysis, and/or some combination of the two schools of investment thought? These and other considerations will be addressed as we study investments. However, for now, it is necessary to recognize that both the company and the stock need to be examined. A good company is not necessarily a good stock. Additionally, a more extensive view also looks at which assets to select, how to value them, and how to combine them together to maximize benefits for risk undertaken.

****

Investment Managers
- Investment organizations differ in size and degree of specialization
- Size does not necessarily imply wise investment decisions nor understanding of the market place – ditto for longevity
- Approaches to investments analysis and portfolio management differ for different investors and managers based on their abilities, including forecasting
- A trend toward greater structure and discipline in investment process, as well as greater use of systematic approaches to investing continues to build momentum
- Discipline is required for success!

Investment organizations, from investment bankers and commercial banks to brokerage firms and financial advisors, are the middleperson that allows for efficient and fair capital/financial markets. They obviously differ in size from an entrepreneur to large firms with thousands of employees. The vast majority of the participants carry out their functions in an honorable and ethical manner. Unfortunately the few who do not behave ethically get the attention in the media and give a 'black eye' to the profession.

Systematic investing refers to a style of investment where financial theory is put into practical application. Alternatively, systematic investing is the tendency toward greater structure and discipline in the investment process and toward greater use of orderly approaches, both quantitative and qualitative, to investing. Moreover, discipline in both buy and sell decisions is required. Along with the greater structure, behavioral aspects of investing and the market place are gaining recognition and acceptance – in both the academic and pragmatic worlds. As we explore investment styles and investing concepts in the rest of the book these ideas are fleshed out.

Forces for Change
- Theoretical breakthroughs
- Development of data-bases, low cost, ease of access and ease of use
- The Internet
- Tools of analysis
- Information, not answers

The forces of change propelling systematic investing (and portfolio management) include:
1. development of strategies, models and techniques based on powerful financial and economic theories that began emerging some 50-70 years ago

2. growth of financial and economic databases, and their availability to the average investor via the Internet
3. statistical tools, technological breakthroughs in the areas of computers and telecommunication
4. the Internet plus greater transparency and lower transaction costs

Each of these forces for change is detailed below.

Government rules and regulation, along with litigation, assists systematic investing by providing a level playing field, and a sense of fairness in financial markets. Additionally, more people are earning master degrees (e.g., Master of Science in Finance [MSF] and Master of Business Administration [MBA] degrees) and professional certifications are becoming more popular (e.g., Chartered Financial Analyst [CFA], Certified Financial Planner [CFP], et cetera).

Financial models, by definition, do not provide answers. Investment and security valuation models, regardless of their sophistication, only provide information for the investor, or portfolio manager, or analyst so they can make better, more informed, intelligent decisions. The reason for this fact is two fold: (1) finance deals with the future and the future is not known, and (2) finance is not an exact science like physics or mathematics, instead we make assumptions (e.g., constant growth, homogeneous expectations, et cetera) so the pragmatic world can be modeled. Finance involves forecasting future cash flows and the risk thereof. The output of the model(s) provides a solid foundation for good decisions. However, we need to recognize that the information provided by the models is subject to human interpretation about what the information implies and means. Also one has to be careful of the quality/accuracy of the input data. While this ambiguity may pose a challenge to a new student in finance it provides the thrill and excitement to the people in the field.

Theory and Application

- Investment and portfolio theory
- Capital market theory
- Security valuation
- Market efficiency, efficient market hypothesis and pragmatic efficiency
- Derivative security valuation

The major theories that have most influenced the evolution of investing are modern portfolio theory, capital market theory, security valuation, market valuation, market efficiency, and derivative securities valuation. For example, portfolio theory defines the practice of formally determining an asset allocation. Databases and statistical analysis allow for solid decisions based on theoretical concepts. Investors need to have a firm grasp of asset allocation as they invest funds.

Capital market theory has inspired the development of an objective basis for investment analysis as well as improved methods of measuring the performance of investing for both individual investors and portfolio managers. Theoretical developments in security valuation have led to models such as the dividend discount models, the security market line, and the capital asset pricing model. Derivative valuation models have spawned a variety of option and future-related strategies.

Market efficiency is discussed in greater detail later in this chapter. The efficient market hypothesis [EMH] has three forms and simply contends that one cannot consistently outperform the market based on various levels of information. EMH does not say one cannot outperform the market, it just says not consistently. For example, Bill Miller of Legg Mason Management Value Trust fund outperformed the market (as measured by the S&P 500) for fifteen consecutive years. The fifteen-year record is rather phenomenal and can be attributed to superb skill along with a touch of luck. In the sixteenth year he did not outperform the market. Pragmatic efficiency refers to the actual operations of the market place and the transparency of information.

Databases
- Data is becoming readily available for all investors
- Cost ranges from free ones such as Yahoo Finance to high price ones such as WRDS and even higher priced sophisticated data bases used by professionals (e.g., Bloomberg)
- Period of analysis – depends on time horizon and data base
- Security and accuracy – user/buyer beware, especially for free ones
- Uses of data
    - inputs to models
    - better understanding of the market and its individual components
    - testing theory and applications
    - identification of investment opportunities

Databases can help investors in innumerable ways. They are used in testing, as inputs to models, utilized in tests of efficacy of the theories as well as in the development of new theories and analytical techniques. Additionally, they provide the input into the models that generate information that investors and portfolio managers use to make better, more informed decisions. Databases such as Morning Star Library Edition, Value Line, or Yahoo Finance are not only excellent sources of financial information, but they also provide opinions about the investment "quality" of many securities. Universities and colleges carry many of these bases for students to use as they learn about investing and portfolio management. Many databases are also readily available via the Internet and useable in Excel (see Appendix A).

Tools of Analyses
- Statistical and other quantitative methods
- Computational power and speed – continuous improvement
- "Black box" concepts make it easier for investors to use various analytical tools
- Excel and other statistical packages have many finance models
- Basis for
    - objective and efficient evaluation of whether or not financial and economic data are useful in investment process
    - testing of new strategies and techniques

- performance evaluation
- Forecasting: past is helpful for generating better forecasts, but one needs to be sure to recognize changing conditions.
- Need to be aware of the GIGO convention (Garbage In Garbage Out)

Quantitative techniques and computer technology provide the basis for an objective and efficient evaluation of whether financial and economic data are useful in the investment process. Statistical techniques and computer software (e.g., Excel) also provide the means for testing the efficiency of newly developed strategies and techniques of portfolio management. Finally, the tools and models allow for efficient evaluation of the success of the investment, whether systematic or not, in achieving performance objectives. Once again, it is necessary to recognize that forecasts of future events are based on the inputs and the output of the model is only as good as the input. Furthermore, the output only provides information and not exact answers.

Participants and Investment Activities
- Investment/portfolio managers and individual investors
- Financial analysts
- Portfolio investors [from individuals to giant plan sponsors]
- Investment consultants
- Evaluators of performance

Professional investment managers are responsible for security selection (discussed in Chapter 6) and active weighting shifts across asset classes (see Chapter 7). Security selection and weighting shifts across asset classes depend on the objectives of the investment. Objectives or goals are normally based on the investor, or set by the plan sponsor (e.g., mutual funds). For an individual investor the objective should be based on their risk tolerance. For mutual funds, plan sponsors set the goals, assist in asset allocation and are often advised by investment consultants. Investors or their advisors, before investing, need to determine if the mutual fund is appropriate for the risk tolerance of the investor. Financial advisors provide recommendations regarding possible investments. Financial analysts, such as CFAs, evaluate financial, economic, accounting, and qualitative information to arrive at investment recommendations. Investment consultants help plan sponsors in setting goals and asset allocation and usually provide input into the selection process of investment managers. Evaluators are involved with measuring the performance of financial analysts and investment managers. Individual investors play an important role in the market place, and are involved, either directly or indirectly, in all aspects of the investment process. All participants, from plan sponsors to individual investors, should recognize the influence of behavioral aspects in the market place.

Asset Classes
- An asset class is comprised of securities that have similar characteristics or features
    - equity: common stock and preferred stock
    - bonds/debt instruments

- money market instruments (debt instruments with a maturity less than one year such as T bills, certificates of deposit, commercial paper, et cetera)
- derivatives
- real estate
- real assets
- venture capital or private equity
• An asset class has similar characteristics
• Data (e.g., returns and standard deviations) exists for many of the asset classes
• Global securities are an asset class unto themselves (it should be noted the discussions in this book are from the viewpoint of the U.S.A., Chapter 9 presents a brief overview of global investing)
  - they can be divided along the same lines as the list above
  - they are also divided by country and/or region of the world

The first three categories – common stocks, bonds, money market instruments – are large, highly marketable, and traditionally considered the "normal" investment instruments for individuals. Derivatives are becoming more popular in investments of individual investors. Common stocks can be divided into domestic and international categories. Equities and investment strategies are also classified based on market capitalization (e.g., small cap, mid cap or large cap), or value and growth stocks. International equities can be classified into major country markets and emerging markets. Bonds (debt instruments) can be divided into: government, corporate, mortgage backed securities, international, and municipal classifications. Money market instruments can be divided into: Treasury bills, certificates of deposit, commercial paper, and guaranteed investment contracts. Bonds that have a maturity of less than one year are also considered money market instruments. Derivatives, by nature of the instruments, are risky. However, they are becoming more popular and the key is how they are used – to hedge (reduce risk) or enhance return (gamble).

While real estate is a large investment category, it has received relatively limited direct investment from investors due to its lack of liquidity, the difficulty in valuing the investment, limited understanding of its risk character, and relatively high cost of management. However, when real estate bubbles occur a lot of investors enter the game and hope that they can turn over the properties quickly and not be the last one who purchased the property. Slack lending standards coupled with easy money and government blessing led to the last bubble in the mid '00s. These conditions lead to a lot of sub-prime loans, and not surprisingly, lo and behold, people who never should have been given the loans started to default on their loans – the start of the subprime mortgage crisis. The resulting crisis is still far from over in 2013 as foreclosures work their way through the market place.

Real estate can be added to a portfolio via real estate investment trusts (REITs) that are traded on various stock exchanges. Besides not having a "common market" real estate value is influenced by location. As the saying goes, "the four most important considerations when valuing real estate are location, location, location, and location." For many investors the best way, besides their own personal home, to add real estate to their portfolio is via REITs. REITs typically provide a diversified set of real estate and are professionally managed.

Real assets, such as collectible items that range from comic books, coins, and fine art to baseball cards, stamps, and wine. Real assets are even more of a challenge to value than real estate. Location also plays a role in valuation; for example, a Cal Ripken baseball card is likely to have a higher price in Baltimore, Maryland, where he played his whole career ,than in Seattle, Washington. Additionally, transaction costs are relatively dear (i.e., twenty to thirty percent or higher is not unheard of). Precious metals such as gold and silver can also be considered a collectible item. In tough economic times, or in periods of social unrest, precious metals become popular and prices increase.

Venture capital and equity capital are smaller and potentially highly rewarding categories, but suffer from the same problem as real estate (e.g., lack of liquidity, difficulty of valuation, and high cost of management) plus highly risky. Equity or private capital has become more popular in the 21st century and hedge funds are becoming trendy and many individual investors are adding them to their asset mix.

Data for the asset classes exist, and extensive databases exist for the more traditional asset classes (i.e., bonds, equity and money market instruments). In fact as time goes on databases for all asset classes, whether domestic or global, are improving and becoming readily available. International securities that have the same asset classification as above should be treated as separate asset classes because they have different risk characteristics then their U.S. counterpart. Additionally, each country is different from every other country so one should not consider stocks in Germany the same as stocks in Australia, Spain, or Hong Kong. As we discuss investments the differences and benefits of investing on a global basis are presented.

Risk-return tradeoff
- Manage risk, return follows
- Risk and return are directly related: expected return E(R)
- A linear relationship is 'assumed' (see graph below)

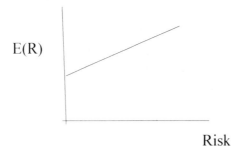

E(R)

Risk

The risk-return tradeoff is a key underlying feature of financial markets. Risk-return tradeoff refers to the return provided for undertaking a given level of risk. Risk and return are directly proportional. Securities with higher risk should generally provide the investor with a higher rate of return, while securities with lower risks would provide lower returns to the investor. Capital market theory suggests that only by taking a higher risk can one hope to generate a higher return. This feature is important in investing, as it is the job of the investment manager or financial advisor to assess the risk profile or risk tolerance of the investor and then select assets to generate returns on the investments that match the risk profile. An investor considering purchasing a mutual fund should be aware of the risk level and objective of the mutual fund and be sure they are in line with their risk tolerance. Risk tolerance is a function of an investor's like or dislike of risk, and <u>not</u> on their ability to bear risk. The key to good investment management is to manage risk; the returns that are generated should be commensurate with the risk undertaken.

Markets and Market Efficiency

- Financial/capital markets range from small to large, have various efficiencies and have global considerations
- *Efficient market:* one in which price corresponds to value (price reflects value)
- Prices change only when new information becomes available
- Speed of adjustment depends on availability of information and competitiveness of the market
- Three degrees of efficiency (Efficient Market Hypothesis [EMH], theoretical concept) which are based on level of information
  1. weak form
  2. semi-strong form
  3. strong form
- Markets are "rational" and securities reach equilibrium over time
- Pragmatic efficiency
  - sense of fairness in the marketplace
  - transparency
  - low costs
- Market anomalies – based on empirical tests of the EMH, include the following:
  - January effect: small-cap and last year's securities that did not do well outperform during the month of January
  - small firm effect: small-cap outperform large-cap
  - momentum: stocks will continue to do well in the next period (support for technical analysis)
  - IPO (Initial Public Offer) effect : under perform, except for first day, for three to five years
  - insider trading: future movement of securities follows lead set by net purchases or sales by insides

The more developed countries have relatively efficient markets, and are hard to outperform on a consistent basis. Developing countries as they are integrated into the global economy and experiencing the inflow of foreign capital their markets are becoming more efficient. Globalization and arbitrage naturally forces emerging markets to become more efficient so no one investor has consistent advantage over other participants.

The Efficient Market Hypothesis [EMH] is based on the Random Walk Theory [RWT]. RWT simply says that stock prices move in a random fashion, and by implication that one is not able to predict future price movements. The foundation of the RWT is that information enters the market randomly and prices only move because of new information, therefore, stock price movements are random. The EMH typically takes three forms:

1. weak form: using only market statistics (price and volume) one cannot consistently outperform the market
2. semi-strong form: using all public information one cannot consistently outperform the market
3. strong form: using even private information (insider information) one cannot consistently outperform the market.

The key difference between the levels is the level of information. A major concept between the levels is the idea of consistently. The EMH does not say one cannot outperform periodically, rather it says not consistently. Additionally, it does not imply that prices are correct or that dollars flow to the areas of most need.

An efficient market is one where price corresponds to value, which is based on all available information, and prices react to new information immediately. A perfectly efficient market, in a theoretical concept, is one where price corresponds to value at all time. It is important that participants in the investment decision process develop a viewpoint as to the efficiency of the market. For investors, it is a critical consideration in determining the funds to be committed to active efforts in changing asset class weightings and security selection. Market efficiency is also a prime determinant for investment managers in developing strategies and designing the investment process. Investment consultants need to have a viewpoint in order to advise investors and to select investment managers. Performance evaluators, as well as consultants, need to appraise the significance of investment performance in the context of the efficiency of the market. In general, the theory is important to market participants because it provides a value base to evaluate. In order to increase investment value/returns, the investor can alter weighing across asset classes or choose securities that are mispriced.

It is interesting to note that even the Federal Courts have gotten into the efficient market controversy. A recent incidence is in re Polymedica Corporation Securities Litigation, 2006 U.S. Dist. LEXIS 70079 (September 28, 2006) where the federal district court spoke on what makes a public market efficient in terms of information and value. It should be noted that subtle differences between the two and the need for appropriate statistical data analysis when one wants to prove either portion. The court indicated an "efficient market is one in which the market price of the stock fully reflects all publicly available information." Chalk one up for academics and theory since it implies that ordinary investors cannot profit off the use of such information. However, the court indicated it was speaking to only informational efficiency and not fundamental value efficiency. Down one for academics and theory since this implies that market price may not be the best estimate of the stock's "actual value."

It is the job of the investor to assess how quickly the value of new information has been assimilated in the price and whether or not the value of the information has been interpreted correctly. Based on the assessment, he/she may choose to invest in or divest that security. Also, the investor knows that all markets are not equal in terms of efficiency. The developed capital markets (e.g., U.S., Japan, London, Germany, Hong Kong, Singapore, et cetera) generally exhibit high levels of efficiency, while developing capital markets (e.g., India, Thailand, Chile, China, Poland, et cetera) are generally not as efficient in incorporating the value of new information into the price of the security. Inefficiencies may give rise to opportunities to "beat" the market and earn more than average returns. If one is not aware of the inefficiencies, or the degree thereof, or the types of inefficiencies the result may be losses.

Efficient capital market theory hinges on the point that investors are rational, at least on average, so that their activities of buying and selling will move the prices towards the intrinsic value of the security. We would also expect that the speed of adjustment to equilibrium depends on the availability of information and competitiveness of the market. Weak form efficiency contends that the current prices fully reflect the information implied by market statistics (price and volume) and investors cannot consistently outperform the market using only these statistics. Semi-strong efficiency implies that current prices fully reflect all public information and investors cannot consistently outperform the market using this information. Strong form efficiency asserts that even using insider information the investor cannot consistently outperform the market. The key concepts behind these three hypotheses are (1) an investor cannot **consistently** beat the market – this does not imply that the market cannot be beaten periodically, just not consistently, and (2) the level of information.

Academics have studied and empirically tested all three forms of EMH. Empirical studies generally support the weak form EMH; however, technical analysis indicates that this theory may not be infallible. The semi-strong hypothesis has had mixed results. Studies of economic events such as stock splits and IPO's tend to support the hypothesis while predictions based on earnings and ratios tend not to fully support the hypothesis. In fact, some studies that look at surprise earning announcements indicate that investors who implement strategies based on these announcements can earn 'abnormal' returns. Research that looks at publically available insider trading information also indicates that one can earn excess returns. Additional studies that examine the "Value-Line enigma," as well as other top producing portfolio managers tend to contradict the hypothesis (unless, of course, you define consistent as being 100 or more years). The American Association of Individual Investors [AAII] also has a record of investment success.

Testing the strong form creates challenges because if the investor has access to private information then he/she is an "insider" who is not supposed to trade on that security in the market. It is thus not possible to truly "study" the strong-form EMH since it would be illegal for someone to trade with knowledge of private information and if they are doing it they would certainly not advertise the fact and say come see me. Given the fact that insiders who do get caught have made significant gains it would seem that the strong form does not hold in the pragmatic world – of course, those who trade on insider information and do not make gains are not caught. Hence, the observation is far from complete.

Anomalies present a significant challenge to the EMH theory. Patterns have been observed, on a historical basis, which could have lead to excess returns and contradicts theory. True believers will dismiss the anomalies as one-time aberrations. Nonetheless, many of the observed patterns repeat themselves; hence, they cannot be so easily dismissed. However, as in all financial matters, just because it worked in the past is no guarantee it will hold in the future. Some anomalies suggest that investors are not always rational, and fail to consider all available information. Behavioral finance can perhaps explain some of the anomalies and why they continue to persist.

An anomaly that continues to exist is value stocks outperforming growth stocks. This phenomenon has existed over the years and even extends to global markets, but it is more difficult to get true measures in less developed countries. Either there is an anomaly, or there is more risk in value stocks that is not being picked up by the empirical models that researchers use. We discuss risk in greater detail in the Section II as valuation and risk concepts are presented. In any event, since value stocks outperform growth based on current risk knowledge value stocks are a good investment if you want to outperform benchmarks such as the S&P500.

Fortune magazine provides a yearly list of most admired companies in the US. A study by Anderson and Smith showed that investing in these companies and rolling over into the next list each year from 1983 to 2004 would have generated an average annual return of 16.5 percent versus the S&P500's return of 10.3 percent. While not risk adjusted the study does present a useful strategy, especially if it continues to work in the future. Additionally, it presents evidence that the efficient market hypothesis may have some shortcomings since it appears that similar to earnings announcements information is not completely incorporated into the stock price.

Pragmatic efficiency is also important. Investors need a sense of fairness in the marketplace so they will enter the game. Reasonable levels of legislation and regulation help protect the smaller investor and enhance the sense of fairness. The key concept is transparency of the information that is driving the prices in the market place – e.g., accounting and financial information that is prepared according to standards and available to all in a timely fashion. Costs are also an important factor – if costs are high, from transaction expenses to obtaining information, the market will not be "fair" since all investors will not be able to partake. If costs are low, all serious investors are able to obtain the necessary information to make investment decisions. This does not imply that pragmatic efficiency leads to wise investment decisions or provides positive returns. Investors in an efficient market need three elements to be successful in investing: (1) capital, (2) knowledge, and (3) time. Having luck, often overlooked (especially in Western cultures), is a nice fourth element to have when investing.

Summary
- Investment management has evolved over the past three-quarters of a century
- Greater structural complexity exists
- Need to establish goals or investment objectives in terms of risk
- Select investments to achieve highest expected return at the desired risk level
- The Internet has increased market transparency and "efficiency"
- Empirical tests indicate that anomalies do exist

Financial markets, techniques and strategies are constantly changing and evolving. It is necessary to develop a systematic and discipline approach to investing. At the same time, there is a need to monitor events and coordinate the information gained. Generally speaking, the market place needs to be viewed as being efficient – basically prices are correct and that beating the market is not easy. As Bill Miller of Legg Mason would indicate, if you think your estimate of value is correct and the market price is "wrong" you should be able to explicitly and succinctly state why. If you cannot express the key underlying difference between your valuation and the market value you are praying for luck – praying for luck is typically a losing strategy. If the market was not efficient the performance of mutual funds would certainly be better. Over seventy-five percent of mutual funds under-perform their benchmarks. The key to success is forecasting ability, buy and sell disciplines, and having a fortunate dose of luck is always helpful.

The first key accomplishment in investing is to establish the goal/objective of the investment and communicate it to all who are involved. The objective should be set in terms of risk and relate to the risk tolerance of the investor. In January 1998 the Securities Exchange Commission [SEC] adopted the "plain English rule" for prospectuses. This rule requires, among other things, that a fund's objective and strategies are presented in plain English and not legalese, the same goes for statistics on past performance and on how to invest in the fund.

CHAPTER 1
THOUGHT QUESTIONS

1. Identify the two critical underlying features of financial markets and relate them to the main activities investing.

2. Review the basic foundation of risk and return and tradeoff thereof. Do you think it is reasonable? Why or why not? Where would you place yourself on the risk return continuum – conservative, moderate, aggressive, or ...?

Questions

1. Indicate what the major activities of portfolio management are. Which one is the main driving force and how does it relate to risk?
2. Indicate the forces of change and how they relate to investing.

3. Why do financial models not provide "answers?" What do they provide?
4. What is the notion of a risk-return tradeoff and why is it important?
5. In what ways are data bases utilized, and how can these be helpful in investing.
6. What are the major asset classes, and how do they differ?
7. Which asset classes are considered "normal" investment instruments for individual investors? How do they differ from the other asset classes?
8. What role do quantitative techniques and computer technology play in the investment process?
9. Identify the major groupings of participants and how they interact in the investment process.
10. Briefly discuss efficient markets, include the differences between the different levels and the implications thereof. Relate the Efficient Market Hypothesis to pragmatic efficiency.

Chapter 2: Behavioral Aspects

CHAPTER OVERVIEW

Behavioral finance is relatively new to the academic field of finance and recognizes that not all investors are rational, and that emotions impact investment decisions. Market efficiency in the form of the efficient market hypothesis [EMH] concerns the level of information available to the market and the ability of investors to consistently outperform the market on a risk adjusted basis. Given the anomalies found in the market place, which should give one pause to blindly accepting the EMH, it is reasonable to believe that investors psychology characteristics may play a role in security pricing. After all, I know of only two rational people: "thee and me, and at times I doubt thee." This chapter presents several psychological factors and some "deadly sins" of financial decision making. These elements help to create trends in prices. If behavioral aspects influence financial markets, the question then becomes how can one measure the influence? One possible answer is technical analysis; hence, as part of the behavioral aspects, a brief overview of technical analysis is presented.

Introduction
- Behavioral finance – human emotions impact investment decisions
  - at times decisions seem to defy logic
  - investors act irrationally, and perhaps predictably so
  - may help explain the anomalies found in the market place
- Human emotions are real and create psychological "factors" and "deadly" sins
- Technical analysis can be used to gauge the emotions in the market

Behavioral finance is in its early stage of development, growing rapidly but still relatively young. Academics and the financial markets are still trying to learn what behavioral biases people have, how to react to them and how to avoid them so better decisions can be made. If you understand the emotional tendencies of investors and the market place, and have an idea of future reaction to an event, based on past behavior to similar events, you are ahead of the game. Behavioral finance tries to explain anomalies by using physiological concepts to explain why investors engage in activities that academics consider systematic errors, as opposed to the assumed perfect markets and rational investors that underlie theoretical models.

Academic Theory Meets Behavioral Aspects
- Academics provide a roadmap and a base to judge from
  - build on modern portfolio theory and traditional valuation models
  - usefulness in pragmatic settings is subject to question
  - numerous anomalies exist and some are persistent
- Financial institutions and practitioners provide means and ways of investing
- Neither group is unbiased in their opinions

- Financial markets are governed by:
  1) rational forces
  2) emotional responses (mood of investors)
- Unlike traditional finance, behavioral finance does **not** assume
  - perfect markets
  - people are perfectly rational
  - that market irrationality is due to imperfections in market mechanisms
- Need to recognize that investors do not always make rational decisions
- Need to accept that people are not unbiased in forecasting or in the way they process information

Behavioral finance examines a larger picture than the more traditional finance which has a tendency to focus on specific models and assumes away difficulties that behavioral finance addresses. The two fields are linked together. Especially, behavioral to traditional, because without traditional finance and modern portfolio theory behavioral would not have a standard to compare against, nor models to use in the selection of securities and the procedures to build portfolios.

Mood does impact perceptions in the marketplace and perhaps performance of securities. Studies from the impact of the Super Bowl to soccer and cricket matches show that mood can affect stock returns. Mood variables are events that impact the frame of mind of a large portion of the population in a similar manner. For example, a soccer match in the World Cup influences the mood of the nation, especially if it is a loss to a keen competitor. On the other hand, efficient market supporters would argue the market place would be quick to capitalize on this information and possible market moves, which, in turn, would neutralize the expected results. However, research looking at correlation does support the Super Bowl anomaly and negative returns with losses in major sporting events. Obviously, correlation does not mean cause and effect. As an investor, regardless of cause and effect, if correlations persist over time it is additional information that an investor should use when making decisions. Moods influence behavior, and one should not discount behavior in financial markets. In academia, many theories and models are based on rational investors. How many 'rational people' do you know?

Behavioral Finance
- Assumes that markets are composed of imperfectly rational "players" in imperfect markets
- Recognizes investment principals based on
  1) risk
  2) return
- Recognizes that financial markets are driven by
  1) financial information
  2) human emotions
- Believes in the pragmatic efficiency of financial markets
- Human emotions are real and create "psychological factors"

- Moods exist and can influence investment behavior
    1) of individuals
    2) on national levels
- Emotional cycle
    - cycle from fear to greed to fear to greed to …
    - the upswing from fear to greed involves ego
    - the downswing from greed to fear involves wishful thinking

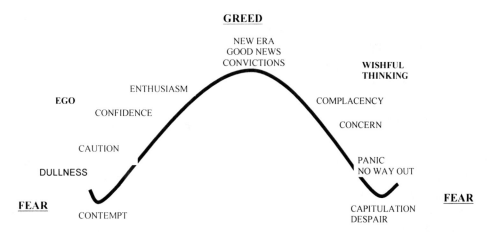

Behavioral aspects, including moods, also influence professionals, from financial advisors and traders to analysts and portfolio managers. Professionals are impacted by crowd mentality (herding) and at times put excessive weight on what has happened or who did what (e.g., What did Goldman Sachs do? What did Warren Buffett do? What did the FED say?). To avoid these challenges one has to develop a discipline and not let irrelevant noise and peer pressure influence the decision making process. One has to build on their strengths and minimize their weaknesses. Regardless of the strategy developed any changes should occur slowly, with reason, and without emotions.

The emotional cycle leads to bubbles and busts in financial markets. History is filled with bubbles and crashes that follow; for example, the Roaring 20s followed by the Great Depression of the 30s. More recent examples include the dot.com bubble in the late 1990s and the real estate bubble in the mid 2000s. The greed-fear cycle and psychological factors are not unique to the United States: they affect all humans, regardless of race, culture, color, or creed. It would be nice to think that we should learn from these past examples and avoid them in the future, but humans will be humans and fall prey to greed and fear. Biochemistry, hormones and physiological aspects impact our brain and financial decisions. One needs to recognize these influences and develop disciplines and strategies so they are "under control." Let us now turn our attention to some of the psychological factors that researchers have examined and how they affect our decision-making, investing and portfolios.

Psychological Factors

Psychological factors impact an investors behavior when investing – this is true for individuals as well as professionals. The factors include overconfidence, disposition, cognitive dissonance, mental accounting, shortcuts, and herding. Having an understanding of these six factors allows one to better understand "less than rational" behavior in financial markets.

- Overconfidence
  - misinterpret accuracy of information
  - misguided convictions
  - overestimate own ability
  - illusion of knowledge and control
  - implications
    o trade too often
    o incur more transaction costs which reduces return
    o belief they will be successful while others will not (also known as self-attribution bias)
    o failure to recognize theory and lessons gained from it

Differences between sexes do exist regarding investment decisions. For example, men are generally more confident and hence have a tendency to trade more often while women follow more of a buy and hold philosophy. Trades have an impact on returns due to the extra costs of trading. Men also have a tendency to take on more risk. However, it should be noted that as women become more knowledgeable they accept more risk – nonetheless, differences do continue to exist. A workable strategy for a couple might be to make investment decisions together so they avoid some of the psychological factors (i.e., overconfidence and disposition factors which are discussed below). Professionals and individuals need to be aware of the traits that are inherent and develop disciplines to avoid pitfalls.

Research studies have shown that investors who are most overconfident perform worse than those who do not have as much confidence. Highly overconfident investors trade the most and underperform the market by 10%; which is worse than those who traded less.

- Disposition, or regret and pride
  - sell winners too early and hold losers too long
  - regret: emotional pain of taking or not taking an action
  - pride: emotional joy
  - losses are only "paper losses" until the security is actually sold

Implications of regret and pride include the failure to act because investors want to avoid regret (i.e., not sell losers). The emotional pain of selling losers is about twice the joy of selling a winner. Investors also seek pride because they want to have joy and therefore sell winners too soon. When this behavior occurs, before you realize it you have a portfolio of losers. Obviously, this is detrimental to investment performance and to wealth maximization. To avoid or minimize the negative consequences of this factor it is important to have a sell discipline along with a buy discipline.

- Cognitive dissonance: past unduly influences future
  - risk aversion is the norm for investors
  - recent experiences influence degree of risk aversion
  - house money effect: after winning investors on average are more willing to assume additional risk
  - snake bite effect: after losing most investors will assume less risk
  - however, double down in the hopes of recovery – implies additional risk
  - memory is also an emotional experience and perceptions change over time
  - change beliefs to avoid negative and increase self image

Implications of disposition and cognitive dissonance are many. They help point out why investors buy high and sell low, or buy on the way down in the emotional cycle and eventually panic and sell as fear takes over. Investors also have a tendency to avoid risk unless they think they can breakeven or they want at least an even chance of having joy. Hence, when one invests in a known financial loser such as the lottery it is due to the emotional joy of thinking what they would do with the winnings being equal to or greater than the dollar cost. Of course, the tendency is tempered by the risk averseness of the investor and the amount of money involved. Cognitive dissonance helps to explain why investors avoid buying on the way up in the emotional cycle – they are overly influenced by the most recent downturn. Cognitive dissonance, along with regret and pride, helps explain bubbles and why lessons learned in bubbles are forgotten in a short period of time. The most recent success is what is remembered and it leads to enthusiasm.

- Mental accounting or narrow framing
  - compartmentalize budgets and funds for various items (see figure below)
  - narrow framing – putting labels on money and avoiding mixing mental accounts
  - purchase, especially necessary items, is similar to financial loss
  - consuming, for example a holiday, is similar to joy of financial gain
  - increases regret of selling losers

Mental accounting has each investment contained in a separate "mental" account as shown in the pyramid above. In such cases, the investor does not take advantage of diversification benefits (i.e., over- or underweight asset allocations). The way investments correlate with each others impacts investment performance. Additionally, it is easy to misperceive overall risk because mental accounts do not interact. For example, as shown in the pyramid of assets, an investor will not use funds from a MMF earning

3% to finance the purchase of a car at 8% interest and then pay back the 'loan' to the MMF account. Of course, this may happen due to other behavioral traits; for example, feeling obligated to payback the bank but the obligation is not as strong to pay yourself. In any event, the net result is detrimental to investment/portfolio performance.

- Shortcuts
    - arriving at a solution without analyzing all available information
    - reduces the complexity of analyzing relevant facts and figures
    - use rule of thumbs
    - representativeness
        o believe past performance is equal to the future performance
        o ignore contradictory information
    - familiarity
        o prefer things, investments that you are familiar with
        o home bias
        o assume something is true without all the facts
    - implications
        o organize and quickly process information
        o difficulty analyzing new information
        o may lead to wrong conclusions
        o underdiversification – home bias, avoidance of unfamiliar

Shortcuts fly in the face of economic theory that say investors process all the information they need and act in a rational manner. First of all, we generally only have access to a limited amount of information, which is true even with access to the Internet and other sources. Second, do we process what we have access to or do we use shortcuts, familiarity, and representativeness to make decisions? Correct, we take the easy way and make decisions without processing all the information – it is easier not to do a full analysis. For example, it is a good company, thus it is a good stock or visa versa.

Implications for investing are that shortcuts allow investors to process and organize information quickly. However, it may not be correct and it is difficult to accurately analyze new information, especially if it is contradictory. Additionally, objectivity can be lost and wrong conclusions drawn. Research has shown that shortcuts lead to a home country bias and underdiversification.

- Herding, or social culture/pressure
    - everyone owns stock
    - popular consensus: creates doubts if you disagree and adds confidence is you agree
    - "groupthink" bias
    - part of everyday life
    - magnifies psychological biases (under and overreactions)
    - implications
        o market mania, emotional cycle
        o irrational exuberance or fear

o   short-term focus
o   social validation

Humans have a tendency to want to follow the crowd regardless of where the crowd is headed. We feel a safety in groupthink as compared to independent thought that may make us stick out from the group. This is true even though we admire thought leaders. In essence, we are not willing to take the risk of being the leader due to the possibility of loss – think back to the emotional pain of loss discussed earlier (emotionally, pain is twice joy). An obvious downfall is that following a group leads to overconfidence and overreaction, up to and including bubbles. When you hear everyone saying the same thing and taxicab drivers providing investment advice, you know the markets are in trouble.

- Psychological factors
  - are interrelated
  - do not explain all observed behaviors
  - affect investors and the financial market place

Behavioral finance recognizes that there is risk and return in the market that is driven by the financial performance of the firm and human emotions. Human emotions are real and exist in every investor. It is extremely hard for an investor to control their emotions. If they do not have discipline the emotions can get the best of the investor and the consequences can be devastating. Some factors of human emotion that are disadvantageous include:
- overconfidence: potential pitfalls can be too much selling and thinking that they cannot lose and that everyone else will lose
- disposition: regret taking actions quickly or not quickly enough
- cognitive dissonance: doubt that occurs after purchasing a security and selling or buying at a bad point in the emotional cycle
- herding: short term focus, creates bubbles, information cascades

Behavioral concepts can be used to recognize human psychology in reviewing behavioral finance. The various human emotions presented above display an investor's psychology. In recognizing these human behaviors in the financial markets, an investor can better manage his or her portfolio. These behavioral factors can cause someone to trade too often, sell too early, hold losers, avoid regret, seek pride, have debt aversion or risk aversion, and preferences which are not necessarily rational. Some other psychological aspects influence investment decisions and are presented below in "deadly sins." However, you should recognize that the factors and sins are not independent and that there is a lot of overlap between all of them.

"Deadly Sins" in Financial Decision Making

Deadly sins, similar to psychological factors, influence investors behavior. The sins include confirmation bias, optimism bias, faulty calibration, mistaken beliefs and framing. While there is overlap with the factors the deadly sins provide additional insight into investor behavior and "less than rational decisions."

- Confirmation bias
    - bias in hypothesis testing (design test to confirm)
    - looking for support
        o what we are familiar with
        o the decision we desire
    - lots of data available in financial markets to support almost anything
    - ignore information that contradicts or questions original opinion

It is 'easy' to prove almost anything. As the saying goes, "lie with statistics." One way to avoid this pitfall is to disprove something instead of proving it. Various experiments have shown that profits of arbitrage go to those who are free of confirmation bias. When you analyze something do you typically identify items to confirm, or do you try to disprove? If you try to disprove, you are rare, and probably a step ahead of many others when it comes to investing.

People tend to take any information as confirmation of their mental models. We believe we see the world as it is, and tend to ignore 'truth.' This is especially true when the popular media is pushing a point of view, or politicians are trying to sell what will get them elected again. While it is important to have an investment plan be aware that under the influence of a plan it is easy to see what you want to see.

- Optimism bias
    - belief that you are better than average
    - belief that misfortune befalls others
    - similar to overconfident
    - illusion of control
    - cultural differences, and well as sexual differences

When students are asked if they believe they are better than the average driver, the vast majority of their hands go up. It is not atypical for people to believe that misfortune will befall others and not themselves – for instance in starting a business, they believe they will succeed while someone else will not be as successful. This sin is similar to the overconfident factor presented previously.

An example of illusion of control: if you provide a random lottery ticket to an individual along with one where they chose the numbers rationally they should have the same value. However, when you ask the individual to sell the lottery tickets, they will demand more money for the ticket where they selected the numbers. This same phenomenon leads to day trading, especially by males.

Different cultures have different outlooks – have you known people who are always optimistic? Have you known people who are always pessimistic? Most people respond positively to these two questions. Obviously, the way one views the world has an impact on their behavior and investment decisions. If you think positively you are more likely to invest than when you think you are going to lose if you invest.

- Faulty calibration
  - linked to overconfident factor
  - hindsight bias
  - failure to learn from feedback
  - failure to recognize that results can be from chance, ability, or situation
  - cultural differences, especially regarding chance and situation

Hindsight is 20/20, while forecasting the future is filled with doubts; hence, investors tend to focus on the past. However, they fail to learn from mistakes, their own or others, and hence will fall into the same error again. Asian cultures have a tendency to appreciate the role of good fortune, while Western cultures underestimate the role of situational factors as causes of outcomes. For example, if you are assigned to the 'petroleum desk,' you will most likely add more to the profits (or losses) of the firm than if you are assigned to the 'copper desk.'

- Mistaken beliefs
  - illusory or invisible correlation
    o Super Bowl effect
    o hemlines
    o presidential cycle
    o years divisible by 5
  - leads to failure of not recognizing 'true' interactions (cause and effect)
  - simple but smart heuristics can be missed
  - overrate performance and fail to recognize chance or situation

The Super Bowl effect relates to the phenomena that if a NFL team wins the market will be up for the year. The relationship has been true over ninety percent of the time. Another correlation is the higher the hemline on women's dresses the higher the stock market. History has shown that during the last two years of a presidential term the market has performed better than the first two years as the President and Congress try to elect a president from their political party. It is well known that the economy and unemployment rates impact elections. For the past 50 or so years, if the year was exactly divisible by 5 the market was up the vast majority of time. These are correlations, not necessarily cause and effect relationships. However, if they hold do you ignore the information or do you recognize and make use of the information? Are the correlations an indication of a mood variable? Additionally, if an "unfounded" belief is stronger then knowledge/discipline then the investor is doomed to make poor decisions.

- Framing
  - how the question is framed impacts the outcome
  - technique used all the time in surveys (especially political ones)
  - related to disposition effect
  - related to mental accounting
  - plays a role in merger and acquisitions
  - related to agency question

As any pollster knows, how you shape the question drives the answer. Consider the following question, Which would you chose: (A) a sure loss of $30,000 or (B) a 20% chance of losing nothing, and an 80% chance of losing $40,000? Which did you pick, A or B? Typically, students and others pick B. What are the expected outcomes: for A, a loss of $30,000; and for B, a loss of $32,000 (0.80*$40,000 = $32,000). Was your answer rational? Did the framing of the question influence your decision?

Behavioral Finance – Factors and Sins
- Little doubt other factors and sins exist
- Impact depends who frames the question and the answer
- Culture differences exist and need to be accounted for
- Need to resolve the mental errors and emotional pitfalls
- Risk return relationship holds!!
- Need to recognize the benefits of investment theory

The deadly sins are companions to the psychological factors discussed previously. They are not unique nor mutually exclusive, rather there is significant overlap between the two groupings. Moreover, there may be other factors or sins that have not been identified and will eventually be recognized. Some of the best ways to avoid the pitfalls of human emotions include:
- being disciplined in both your buy and sell decisions
- recognize that you and others have emotions that drive investment decisions
- consult with another person who can help you recognize and control your emotions

Behavioral concepts can be very valuable to an investor trying to understand trends in the market. As much as someone would like to deny it, markets are very strongly affected by investor behavior and the overall psychology of the market. Although something like a terrorist attack would likely not cause every security available to crumble, investors will still pull their money out of markets as quickly as possible only because of fear. Fear is one of the major drivers of large moves in the markets. Anticipation of this type of behavior, but on a smaller scale, could really help investments perform better. It is important to recognize when the market is overreacting to news of some event and to make a move on the market. It is also important to realize when the market is overreacting on the positive side. If an investor can get in on a number of securities when they are low and/or exit when they are too high, then that person's investments will be extremely successful. This also assumes that the investor can overcome their own psychological intuitions of the market. Keep in mind that studies have shown that it is difficult to time the market.

Behavioral Aspects and Ethics
As the above indicates human emotions play a role in investing. Ethics can also have an influence when investing, especially if you are relying on others or the playing field is not a fair game because someone is being unethical (e.g., a Ponzi scheme, the media

reporting a rumor as a fact, incorrect or incomplete accounting statements, falsehoods by executives, the media reporting mob/herding as 'truth' and not mob behavior, et cetera).

On a smaller scale, if a financial advisor makes a recommendation does she or he receive a benefit? Is their judgment cloudy because of a "gift" they received? Studies have shown that while one group (say financial advisors) believes that gifts such as coffee mugs, a round of golf, lunch, dinner, calendars, or educational retreats would not compromise their judgment another group of professionals (say doctors) should not receive gifts because their objectivity could be impacted. It is easy to say other people are influenced by conflicts of interest, while we are above such basic human emotions. Bottom line, buyer beware!

****

Personal Finance

An individual needs to be aware of the behavioral concepts presented in this chapter and determine how they "fit them." Additionally, it needs to be recognized that the investment theory and applications presented in the text apply to both individual investors and professionals. The book lays out the foundation and the investors are the ones that must implement a plan whose objectives are based on their risk tolerance. Easier said than done, and in many cases individuals seek outside assistance for advice and wise financial decisions.

Seeking outside assistance raises the challenge of which broker or financial advisor to use, especially when the media is filled with stories about how investors were taken advantage or how brokerage firms were engaged in unethical practices. Besides asking your friends and colleagues two reliable Internet sources to check are:
  1) brokercheck.finra.org
  2) nasaa.org
These sites provide information regarding any disciplinary actions and employment records. Additionally, investors can also use the Internet as brokers do to find potential investments. Look yourself up at these two sites:
  1) zoominfo.com
  2) jigsaw.com

The Internet can also provide guidance to typical retirement/investment questions: for example, Morngingstar.com, TRowePrice.com, Fidelity.com and annuities.com. Appendix B provides a series of Internet sources that an investor could use to make better decisions. Some additional general information regarding personal finance is presented in Appendix C.

*Last, but certainly not least, if it sounds too good to be true it is **not** true!*

****

Technical Analysis
- Can be considered the study of investor psychology
- Represents the interaction of supply and demand
- Provides an "unbiased" opinion of security
- Focus is on price not value
- Forecasts price movement of securities
- Valuable source of information
  - in timing decisions (when to avoid a large loss)
  - overall market conditions
- Fundamental analysis
  - good company (assuming the information examined is correct and the analyst is unbiased in the evaluation)
  - examine economy, industry and company
  - requires use of accounting data (denotes choice since it is based on GAAP)
  - subjectivity is involved
- Technical analysis
  - used to identify a 'good' or 'bad' stock
  - "only" looks at interaction of supply and demand for security
  - uses 'only' market statistics of price and volume
  - subjectivity involved regarding technique to use, such as:
    o point and figure
    o patterns in line graphs
    o bar charts
  - concentrates on detecting trend changes early or determining extreme conditions that are indicative of overbought or oversold market
- Technical analysis is slowly being accepted in academia, and recent studies indicate that it does provide useful information

The primary tool used in technical analysis is the trend chart that simply plots price over time. Analysts look for overall trends, sub trends, recurring patterns, and support and resistance levels. Technical analysis can complement fundamental analysis by removing some of the subjective decisions utilized in fundamental analysis. Once fundamental analysis deems a firm to be attractive, technical analysis can aid in determining the timing of purchase, and levels for buy and sell decisions. Technical analysis can also be used to identify which stocks are ready to decline. Even with technical analysis there is subjectivity, just 'not as much' as in fundamental analysis.

Charting can help remove some of the psychological factors involved in buy and sell decisions, which in turn can help protect the investor from suffering large losses. The key to investing is to avoid a large losses. To recover from a large loss means superior investing to just breakeven.[1] Technical analysis supports the theory that behavioral aspects are involved in the marketplace. Support levels, resistant levels and price bottoms seem to be psychological barriers for investors; and hence, influence their buy

---

[1] Losses and returns needed to breakeven are presented in Chapter 6.

and sell decisions.   By identifying these levels, the technical analyst can predict secondary trends in a stock's price movement.

Point and figure charting [P&F] is one of several ways to plot price movements to identify trends using technical analysis. As compared to line charts, bar and candlestick charts, P&F charts "ignore" the element of time (see P&F sample below). Typically X's represent rising prices and O's represent declining prices. Each column consists of Xs or Os, and alternate. Xs mean the demand is greater than supply and Os mean that there is an excess supply.

The size of the box is set by the investor and is normally based on the current stock price [e.g., low price stocks (less than $20) may have a box size of $0.50, higher priced stocks (say $20 to $100) may have a box size of $1, and at high prices (greater than $100) a $2 box is reasonable, and at very high stock prices you may have a $5 box size]. The size of the box is to remove minor variation of stock prices and to help focus on the trend. Before moving to a new box the new price must be reached and if small or no price change occurs the chart is left untouched. If using a three-box reversal chart a price needs to move three boxes before you move to a new column – e.g., assume a $1 box, if in a declining column at $41 before moving to a rally column of Xs the stock price must reach $44. Common practice is to use high and lows during the day and not just closing prices. With a three-box reversal chart each column must contain at least three Xs or three Os. Xs and Os will not appear in the same column.

Point and Figure Chart
Double top breakout
Three box reversal chart

49				4		
48				X		
47	O			**X**		
46	O	X		2		
45	8	X	O	X		
44	O	9	O	1		
43	O	X	O	X		
42	O	X	B	X		
41	O		O			
40						
	12			13		

What an investor sees when looking at a P&F chart is the underlying supply and demand of the security. Time can be included by having the year on the bottom of the chart, the first nine months (January through September) of the year represented by the numbers 1 through 9, and then A, B and C for October November and December, respectively. All months may not be recorded – if there is no new price movement there is no new box and the month is not recorded.

Support and resistance levels can be identified on a P&F chart, along with price objectives on either the upside or downside trend. Trend lines, volume, moving average and other technical measures can be included to help identify buy and sell signals. Point and figure technical analysis is based on the simplest, most basic law of economics – supply and demand. StockCharts.com is an excellent reference for point and figure charts.

One of the P&F technical indicators used by James Gautier when he was the Managing Director of Legg Mason Trust Company is the New York Stock Exchange Bullish Indicator. When seventy or more percent of the analysts have a buy recommendation it is a sign that the market is entering an overbought zone and that the downside risk has increased. When the indicator is less than thirty percent it is an indication that the market is in an oversold zone and that upside potential has increased. Another way of looking at this is that when the market reaches an overbought zone, greed is dominating investment decisions. Similarly, fear is prevalent when the bullish indicator is under thirty percent. A saying in the market place that support this concept is: "when everyone is buying it is time to sell and when everyone is selling it is time to buy."

Research by Odders-White and Kavajecz suggests that using support/resistant levels and moving averages technical analysis conveys important information about the order book. Having the ability to forecast information about the specialist order book provides useful information regarding buy and sell decisions since it can help predict future price movements. In essence, the forecast predicts future supply and demand which is only known by the specialist.

Market place
- Fast changing and increasingly competitive
- Company is still the most studied, yet it generally accounts for lowest cause of changes in market price (overall market and extra market/group account for the majority of the price movement)
- Emotions (e.g., fear and greed) move financial markets
- Emotions influence investor's behavior regarding market conditions (from irrational exuberance to over or under reaction)
- Psychological as well as financial factors impact value, price and risk undertaken
- Excesses do exist and will continue to occur in the future
- Risk and return relationship exists and is valid, especially in the longer term
- Use a combination of both fundamental analysis and technical analysis in portfolio decisions and strategies
  - fundamental analysis provides benefit regarding value of company
  - technical analysis allows for the recognition of psychological factors that impact risk and return undertaken
- Some professionals do not always act in the best interest of their client(s)

- Diversification (Markowitz's concept of combining securities that are less than positively correlated, better known as modern portfolio theory) does work!! (for more information see Section V: Modern Portfolio Theory and Evaluation)

Not discussed in the factors and sins is "career risk" or "career bias" which is the behavioral trait that professionals act to maintain and promote their careers or to increase their own wealth. In corporate finance it would be called "agency theory." This implies that some decisions are not necessarily made to maximize risk-adjusted return for the investor, but rather to minimize the advisors own downside risk. Remember financial markets are basically efficient in that they are difficult to beat on a consistent basis. While in some ways one cannot blame advisors for having a self serving attitude since they operate in a highly challenging and not always rational market (e.g., dot.com bubble in the late 1009s) it is not justification for misappropriate behavior. One should **always** be ethical and honest in their dealings with others.

From a fundamental analysis viewpoint, an investor needs to consider the source of information and make judgments accordingly. Research, for example, from Wall Street or the City (financial district of London), is based too often on corporate relations personnel that communicate with securities analysts. As such, the research is not via a truly independent analysis of the firm. The Sarbanes Oxley legislation addressed this issue to some extent, but corporate spin still exists and one should not believe that all research is without bias. All too often the need to recommend something sellable carries the day. Instead, an investor needs to look at items such as quality, cash flow, balance sheet, insider behavior, industry, and overall economic outlook. If one does not take an independent look and just buys securities that are popular they are usually at premium prices and probably do not represent value. However, if one uses technical analysis they may be able to identify a trend, ride it, and then sell before it crashes. Remember technical analysis does not 'worry' about value, instead only price and the trend thereof is of import.

Recognizing human behavior helps explain some of the excesses and fraud that occurs in the market place. While Sarbanes-Oxley addressed some of the fallout of the excesses of the late 1990s it did not confront some of the causes that changed the attitude of top management and board of directors. Some of the causes include the failings of competitive advantage where big is considered better, tax laws that encouraged management to use options for compensation, and the change to the dominance of institutional investors who want quarterly performance results more so than long term results. Recognizing these structural changes from a behavioral perspective show that greed, coupled with pride and shortcuts could help identify dangerous situations and investors could avoid some of the worse cases of abuse. We also need to recognize that many individual investors are also guilty of greed and abuse: for example, people who purchased houses in the early mid 00s that put nothing down to purchase the property and had no demonstratable means of repaying the loan. This greed was done with government encouragement and blessings (everyone had the 'right' to own a home). It should be noted that after ten years of study the Federal government could finally draw the conclusion that if someone has no down payment and has no demonstratable means of repaying they are likely to default.

Our behavior is influenced by the mood we are in, and the mood depends on how we have done recently in the marketplace. If we have had recent success (somewhat similar to using house money) we have a tendency to be optimistic and overlook things, while if we had losses we tend to be upset (similar to snake bite) and question more. For example, after the dot.com bust alleged frauds revealed in late 2000 to 2001 received a lot of response from individual investors, regulators and even Congress. However, after being up by 10 or 20 percent alleged fraud revealed in 2003 did not receive as much attention. Additionally, at the end of 2006 the SEC eased guidance on portions of the Sarbanes-Oxley Act and the Department of Justice renounced some of the tactics it used to prosecute companies. The bursting of the housing bubble followed a similar pattern; even if it is taking longer to clear because of foreclosures and a poorly performing economy.

Summary
- Behavioral finance is important in investing and investment management
- Need to recognize that factors and sins exist, and develop strategies to
  - capitalize on them in the market place
  - develop strategies to avoid falling into the same traps
- Investors need to have buy and sell disciplines
- Technical analysis can provide information regarding behavior
- Risk, return, and diversification are all valid and important concepts

Behavioral finance recognizes that not all investors are rational. The irrational and speculative behavior of these investors is not accounted for in the efficient market hypothesis. Because of this it is important that investors understand human psychology and develop strategies to capitalize on, or at least consider, its effect on the market. This effect exists in the pragmatic world but not in the theories or models most commonly used in financial modeling.

Not all investors act rationally to changes in the market place, or changes within a particular security. Human psychology plays a role in helping explain movements within the market as the result of new information being introduced to the public. There are six main factors that will affect investors and the market place. These include investor overconfidence, regret and pride, past/memory elements, mental accounting, shortcuts and social culture. Behavioral finance includes all these factors and helps determine how human emotions will impact investment decisions. Recognizing these factors and their effect helps improve investment results. Behavioral finance helps identify emotional pitfalls of markets, explain irrational movements in financial markets, which includes bubbles and underperformers. You should also keep in mind the necessity to have buy and sell disciplines, and the need to stick to them.

There is an emotional cycle that goes from caution, to confidence, to enthusiasm, to greed, to complacency, to concern, and finally to panic, no way out before moving onto caution and repeating the cycle. It is important for investors to take these factors into account and by doing so will improve the way they manage their investments. Technical analysis is a tool that can be used to help judge the emotional conditions of the market place, and the desirability of investing in individual securities, sectors, groups or the stock market as a whole. This in turn relates to the major activities of portfolio management presented in Chapter 1: asset allocation, weighting shifts across major asset classes and security selection within asset classes.

We should recognize that behavioral finance is not antipodal to theoretical finance and valuation models presented in this book. Instead one can view that capital market theory and efficient markets represent the mean or average over long periods that allows for the development of rational models to help in the understanding of financial markets. The models act as a benchmark on which various behavior, irrational or not, can be identified and judged. Neither behavioral aspects nor theory provide answers, instead they work hand-in-hand to help the investor make better investment decisions.

CHAPTER 2
THOUGHT QUESTIONS

1. Discuss how psychology can help explain investor behavior, and by understanding the various factors and sins how an investor could improve investment results.

2. Discuss how technical analysis can be used in conjunction with financial/fundamental analysis to invest.

Questions

1. Indicate the major concepts behind behavioral finance, and compare it to traditional finance.
2. Identify and discuss three psychological factors. Why did you choose those three, and not others?
3. Identify two deadly sins and relate them to psychological factors.
4. Discuss the major concepts behind point and figure analysis.
5. Identify and discuss several elements in the market place that investors need to be aware of if they plan to be successful.
6. Are risk and return still a valid concept, or will human emotions override logic and discipline?

Section II: Valuation and Risk

Section I presented the foundation for investing. We now turn our attention to valuation and the risk characteristics of two main asset classes, namely bonds and stocks. Both classes are large, global, part of "everyone's portfolio," and they are the basis for many derivative instruments.

Chapter 3 presents bond valuation, from basic valuation and bond pricing theorems to duration and convexity. Fundamental sources of risk are discussed along with bond ratings and yields. It should be noted that bonds are normally purchased based on yield and not price (a dollar amount). In Chapters 4 and 5 equity valuation and risk analysis is presented. We start with the underlying theory of equity valuation and move to more advanced models before considering modifications and applications. The framework presented is tied to capital markets and the CAPM (Capital Asset Pricing Model).

The primary reason for investing is to make money, or receiving a future return for the risk undertaken. The easy answer to making money is rather simple – buy low, sell high; or vice versa; sell high, buy low. Unfortunately investing is not so easy. In a more complete picture, investing, from investment management to portfolio management, is daunting, challenging and fun. The financial environment and investment opportunities are constantly changing; plus, as discussed in Chapter 2, emotions are involved and impact investment decisions.

Investment management's focus is on how to value assets/securities and recognizing the difference between market price and value. Portfolio management deals with how to combine the securities and assets into efficient portfolios. It is also essential to recognize that the market and/or individual investment is often driven by greed and fear. Emotions are important and overreacting is contagious. Value is, or should be, based on cash flows generated discounted to present value according to the degree of risk – likelihood of flows, both negative and positive.

Valuation is difficult and always has been. Cash flow is based on assets (real or financial) and the earnings and capital gains/losses they generate. An investment strategy should be based on a well-defined discipline. Logically the discipline should be based on areas of competence and forecasting ability. Forecasting, whether cash flows or market moods, is the true key to successful investment and portfolio management. With the above being said, let us now move into the exploration of valuation and risk of bonds and equities.

Chapter 3: Bond Valuation and Risk Analysis

CHAPTER OVERVIEW

The valuation of bonds is important for determining the attractiveness of bonds to other investments – from both risk and return perspectives. Two basic sources of risk for bonds are variation in interest rates and credit risk [possibility of default]. In this chapter, we describe approaches to valuation of bonds and how these approaches are applied in practice. Measures for analyzing risk are also introduced in this chapter. Duration is also explored in some depth, including the concept of convexity. How debt instruments/bonds can be used in positioning investments is also discussed. The chapter then goes into credit risk across the quality spectrum, and how returns relate to "risk-free" government bonds. Additional bond concepts and the yield curve are presented in Section III, Strategies and Applications, Chapter 10, and is based on the valuation and risk concepts discussed below.

Introduction
- Bond, an interest bearing security with a time horizon greater than one year
  - requires the issuer to pay the investor a set or variable amount at specified times
  - principal (or face value, or par value, or maturity value) is paid at maturity
- Relative attractiveness of bonds in a comparison universe is based on
  - time horizon
  - risk tolerance
  - interest rate environment
  - tax considerations
    - o municipal (public purpose) bonds: exempt from Federal taxes and from state and local taxes in which they are issued
    - o treasury bonds: tax-free from state and local taxes
    - o municipal (private purpose) bonds: taxable unless specifically exempted
    - o corporate, taxed at all levels
- Risk of bonds
  - interest rate risk (the primary source of risk for bonds)
  - default risk (credit worthiness)
- Bond terms need to be understood to avoid confusion
- Bond valuation concepts and models
  - present value concepts
  - bond pricing theorems
- Basic types of bonds include (domestic and global)
  - corporate
  - Treasury or government
  - municipal or munis
- Bonds turn into money market instruments when their remaining maturity is less than one year

Bonds (debt instruments with a maturity of greater than one year) are often overlooked by individual investors in investment strategies – returns are not usually as high as stocks and information is more difficult to obtain. However, financial advisors and portfolio managers recognize the importance of bonds and use them in developing portfolios. Bonds are a significant portion of the financial markets, for example, in early 2007 the overall debt market within the United States consisted of approximately $2 trillion municipal bonds, the corporate market of around $5.6 trillion, and $4.9 trillion of outstanding U.S. Treasury securities. Government debt is increasing and impacts the overall financial markets – in fact, the growth of government debt is reaching a crisis point as the level approaches $17 trillion in 2013 and the debt ceiling needs to be increased once again. Debt instruments offer a wide range of maturities, from money market funds and Treasury bills to thirty year Treasuries and fifty year or longer corporate bonds. Municipal bonds provide a tax advantage for investors.

Risk of bonds is generally divided into two sources: 1) interest rate risk refers to how prices vary as interest rates change and is parallel to systematic risk, and 2) default risk corresponds to unsystematic risk and refers to the likelihood of receiving interest payments and principal in a timely manner. Interest rate risk is driven by general market conditions, and to a lesser extent by extra group factors. Default risk is generally issuer specific, but is influenced by market and sector conditions. The two sources of risk are not independent. The primary method of valuing bonds is to calculate the present value of expected cash flows discounted by an appropriate rate based on perceived risk of the flows.

As noted above, bonds include corporate debt issues, Treasuries issued by the Federal government, and municipal bonds issued by various state and local municipalities. Terms and models apply to all three types. The same basic classifications apply to global debt issues. Corporate bonds are typically issued by companies that also have publicly traded equity. Treasuries are generally viewed as "risk free" since they are issued by the Federal government which has the power and ability to print money, and hence by definition cannot default. Hence, Treasures have a certain outcome, but it does not mean they are free of risk. Treasuries, as with many investments, face inflation risk, and governments can cause inflation by printing too much money. Treasuries are typically tax-free from state and local income taxes. In recent times the amount of government debt has been expanding 'exponentially' and has impacted the economy, both domestically and globally. The huge increase in government debt has implications for inflation, and as you know debt needs to be repaid which implies future generations of Americans have been saddled with obligations beyond their control.

Municipal bonds are issued by a state or a local governmental unit or an entity provided a "municipal status" (e.g., a new Hilton Hotel built near the convention center at the request of the city). Municipal bonds are often referred to as munis. Municipal bonds are either general obligation bonds backed by the full taxing authority of the issuing municipality or revenue bonds which are backed by the particular purpose of the bond (e.g., revenues collected at toll booths to repay bonds issued to build a bridge or a highway). In 1986 municipal bonds were divided into two groups: 1) general purpose bonds and 2) private purpose bonds. Private purpose bonds are bonds that provide more than a ten percent benefit to private parties. The interest rate on general purpose munis is generally lower then private purpose bonds because they are typically tax-free from Federal income tax and from state and local income taxes. The exemption from state and local taxes is normally only in the state of issue. Hence, if you live in Connecticut and purchase a New York bond you will pay Connecticut income taxes on the interest income. In addition, when comparing yields, especially in pragmatic settings, on the various types of bonds one should compare after tax yields due to the tax exempt nature of some bonds.

Bond Terms
- Differences between fundamental interest rate terms exist
- As in all areas of finance when communicating with others be sure to define terms since just saying premium can imply several meanings
- Key bond terms include the following:
  - nominal rate is the real rate plus an inflation factor
  - the real rate is the nominal rate less the inflation factor
  - yield to maturity [YTM], the expected yield if one holds the bond to its maturity date, and is the same as the internal rate of return which equates all future flows to the current price in present value terms (a future value concept and term)
  - coupon rate, c, is the annual payment of interest divided by the par value
  - required return, r, the discount rate that reflects the risk of the debt instrument
  - call feature, ability of the issuer to pay off the debt before maturity
  - put feature, ability of the investor to redeem the debt before maturity
  - duration can be viewed as the "weighted average time" to recover cash outflow
  - premium bond sells at a price above maturity value
  - discount bond sells at a price below maturity value
  - zero coupon bond – sells at a deep discount because the 'coupon rate' is zero and the implied rate is paid at maturity
  - original issue discount bonds [OIDs] – the coupon rate is lower than what the market expects for the risk of the instrument; and hence, it sells at a discount
  - inflation premium represents compensation for inflation risk
  - risk premium consists of four elements: 1) interest rate risk, 2) purchasing power risk, 3) business risk, and 4) financial risk

As investing in bonds is discussed below these terms are fleshed out in greater detail.

Valuation Theory
- All investments derive value from the cash flow they are expected to generate
- Present value of security is cash flow received over the time horizon, discounted back at the rate 'r' (the required return)
- Required return consists of risk-free return (real return plus inflation premium) plus risk premium (interest rate risk plus business risk plus financial risk)
- Required return, r, is based on the level of risk and represents the discount rate
- Valuation of a perpetuity
  - perpetuity pays out a fixed amount over an indefinitely long period

- price, P_0, is simply fixed cash flow (interest payment 'I') capitalized by the discount rate (r)

$$P_0 = \frac{I}{r}$$

- Bond Valuation (present value)
  - price, P_0, is the present value of future cash flows – coupons or interest payments (I) plus principal (P_n) discounted to present value by the discount rate (r)

$$P_0 = \sum_{t=1}^{N} \frac{I}{(1+r)^t} + \frac{P_N}{(1+r)^N}$$

  - the discount rate, r, is also referred to as the yield to maturity and reflects the risk of the bond
  - maturity and interest rate sensitivity impact valuation
- Excel has valuation models and data can be obtained from Internet sources
- A template for bond valuation is presented at the end of the chapter

The present value [PV] method of bond valuation calculates the present value of expected cash flows (coupon payments and the repayment of principal) using a discount factor equal to the required rate of return. The computed PV indicates what an investor would be willing to pay for the bond to realize a rate of return that typically takes into account the risk-free rate, including the expected rate of inflation, and the risk of the bond. A second approach is to compute the internal rate of return [IRR], which is the discount rate that equates the present value of cash outflows for an investment with the present value of its expected cash inflows. The IRR is an implied yield to maturity [YTM]. If the YTM is higher or equal to the risk factor of the bond, the bond would be considered a candidate for investment subject to portfolio factors [from objectives to correlation considerations]. PV and IRR are both present value concepts. The same basic equation is used to solve for both PV and IRR, the only difference being which variable is the unknown (P_0 or r).

Generally. bonds are purchased on yield and not a dollar amount. In fact, bond prices are quoted as a percent of par value. For example a price of 99 would mean 99% of par, so for a typical $1000 par value bond the market price would be $990. Zero coupon [ZCB] and original discount bonds [OID] differ from the traditional bond that pays a coupon that is indicative of the risk as measured by the discount rate, or the coupon rate is close to the discount rate ($c \approx r$) when the bond is first issued. For zero coupon bonds the coupon rate is zero ($I = 0$); hence, the maturity value represents the only cash inflow. The price of the bond reflects this situation, for example, a ZCB with a face value of $50,000 maturing in 30 years may sell for, say, $4,100 (the actual price would depend on the discount rate – see present value formula above – the higher the discount rate the lower the present value of the maturity value P_n). For OID bonds the coupon rate (c) is much lower then the discount rate (r) and therefore the bonds sell at a 'large' discount. For example a 30 year $1,000 bond with a coupon of $20 (or c = 2%) that has a risk factor of 5% would sell at a large discount – using the present value above with I = $20, n = 30, P_n = $1,000, and r = 5% the present value P_0 = $538.83. ZCB and OID bonds face special tax considerations in that the discount needs to be amortized over the life the bond according to tax tables provided by the Internal Revenue Service. A general rule of thumb is that for taxable accounts ZCBs are not advisable and OIDs are questionable.

Bond Pricing Theorems
- Bond Pricing Theorems (also known as Bond Value Rules): relationship between price and interest rates. A portfolio manager uses the bond pricing theorems to help assess interest rate risk of debt securities and desirable characteristics of debt instruments to consider investing in given an interest rate forecast. The five theorems are:
  (1) bond prices move inversely with interest rates
  (2) bond prices vary directly with term to maturity
  (3) bond price sensitivity to interest rate changes increases at a diminishing rate as time to maturity increases, or the rate of price change in (2) increases at a decreasing rate
  (4) for a given change in interest rates, decreases in yields cause price rises that are larger than price losses resulting from increases in yields
  (5) bond price volatility is inversely related to its coupon rate, or the lower the coupon rate the greater the volatility for a given change in yield

Bond pricing theorems assist a portfolio manager in deciding on the type of bond to purchase in a forecasted interest rate environment. For example, if the portfolio manager had to invest in bonds and interest rate is expected to increase what type of bond should be purchased? The purchase of a short-term, high coupon bond would be more desirable than a long-term, low coupon bond. The reasoning follows: based on theorem (1) with an increase in interest rates the value would decrease, and the investor would want to minimize the loss of value. Based on theorems (2) and (3) the shorter the term to maturity the smaller the price change. Lastly, based on theorem (5) a high coupon bond would have a smaller change in value than a low coupon bond. The opposite would be true if the forecast was for interest rated to decrease. Of course, to be considered eligible for investment a bond also has to meet the objectives of the investor and the correlation to the other securities held by the investor should also be considered.

Duration
- Duration is a measure that allows one to evaluate the relative exposure to interest rate risk of securities with differing patterns of cash flows
- Duration is a better risk measure than maturity or average life since it accounts for time value
- Duration [d] is a measure of the time to each payment weighted by the present value of that payment

$$d = \frac{\sum\limits_{t=1}^{n} \dfrac{I_t(t)}{(1+r)^t} + \dfrac{P_n(n)}{(1+r)^n}}{\sum\limits_{t=1}^{n} \dfrac{I_t}{(1+r)^t} + \dfrac{P_n}{(1+r)^n}} \quad \text{or} \quad d = \frac{\sum\limits_{t=1}^{n} \dfrac{I_t(t)}{(1+r)^t} + \dfrac{P_n(n)}{(1+r)^n}}{P_o}$$

- Duration has the measurement of time
- Duration "combines" the bond pricing theorems into a single number

- Zero coupon bonds have duration equal to their maturity
- Securities making interim payments have durations that are shorter than their maturity

The duration concept was developed by Frederick Macaulay in 1938 to capture interest rate risk. Duration is a measure that allows one to evaluate the relative exposure to interest rate risk of securities with differing patterns of cash flow, because it specifically takes into account both interim and final cash flow payments. The numerator has the cash flow weighted by the time period in which it flows. The denominator is just the present value of the bond. Hence, Macaulay duration, or just plain duration is considered a time weighted average of the bonds risk. Basic duration relationships include the following:

1) Duration is less than maturity because duration is the weighted average time to "full recovery" of the initial investment – a coupon bond will always have duration less than its maturity.
2) Duration is a composite measure that considers both coupon and maturity flows. It is better than maturity because the price volatility of a bond varies inversely with its coupon and directly with its maturity. Therefore, it is better to use a measure that is a combination of both relationships.
3) If a coupon is lower, duration increases because there is an inverse relationship between the two.
4) If the YTM is smaller, the duration is greater because there is an inverse relationship between the two.
5) If the maturity increases, duration will also increase because there is a direct relationship between the two.

Note: Bond Pricing Theorems can be used to help explain these relationships.

- Duration and interest rate sensitivity
    - while duration combines coupon and maturity, the two key variables that investors must consider in response to expected changes in interest rates, it does not allow us to make direct statements about the expected price change for a change in yield
    - modified duration (d_m): defined as duration divided by 1 + yield to maturity, allows one to make direct statements
        - percent change in price = [-(duration*change in yield)/(1 + yield)]*100
        - or percent change in price = -(modified duration)(change in yield)*100
        - Example: Consider a 9%, 25-year bond selling to yield 7% with a modified duration of 10.62. If yields increase instantaneously from 7% to 7.10%, a yield change of 10 basis points (+.0010), the approximate percentage price change is:
            % change in price = -(10.62)(+.0010)(100)
            % change in price = -(.0106)(100)
            % change in price = -1.06%
    - the negative sign in front of the right side of the equation represents the inverse relationship between yield and price (bond value rule one)
    - works best when gauging relatively small changes in interest rate and when evaluating changes over shorter intervals
    - direct relationship to risk
    - one needs to be careful to not interchange duration and modified duration

Because the price volatility of a bond varies inversely with its coupon and directly with its term to maturity, it is necessary to determine the best combination of these two variables to achieve your objective. Duration of a security is a composite measure that considers both coupon and maturity. The duration of a bond is a more appropriate measure of its risk characteristic than the term to maturity, because duration takes into account both the repayment of capital at maturity and the size and timing of coupon payments prior to final maturity. An adjusted measure of duration, called modified duration, can help estimate the price volatility of a bond. Modified duration (d_m) is defined as duration/(1+yield), which in turn implies $\%\Delta P = -d_m(\Delta r)(100)$. It has been shown, both theoretically and empirically, that bond price movements vary proportionally with modified duration. Modified duration is used 'only' to estimate percentage price change for a given change in yield. Modified duration is only an approximation because it does not consider the curvilinear nature of the price yield relationship (see below).

To minimize interest rate risk, a duration-matching strategy is superior to a maturity-matching strategy because duration incorporates the interim cash flows in its formula. In so doing, measuring a bond's sensitivity by way of duration is more precise and reliable than a bond's sensitivity by way of maturity to the relative exposure of a given bond to interest rate risk. When duration matches the investment horizon, price risk and investment risk will offset each other and the net effect of interest rate swings is minimized. See the immunization discussion presented later in this chapter.

Convexity
- Modified duration is a linear concept for a curvilinear relationship
- Asymmetry in price responsiveness to changes in interest rates is known as convexity
- Price of bond will increase a greater amount from a decrease in interest rates than it will decrease in price from an equivalent rise in rates (bond value rule number four)
- Duration interest sensitivity equation can be adjusted to correct for convexity "errors" – becomes relatively more important at more divergent interest rates
- Determinants of convexity
  - larger as maturity of bond increases
  - lower at higher coupon levels

Modified duration assumes a linear relation between price and yield, while the actual relationship is curvilinear (see graph below). Therefore, recognizing "convexity" provides better information.

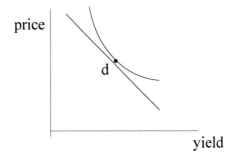

- Adjusting for Convexity:
  - need to adjust duration for curvature of relationship by adding a quadratic term
  - able to better estimate price change for a change in interest rate
  - becomes more important at more divergent interest rates
  - to account for convexity in the percentage change formula another term needs to be added:

$$\% \text{ Change in Price} = \left[\frac{-d * \Delta r}{1+r} + cv * \left(\frac{\Delta r}{1+r} \right)^2 \right] * 100$$

  - where the cv (convexity) term is:

$$cv = \left(\frac{1}{2} \right) \frac{\sum_{t=1}^{n} \frac{C_t(t)(t+1)}{(1+r)^t}}{P_o}$$

The example below shows the relative impact of terms if we assume an instantaneous change of interest rates from 7.5% to 7.0% for a 20-year maturity, zero coupon bond.

	t = 0	t = 1		
Par Value	$1,000.00	$1,000.00		
Coupon	None	None		
Maturity	20	20		
Yield	7.5%	7.0%		
Price	$ 235.41	$ 258.42	9.77%	actual change
Duration	20	20		
Convexity	210	210		
duration impact (d_m)		9.30%		
Convexity impact (cv)		0.45%		
Modified duration & convexity impact		9.76%		
The modified duration related impact of 9.3% is less than the actual 9.77% price change. This is explained by the failure to include the convexity impact, whose 0.45% impact accounts for the difference. As interest rates become more divergent, the convexity estimate must be included with the modified duration based estimate to arrive at a closer approximation of the actual price change. Note: rounding differences impact the numbers above.				

It should be recognized that even with the convexity term added it is still an estimate of the expected price change. In the example above the estimated percent price change is 9.76% while the actual price change is 9.77%. With larger interest rate changes the difference between estimated and actual change increases.

- Determinants of Convexity
  - maturity, direct relationship
  - coupon, inverse relationship

The major determinants of convexity are similar to those of duration. The bond's maturity and coupon are the two intrinsic principal determinants of a bond's convexity: (a) the longer the maturity the higher the convexity, and (b) the lower the coupon the higher the convexity. The general level of interest rates also plays a role. If interest rates are high convexity levels will be lower. Convexity is a measure of the curvature of the price-yield relationship and shows how a bond's price-yield curve deviates from a linear approximation of that curve (see the graph above).

Mathematically, convexity is the second derivative of price with respect to yield divided by price. For noncallable bonds, convexity is always a positive number, implying that the price-yield curve lies above the modified duration line. Duration of the bond is the tangent point of the price yield curve and the modified duration line. In essence the modified duration line is the slope of the price-yield curve at the current yield and price of the bond. Because of the convexity relationship, as the yield increases, the rate at which the price of the bond declines becomes slower. Similarly, when the yield decreases, the rate at which the price of the bond increases becomes faster.

- Investments in bonds – basic strategies as part of a portfolio
  - three approaches
    - maturity-concentrated
    - laddered
    - barbell
  - important to have a forecast of general trend of interest rates before deciding on structure of bond investments

Investment maturity profiles are based on interest rate forecasts, investment objectives, and convexity analysis. Three general types are:
1. Maturity-concentrated: the investor would have a strong interest rate opinion and would tailor the investments accordingly. If rates are going to fall, buy longer maturity bonds; if rates are going to go up, buy shorter maturity bonds.
2. Laddered: no real interest rate forecast. This provides average returns over an interest rate cycle.
3. Barbell - have both short and long term bonds, and few if any intermediates. This investment can be adjusted to emphasize short or long-term bonds depending on how the investor believes the interest rate is moving. It differs from the laddered construction as it includes both long and short-term bonds, but few or no intermediate-term bonds. It may also be considered more liquid than the laddered portfolio because of the higher concentration in short-term bonds. This type of portfolio is designed to yield higher returns when the yield curve is upward-sloping.

As noted previously, there is an inverse relationship between coupon and convexity and yield and convexity, and a direct relationship between maturity and convexity. Mindful of convexity, an investor would emphasize maturity concentrated portfolios when interest rate directions are apparent. Longer maturity portfolios would be used when interest rates were expected to fall, and shorter maturity portfolios would be used when interest rates were expected to rise. Laddered and barbell portfolios would be used when interest rates were unpredictable. Laddered portfolios have maturities that are evenly spaced so that the same amount matures and is reinvested each year, and provide average returns over the interest rate cycle. Barbell portfolios are concentrated in short and long-term maturities with limited intermediate-term bonds. Barbell portfolios provide a liquidity edge and higher returns during constant (assuming an upward sloping yield curve) and decreasing interest rates than laddered portfolios due to heavier concentrations in short and long-term bonds. Therefore, it is important for the bond portfolio manager to forecast the interest rate trend when deciding upon a portfolio structure.

If the risk profile of the investor calls for buying and holding bonds with short maturities, say less than five years and the average maturity is less than 3 years the duration concepts discussed above are of minimum value. The reason for this is that the difference between maturity measures and duration measures would be minimal and the additional 'cost' of calculating durations may not cover the benefits gained.

"Reinvestment" Rate Risk
- **Only applies to future value**, not for present value
- "Reinvestment" rate risk refers to the ability of earning "interest-on-interest" at the current interest rate structure
- Magnitude of risk to achieve future value increases as maturity of bonds in a portfolio increases

"Reinvestment" risk can also be termed "investment" risk of investing interest payments to achieve a future value. The YTM of a 10%, 5-year debenture purchased at par is 10%. The yield to maturity will be the same regardless of what the investor does with the interest payments. However, the realized yield to maturity (actual realized compound yield) will change depending on what happens to the intermittent interest flows. For the same 10%, 5-year debenture purchased at par if the bondholder consumes the interest payments instead of investing them at 10% the realized yield is 8.4% due to the loss of return resulting from not investing the coupon payments. Or the realized yield, a future value concept, is not equal to the expected yield to maturity, which is a present value concept. Regardless of what the investor does with the coupons the present value of the debenture does not change. A "reinvestment assumption" is not necessary to calculate the IRR or expected YTM.

- Reinvestment risk control
  - reinvestment risk constitutes a problem in achieving target return levels (future)
  - capital gains (or losses) help offset reinvestment risk (gain)
  - discount bonds (especially zeros) are ideal for achieving target rates of return

The components of interest rate risk that a bondholder is faced with are (re)investment rate risk of interest payments and variation in bond prices over the life of the bond due to changes in interest rates. (Re)investment rate risk is the risk that coupon payments cannot be invested at the current market rate of the bond to achieve a target future value; this risk is not applicable to zero-coupon bonds. (Re)investment rate risk can be minimized through a process called immunization (see below). The other risk a bondholder faces entails the bond price changing as market interest rates fluctuate. The risk can be monitored through the duration of the bond and depending upon which way interest rates are suspected of moving, a strategy of buying bonds with a higher or lower duration may be used.

- Immunization
    - depends upon the concept of duration for ensuring that an investment is structured in such a way that any capital losses/gains from interest rate changes will be offset by gains/losses on (re)invested return of interest payments
    - to "immunize" a portfolio against interest rates changing, the manager can match duration to time horizon
    - works well for certain payoffs for terminal periods
    - does not work as well for less defined outcomes

Immunization – structuring a bond investment so that capital gains (losses) from interest rate changes will be offset by losses (gains) on the investment of interest payments in order to achieve a specific dollar amount or rate of return over a specified period of time. A bond portfolio is immunized against interest rate risk when the portfolio's value at the end of the holding period, regardless of interest rate movements, is the same as it would have been if the interest rates had remained constant and interest payments were invested at the same rate for the time horizon. For immunization to occur, any change in interest rates must be the same for all forward interest rates, resulting in a parallel shift in the yield curve. Given this assumption, it is possible to immunize a bond portfolio if the duration of the portfolio is always equal to the desired investment horizon. This is possible because price risk and (re)investment risk caused by a change in interest rates have opposite effects on the ending wealth position. An increase in interest rates will cause an ending price below expectations, but the return from investing interim cash flows will be above expectations. A decline in market interest rates will cause the reverse situation. Mathematically, a coupon bond with a given duration is similar to a zero coupon bond having a maturity equal to that duration. In this way, an immunized bond investor can be confident of meeting a given liability on a predetermined future date. Immunization is a process whereby an investor can "lock in" a specific percentage yield (or dollar value return) over a given period of time. If the assumptions at the beginning of this paragraph do not hold, which is typically the situation in the pragmatic world, the investor will have to follow a more active immunization process. An active immunization process requires adjusting the duration of the portfolio periodically. The adjustment has costs associated with it so, as with any finance decision, the costs should be compared to the benefits and only undertaken when the expected benefit is greater than the cost. In pragmatic settings, the cost and benefits need to recognize behavioral considerations.

A bond manager may want to immunize the investment if he/she knows that, after a certain period of time, he/she needs a certain amount, say $1 million, and to achieve this goal he/she needs to obtain a return of 8.5% during the time period. Use of the immunization process would lock in (if the assumptions hold) to a return over the period and ensure that the desired ending value is achieved within reason (i.e., a 100% guarantee of an 8 1/2 % return is, most likely, not feasible unless the portfolio is a zero coupon bond with minimal likelihood of default and a maturity equal to the time horizon). The actual result will depend on how interest rates changed over the time horizon and how active the immunization process was.

A zero coupon bond (whose maturity inherently equals its duration) is automatically immunized as there are no interim cash flows, no investment rate risk. In order to immunize a bond portfolio over, say a four year period, a coupon paying bond with a duration of four years (which implies the maturity is greater than 4 years), or a zero coupon bond with a maturity (duration) of four years is necessary.

Risk Premium and Bond Ratings

- Government debt instruments [Treasuries] are subject only to interest rate and purchasing power risk
- Corporates are also subject to business and financial risk
- Municipals are also subject to credit risk
- Risk premium is the additional yield on corporates to compensate for added risk
- Yield spread: the difference between rates on various classes or groups of bonds, e.g., the difference between Treasuries and corporates
- Default - the inability to meet interest or sinking fund payments or repayment of principal in a timely manner
- Bond ratings are designed to rank order issues based on the probability of default
  - top four ratings (Aaa to Baa) are investment-quality
  - high-yield ("junk") bonds are lower ratings (Ba or lower)

A credit rating includes a subjective assessment of the strength of the issuer based upon information available in the marketplace. Both corporate and municipals bonds are rated by various agencies (e.g., Standard and Poor's, Moody's, and Fitch). Credit ratings only provide a general gauge as to default risk – the rating should not be thought of as a precise measurement. While they may not be exact, credit ratings are used to help ensure that bonds default risk matches the investor's risk/return objectives. Treasuries are normally rated AAA because they are "guaranteed" by the Federal government to be paid. However, with the excessive increase in debt (over one trillion per year, 2009 – 2012) and the partisan political environment where the President claims default is imminent for certain sectors (e.g., social security) to spread fear and achieve his objectives Treasuries were downgraded by S&P. Soon after the downgrade the government started to investigate S&P – talk about fear tactics and the power of the Federal government. For the time being, or at least until politics goes totally overboard, we will assume that Treasuries have a certain outcome. Even with a certain outcome they still face inflationary risk as well as interest rate risk. One also needs to be sure to recognize the difference between Treasuries and Federal agency paper (i.e., Fannie Mae and Freddy Mac securities).

Municipals are, in many ways, a class onto themselves. Besides being 'tax exempt' defaults are relatively rare. This does not imply that they all have high credit ratings. Revenue bonds (bonds secured by a single project, e.g., golf course or toll road) are riskier than general obligation [GO] bonds (bonds secured by the taxing authority). Even among GO bonds there are differences, cities and towns are generally riskier than states. It should also be recognized that many munis also carry insurance, whether they need it or not. Munis are typically issued as serial bonds, and some have call features which impact the potential yield that an investor may receive. While they are tax exempt from federal taxes, municipal interest can be subject to the Alternative Minimum Tax. Additionally, deep discounted munis face tax consequences as the discount is amortized over the life of the bond. In fact, a zero muni can actually have a negative value if held in a taxable account – there is no interest paid, and the taxpayer has to pay taxes on the increase in the book value of the bond which implies a negative cash flow. The same can also be said for taxable debt instruments.

High yield securities (also called junk bonds) are bonds that are issued by companies with very high levels of business risk and/or financial risk. The variability of operating income, whether based on either internal or external factors, can result in higher levels of default risk. In order to be compensated for this risk, the holder of a junk bond expects to be paid a premium in the form of a high yield. The risk-return premium for junk bonds is approximately the return required on equity. The default rate on junk-rated debt is higher than investment grade bonds but many contend that the risk return relationship is worthwhile, especially during good economic times when default rates for junk bonds is typically less than one percent. During less favorable times default rates could reach the neighborhood of five percent or higher. Those who contend that junk bonds are worthwhile typically assume that an investment is in a well-diversified junk bond portfolio, and not just one or two high yield bonds. Of course, the subprime and liquidity crisis in 2008, and the political climate in 2011 changed many opinions about the riskiness of bonds.

Yield spread is the difference between the yield on corporate bonds and the yield on "default free" government bonds. Why are government bonds considered default free? To pay the bonds they just need to print the money! Of course, that belies the question of impact on inflation. Government bonds are subject to interest rate and purchasing power risk while corporate bonds are the subject not only to these risks, but also to business and financial risks as well. Bonds trade at different spreads to one another based upon the creditworthiness of the issuer and in some instances based upon the supply and demand of particular issuers. The benchmark issue of bonds from which all other bond issues trade is the bonds issued by the Treasury of the United States. The greater the yield spread between a particular corporate issue versus a comparable direct U.S. obligation, the greater the credit risk, all other things being equal. A good investor uses this fact in their judgment of default risk. Primary reasons for changes in yield spread lie in the economic cycle, changes (or expected changes) in inflation, changes in a firm's financials or business opportunities, politics, and other risks that change over time. Variations in yield spreads can be incorporated into investments by determining if the spread is adequate to cover the credit quality of corporate bonds. If the investment is not immunized, the spread could also be used for determining where cash throw-offs (interest payments) are invested.

- Credit quality determinants assist in the development of bond ratings
  - four fundamental financial factors used to asses credit quality
    1) fixed-charge coverage (EBT/fixed interest charges)
    2) level of long-term debt to equity (debt-equity ratio)
    3) liquidity position
    4) size and competitive position of company
  - bond ratings are <u>not</u> a "science," but they also include "art" (subjective factors)

There are essentially four fundamental financial factors that can be used in assessing the credit quality of corporations. The level and trend of fixed-charge coverage, (which is the ratio of earnings available to pay interest to fixed charges), is perhaps the prime measure of credit quality. In stable industries, an earnings coverage of two or more times interest charges may be regarded as adequate, whereas in industries subject to wide fluctuations in earnings a coverage of three, four, or more times may be a good score. In industries sensitive to the business cycle, coverage of fixed charges under recession conditions is the significant ratio.

The second factor is the level of long-term debt in relation to equity, with debt measured by the amount shown on the balance sheet and the amount represented by off-balanced-sheet obligations, such as lease obligations. An analysis of the corporation's capital structure is in a sense a measure of asset coverage, which supplements the measure of earnings coverage. A higher debt to equity ratio is more appropriate for companies in stable industries than for those operating in industries more exposed to the cyclicality of the economy.

Liquidity position, current and prospective, is the next financial factor to consider in evaluating credit quality. Some companies may appear to have satisfactory earnings and capital, yet the holders of their bonds or preferred stocks may not be sure that enough cash will be on hand to pay debts when they become due. Finally, the size and competitive position of the company within its industry is important in assessing credit quality. Generally, there is a good reason to have greater confidence in long-term continuity of companies that are of substantial size and competitive leaders in their industry. Although size alone does not guarantee a profitable level of operations, seasoned firms that are dominant in their industry naturally tend to be better able to withstand adversity. This assumes that companies are not crazed with market share or competitive advantage, but instead they are run by ethical managers whose objective is to maximize the wealth of the owners and all other stake holders are considered in an appropriate manner.

Naturally, there is a cyclical pattern to the quality of bond issued. This is evidenced by the average risk premium which fluctuates over time with the cyclical fluctuation in the economy. Risk premiums widen during troughs in the economic cycle and narrow during peaks in the economic cycle. This appears reasonable given that firms are less able to maintain desired ratio minimums during economic downturns and the risk of bankruptcy increases. Hence, a portfolio manager needs to scrutinize bond holdings for increased default risk, in particular, during recessions.

Bond Yields
- Bonds, unlike stocks, are typically purchased on yield and not price in dollars and cents
- Bond yields
    - current or simple yield

        yield = I/P

    - approximate yield

$$\text{yield} = \frac{I + \dfrac{P_o - P_n}{n}}{\dfrac{P_o + P_n}{2}}$$

    - compound or true yield

        solve for r in the following equation: $P = \sum_{t=1}^{n} \dfrac{I_t}{(1+r)^t} + \dfrac{P_n}{(1+r)^n}$

    - solving for r in the compound or true yield formula is like an internal rate of return calculation in capital budgeting
    - horizon or call yield, when the time in the above formulas is not n but either the expected holding period (horizon) or the time to the first or next call date of the bond

Yields are like the price of a stock, investors normally purchase a bond based on yield not price. Obviously, yields are based on the perceived riskiness of the debt instrument given the state of the economy and business cycle. As can be seen from the formulas above current yield is the easiest one to calculate and compound the most difficult. If the bond is selling at par all yield calculations result in the same answer, and as the price varies from par the differences between the yields increase. Compound yield provides the best information since it accounts for time value and when the flows occur. For bonds selling at a small discount or premium, it is generally not worth the cost to calculate the approximate or compound yield. However, it should be recognized that with technology today there is little or no cost associated with calculating yields. Therefore, it is appropriate to calculate the true yield. Once again it should be noted, Excel has models for these calculations and data is available on the Internet (see Appendix A for sources).

Calculating yield to call (c) or horizon yield (h) is simply substituting a 'c' or a 'h' for the 'n' in the formulas above. What is being changed is the time element and the price of the bond at the end of the time period. When using n in the formulas as presented above it represents the time to maturity and the value at maturity. When using c it is the call price (typically larger then the maturity value), and the time period is to the call date, which is less than maturity. For the horizon time frame, which would be less than the time to maturity, both the time 'h', and the value will have to be estimated since the indenture agreement is not involved. Instead it is dependent on the investor regarding the time period and the anticipated market conditions for forecasting the price. Obviously, the current yield is the same regardless of the time frame.

Fundamental Sources of Risk

- Four fundamental sources of risk: interest rate risk, purchasing power risk, business risk, and financial risk
- Historical relationships are helpful in assessing the extent to which these factors affect the risk and return in the future
- Interest rate risk
  - variability in return caused by changes in level of interest rates
  - part of market rate that affects all securities
  - an element of systematic risk associated with debt instruments
- Purchasing power risk
  - inflation and the expectation of inflation in the future
  - only way to adjust yield in fixed income securities is the price of the security, inverse relationship (see bond pricing theorems presented previously)
  - an element of systematic risk associated with debt instruments
- Business risk
  - uncertainty of income flows caused by the nature of a firm's business
  - generally divided into two categories: internal and external
    o internal, associated with operating conditions that can be managed with the firm (e.g., amount of fixed costs (operating leverage), business and/or services offered and the mix thereof)
    o external, associated with operating conditions imposed on the firm by circumstances beyond its control (e.g., competitor actions, government regulations and general economic conditions under which the firm is operating)
  - higher the quality of the firm the lower the premium for business risk
  - higher the quality of the earning the lower the premium for business risk
- Financial risk
  - arises from the introduction of debt into the capital structure (financial leverage)
  - increased variability of earnings compounds uncertainty of meeting obligations
  - dependent on economic conditions and industry the firm operates in
  - the level and strength of the earnings (cash flow) stream
  - the higher the quality of the firm the lower the premium for financial risk
- Exposure to Risk Components
  - summed ratings across risk categories provide an aggregate measure of riskiness of individual bond classes
  - risk and return are generally aligned over longer periods; however, performance for individual bond categories can vary considerably over shorter periods
  - the structure of the investment/portfolio, from maturity-concentrated to barbell, impacts the amount of risk undertaken
  - various strategies can be undertaken based on the forecasting ability, and the basic sources of risk involved

Besides the positioning of a bond investment in maturity-concentrated, laddered and barbell structures several bond portfolio techniques are available to address risk. Four popular strategies include the following: 1) passive portfolio strategy of buy and hold and/or indexing, 2) active management with interest rate anticipation, valuation analysis, credit analysis, or yield spread analysis, 3) matching fund strategy with pure immunization and horizon matching, and 4) contingent procedure which uses contingent immunization. The most advisable strategy to undertake will be based on forecasting ability. If one is **not** a good forecaster one should not attempt to identify sources of risk and employ a strategy to address it. Instead, the investor should follow a passive strategy. If forecasting ability exists, employing more active strategies are advisable. For example, if one is forecasting a decrease in interest rates due to decreasing inflation or a slowing economy undertaking an interest rate swap by moving from lower duration to a higher duration portfolio would be advisable. If the credit analysis shows a change in the firm or industry one should undertake an appropriate strategy following the logic of bond valuation theorems or duration principals. Additional bond strategies and term structure implications are presented in Chapter 10.

Summary

- Theory of valuation models provides for a greater understanding of fundamental sources of risk which affect the risk-return relationship of bonds
- Risk-return characteristics of Treasuries, corporates and municipals (munis) differ and vary over time, as do their relationships to each other
- Understanding risk-return characteristics of securities is critically important for generating optimal investments
  - knowledge of the bond pricing theorems is fundamental
  - knowledge of duration concepts and relationships are essential

In this chapter, we presented the fundamentals of valuating debt instruments. While the focus is on bonds, which implies longer term, the same considerations apply to shorter term debt instruments. Moreover, the market place is constantly presenting more and varied debt instruments. Debt in various forms from credit cards to home mortgages along with standard fixed income securities like Treasuries are being packaged together and then sliced and diced into various tranches and sold to investors globally. As they are sliced and diced they become more difficult to understand and evaluate. However, the basic principals of cash flows, risk levels, and time value apply to all of them – assuming one can identify the flows and risk associated thereof. Unfortunately in the pragmatic world behavioral aspects get involved and greed takes over and then, sooner or later, fear follows. One of the more recent instances of this is the housing bubble followed by the "subprime crisis" that occurred in 2007 – 2008.

CHAPTER 3
THOUGHT QUESTIONS

1. Describe the underlying model that is used in the valuation of bonds, and tell how the model is useful in providing perspective on the way bonds respond to variations in interest rates and credit risk.

2. Discuss the concepts of duration and immunization. Relate the concepts to interest rate risk, valuation models, and how they are used in practical bond analysis.

Questions and Problems

1. Assume there is a bond paying an $80 coupon with a term to maturity of three years. Calculate the yield to maturity when the bond sells at (a) par, (b) $800, (c) $1100.
2. Determine the duration for the following securities
   a. a bond due to $1200 (interest and principal) at the end of four years and selling at $900
   b. a bond paying a $100 coupon selling at $800 and having a maturity value of $1000 in four years
   c. a "mortgage" type security selling for $1000, and making level payments of $500 per annum over a life of four years
   d. a preferred stock selling at $560 and paying a dividend of $4 per share
3. Determine the approximate price change using modified duration for each of the securities in the preceding problem associated with a +10 basis point change in the YTM.
4. Explain the key differences between terms in each of the following sets:
   a. nominal rate, real rate of return
   b. yield to maturity, coupon rate
   c. duration, term to maturity
   d. discount, premium
   e. inflation premium, risk premium
5. Identify the major types of bonds and the differences between them.
6. What does duration measure? Identify three basic relationships of duration.
7. A 9 year bond has a yield of 10% and a duration of 7.194 years. If the market yield changes by +50 basis points, what is the approximate change in the price of the bond?
8. Why does modified duration (d*) not provide the exact percentage change if bond price for a given change in the yield to maturity? What factors impact the difference between the estimated price change and the actual price change?
9. Identify some basic strategies used by bond portfolio mangers, and relate the strategies to interest rate forecasts.
10. Why does the "reinvestment risk" not apply to present value?
11. What does immunization mean?
12. Identify the credit quality determinant used in the development of bond ratings? What risk(s) does a bond rating try to identify/measure?
13. Identify the fundamental sources of risk.

Bond Analysis/Valuation

Bond_____   Exchange_____   Current Position_____

Maturity Date: _____
Valuation Model Equation:

Financial Variable Values:

r = _____   I = _____   M = _____   n = _____

Valuation Result (*intrinsic value*): = _____

Expected Yield: _____   Does it meet yield requirement?   Yes   No

Current Market Price: P = _____

Duration of Bond: d =   d* =

Current Status of Bond: Overvalued _____   Undervalued_____ Fair value _____

Analysis of Investment Potential:
(include sensitivity analysis)

Investment Action: BUY   SELL   NO ACTION

Rationale for Investment Action:

Chapter 4: Equity Valuation and Risk Analysis

CHAPTER OVERVIEW

This chapter presents the underlying theory of equity valuation models, and how these models can be, and are, applied to solve practical problems of stock evaluation. It is crucial to ensure that the inputs to the models are developed as carefully as possible. A set of principals is illustrated that analysts typically use to develop inputs for equity valuation models. Next, we explore capital market theory which allows for an exploration of the performance of security prices, risk-return relationships and an appropriate index of risk. The capital asset pricing model [CAPM] is presented and used to illustrate a 'practical' method for analyzing the structure and important characteristics of investments and how one can identify investment candidates. Assumptions needed are presented along with uses and limitations. We then describe and exemplify a framework for considering risk and return simultaneously, which is linked to the CAPM. Throughout the chapter the practical problems of developing reliable inputs and using various models are noted. It is important to keep in mind that we are dealing with the future, therefore, the valuation models presented do not provide "answers *per se.*" Instead, they provide information and insight for the investor to make better investment decisions.

Introduction
- Underlying theory of equity valuation models is presented, and the need for specialization is recognized
- Inputs to models are critical, and there is more uncertainty with equity inputs than there was with debt securities
- Risk-return relation can be linked to the CAPM/APT models
- Equity valuation models provide information and insight
- Valuation models typically do not consider behavioral considerations

Equity valuation models are typically built on assumptions that investors are rational and that value is derived from future cash flows discounted back to the present given the expected risk. As with all theoretical developments we need to keep in mind the assumptions and that the models provide information and not answers. Equity models generally have no 'known' inputs, even the next dividend is subject to approval by the board of directors. One must be careful to avoid circular reasoning when using various models as estimates for required return or other variables. Many Internet sources also provide information that can be used to estimate the value of a stock (see Appendix A).

Stock Valuation Models
- More challenging than bonds, since flows and time horizon are not as well defined
- Fundamental determinant of stock value is cash/dividend flow
- Price, or value, is a function of projected dividends to be paid at some future time, and the risk thereof

- The dividend policy of a firm can be a signaling mechanism about future investment opportunities and/or growth rate of the firm
- Dividend Discount Model(s) [DDM] is the starting point for equity valuation

The intrinsic value of a stock is the discounted future dividend stream. The discount rate is based on the perceived risk of future cash flows. If the firm does not pay dividends, earnings or free cash flow is generally used and the discount rate is adjusted accordingly. Furthermore, dividends are a function of earnings, and it should be recognized that sometimes a company pays dividends even though the reported earnings are negative because dividends are from the cash account while earnings are a bookkeeping/accounting number. Earnings, as defined by the DuPont method,[1] are a function of net margin, asset turnover, and leverage. By analyzing each of the three elements an analyst can determine the sources of a company's return and compare it to others in the industry/sector. The margin and turnover are a function of sales, which is generally affected by national and global economic conditions. Thus, economic conditions can affect the intrinsic value of a stock. Additionally, economic factors such as inflation, risk-free rates of return, taxes, and fiscal policy impact required return and the cost of goods and services which in turn impact the value of a firm. For a firm to be successful and to be considered a viable investment candidate having a positive margin is of paramount importance. Margins are the key to generating a positive profit and eventually a dividend stream.[2] One needs to be careful of investing in firms that seem to fail to recognize that the objective of a firm is to maximize the wealth of the shareholders and instead have their primary goal as market share (e.g., firms like GM and Chrysler). Maximizing the wealth of the shareholder is a long term concept which addresses and includes fairness to all stakeholders.

Because dividends are a base for equity valuation models a firm's dividend policy provides useful information. Having a steady dividend, with slow growth is one of the best dividend policies for a firm – it provides stability for equity evaluation. Having a variable dividend policy creates uncertainty for evaluation purposes and generally leads to lower valuations due to perceived increase in risk. A firm that pays no dividends or has a low dividend payout ratio is one characteristic of a growth company, while a firm with higher dividends can be classified as a value company. Let us now turn our attention to dividend discount models.

- Dividend capitalization model
  - general model: price (P) equals all future dividends (D) growing at the rate of (g) discounted to present value by the appropriate discount rate (r)

$$P_0 = \frac{D_o(1+g)^n}{1+r} + \frac{D_o(1+g)^2}{(1+r)^2} + \ldots + \frac{D_o(1+g)^n}{(1+r)^n}$$

---

[1] DuPont method/equation : ROE = (Profit margin)*(Asset turnover)*(Equity multiplier) = (net profit/sales)* (Sales/Assets)*(Assets/Equity) = (net profit/Equity) or return on equity [ROE]

[2] For more information about margin and the impact it has on a firm see *The Power of Positive Profit* by Graham Forster, 2007, John Wiley and Sons.

- simplified version (DDM model):
  o assume constant growth, time goes to infinity, and the discount rate greater than growth rate
  o value of stock is equal to its year-ahead forecasted dividend per share capitalized by the difference between the company's required return (r) and its constant growth rate (g)

$$P_0 = \frac{D_1}{r - g}$$

- the graph below presents a pictorial representation of the DDM model, the growth rate g is a steady state growth rate (g_s)

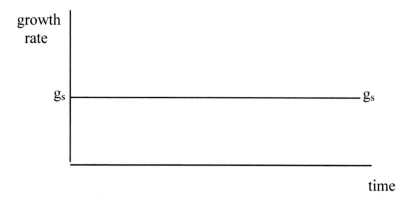

Simplifying assumptions impacts the usefulness of the information gained from the DDM. The assumption that time goes to infinity is reasonable because most firms are ongoing concerns. The assumption that dividends grow at a constant rate forever is not a realistic assumption for many companies, but it does simplify the math. The last assumption that the discount rate r is greater than the growth rate g is realistic for most firms. Additionally, estimates of the required return for a firm generally recognize the expected growth rate of the firm.

Due to the assumptions using DDM may lead to over- or undervaluation of a stock. The usefulness of the simplified DDM depends on the life cycle of the firm. For example, in the early years of a company's life the growth rate may be greater than the long term required return, and if g > r the simplified DDM does not provide meaningful results. Furthermore, it is unlikely that a high growth rate will continue indefinitely, requiring several stages to the discount model. For these types of situations a multi-stage model is necessary to overcome the deficiencies of the simplified DDM. Multi-stage models are presented later in this chapter and in the next chapter. However, if a company is in the stable or mature phase of its life cycle the simplified DDM is an excellent match.

If the model value does not come close to the market price it means that the investor or analyst should do a sensitivity analysis to help in placing a value on the stock. One can do a sensitivity analysis by determining what the variables would have to be to arrive at the market price. For example, an investor, Henry, is trying to determine the value of Anna's Deli and estimates that the required return is 4.7%, growth is 3%, and the current dividend is $1.00 per share. Using the DDM the estimated value would be:

$$P_o = \frac{D_1}{r-g} = \frac{1.0(1+.03)}{(.047-.03)} = \frac{1.03}{.017} \approx \$60.59$$

If the current market price is \$51.50 the stock could be a potentially nice investment. However, before considering the purchase Henry should determine what the numbers would have to be to arrive at a price/value of \$51.50. Let us assume Henry feels good about the current dividend of \$1.00 and growth has been 3% over the past 5 years, but he is less certain of the 4.7% risk factor. What would r have to be to generate a value of \$51.50, or what would (r-g) have to be so when it is divided into 1.03 you get \$51.50:

$$\$51.50 = \frac{1.03}{(r-g)}$$

$$(r-g) = \frac{1.03}{51.50} = .02$$

If (r-g) = .02 and g = .03, then r = .05, or 5%. The question now becomes: is the market estimate of risk correct, or does Henry know something the market has missed that reduces the risk of Anna's Deli? If Henry cannot identify what the market has missed regarding risk he should think long and hard before purchasing the stock. The above also shows how sensitive the model is to slight variations in the input variables. This is true for all valuation models, and one must take upmost care in determining inputs – remember the GIGO convention, Garbage In Garbage Out.

Stock Value and Differing Model Inputs
- Price/earnings (P/E) ratio model
  - a simplification of the DDM
  - assume that g = br', where b = the retention rate and r' = management's expected return; this g is commonly referred to as the sustainable (internal, implied, or normalized) growth rate
  - D_1 = E(1-b), where E = earnings at t = 1
  - assume that the expected return by management is equal to the required return by the investor, or r' = r
  - an estimate of r can be ROE – the return on equity
  - plugging the above into the DDM and simplifying results in the following:
    $$P = \left[\frac{P}{E}\right](E)$$
  - or price is equal to the (P/E) ratio times earnings, which is known as the P/E multiplier model
- The (P/E) model is a function of return on retained earnings and the discount rate
- Price/earnings ratio and the discount rate
  - appropriate indicator of discount rate is the inverse, or the E/P ratio
    - o builds on the DDM, with g = br where b = the retention rate
    - o company can only invest retained earnings at the discount rate
  - no differing growth opportunities, otherwise need to recognize the various growths

- Other multiplier models

  - $P = \left[\dfrac{P}{B}\right](B)$ where B = book value

  - $P = \left[\dfrac{P}{S}\right](S)$ where S = sales

  - $P = \left[\dfrac{P}{CF}\right](CF)$ where CF = cash flow

As noted previously the inputs determine the output and how useful the information is to the investor. To estimate sustainable growth, g, one can use ROE*b, or

$$g = ROE * (1 - \frac{D}{NI})$$

where
  ROE = return on equity
  D = dividend
  NI = net income

If ROE does not make sense, or generate a reasonable growth rate consider using ROC, return on capital, where

$$ROC = \frac{EBIT}{TC} = \frac{EBIT}{Debt + Equity}$$

where
  EBIT = earnings before interest and taxes
  TC = total capital

One needs to think about how reasonable the numbers are compared to others. Additionally one needs to avoid circular reasoning. If your "value" is greatly different than the market price, explain why and/or use sensitivity analysis to identify why and then consider which numbers are "better" before making an investment decision.

The price earnings multiplier model is a simplified form of the DDM. Due to its simplicity and ease of use, it is used extensively in pragmatic settings to get a quick estimate of value. It is important to recognize that the (P/E) ratio is a single number and not two numbers. For example, for company KJR a reasonable estimate for the P/E is 13, and expected earnings are $1.20 so a logical price estimate is $15.60 [P = (P/E)(E) = (13)(1.20) = 15.60]. After the establishment of the P/E model, other multiplier models were developed. Regardless of the variable used, (i.e., earnings, book value, sales, or cash flow) the model only provides an estimate of value. In Chapter 5, we expand on these concepts.

- Estimating the discount rate
  - estimate market conditions as a whole
  - build forecast by recognizing inflation rate and real return
  - estimate the riskiness of the firm
  - useful for stable companies, need to modify for others
- Dividend Capitalization Model: simplified form

- discount rate is a function of expected dividend yield [D/P] plus growth rate of dividend [g]: solve DDM for 'r'

$$r = \frac{D}{P} + g$$

Three factors that must be estimated for any valuation model are the cash flows, the discount rate and the holding period (or time horizon). For many debt securities these values are generally fixed. Generally, cash flows and time horizon are embedded in the bond and a reasonable estimate of the discount rate is the current market rate for the risk class the bond would fall into. However, for equity securities these items are more challenging to estimate. Cash flows are a function of the companies' sales and expenses which are in turn a function of the sector, industry, and economy. These and other factors make the discount rate more challenging to calculate due to the difficulty in assessing the riskiness of the cash flows. Moreover, the investor has to be aware of the objective of the firm and the behavior of the top management and the Board of Directors. For example, does the CEO still receive a bonus when the firm is losing money and/or eliminating thousands of jobs? Is top management working for themselves or for the owners, namely the shareholders and other stakeholders?

After estimating cash flows, growth, and the discount rate the models presented above represent valid ways to estimate equity value. The DDM and multiplier models provide a systematic way to estimate equity value. However, one has to be aware of the underlying assumptions and determine if the model fits the company (e.g., if the firm is in the stable/mature stage the DDM is an excellent model to use).

- Cyclical companies
  - Graham and Dodd: basic process is to adjust earnings of a company to what they would be at the midpoint of economic cycle
  - given a normalized rate of return "r" and a normal retention rate "b," a sustainable growth rate g for normalized earnings per share will be g = br

Cyclical companies and young companies pose a similar challenge – how to estimate reasonable earning streams, dividends, and growth rates? Graham and Dodd presented a method for valuing cyclical companies by normalizing flows and growth rates to provide good estimates of long term value. Normalizing flows and growth rates implies taking an average or midpoint that the variables exhibit over a life cycle. Using rates at the high point or trough of a cycle would provide misleading information. Typically, one can see how the numbers varied over a previous cycle or cycles. The next step is to adjust for expectations about the current or upcoming cycle and make estimates for earning and other variables. Similar to the process for cyclical companies, an investor can make estimates for a new company by comparing the new company to older more established firms. To estimate price one puts the estimated numbers into the valuation models.

Growth Stocks and the Two-Stage Growth Model
- High growth companies or companies in the first two stages of their life cycle
- Model presupposes that growth is at one rate associated with supernormal growth (g_h) for a certain number of periods (say n periods), and then growth is at a steady state rate in line with the general corporate average from then on (g_s)

- Valuating a Growth Stock
  - higher growth leads to higher prices (P_o)
  - the longer the high growth rate the higher the value
  - industrial life cycle or firm life cycle: first two stages characteristically have higher growth rates than the stable/mature stage
  - after time n there is a step-function to the steady state growth rate (g_s)
- Two-stage growth model:

$$P = \sum_{t=1}^{n} \frac{D(1+g_h)^t}{(1+r)^t} + \frac{\dfrac{D_n(1+g_s)}{(r-g_s)}}{(1+r)^n}$$

- The graph below presents a pictorial representation of the two-stage growth model

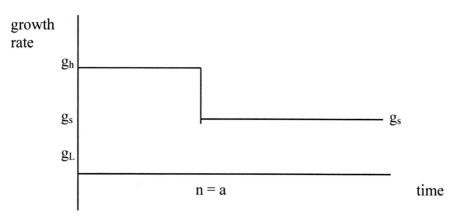

The mathematical formula of the two-stage model includes two terms: the first term represents the value during the high growth period and the second term is the value for the long term steady growth. The first term is the extraordinary growth (g_h) for n periods. The numerator of the second term is simply the long term value as measured by the DDM model. This long term value (P_N) at time N is then brought to present value. For example: Testsoup Inc., a new Internet company that helps people prepare for tests such as the SAT and GMAT, is expected to have a supernormal growth rate of 25% for five years (n = 5) and then decline to a steady state growth of 8%. The risk factor for Testsoup is 12%, and the dividend is $1.00. To estimate the value of the firm first determine the dividends for years 1 through 5 and then discount them back to present value to determine the value of the high growth period.

t	Dividend	Present Value
1	$ 1.25	$ 1.12
2	$ 1.56	$ 1.25
3	$ 1.95	$ 1.39
4	$ 2.44	$ 1.55
5	$ 3.05	$ 1.73

Total present value $ 7.04

Next, we need to determine the value of the firm at n, or t = 5, for steady growth:

$P_5 = D_5(1 + . g_s)/ (r-g_s) = 3.05(1 + .08)/(0.12 - 0.08) = \$82.40$
the present value is $= [82.40/(1 + 0.12)^5] = \$ 46.75$

Adding the present values of the high growth stage to the steady state value we determine the estimate price for Testsoup:

$$P_0 = \$\ 7.04 + \$\ 46.75 = \$\ 53.79$$

Without the high growth, and assuming the steady growth is 8%, the current price of Testsoup would be $ 31.25. So the five years of supernormal growth adds $ 22.54 to the value of the firm.

An increase in a firm's growth rate does not necessarily always mean an increase in intrinsic value. What matters is the spread between the growth rate and the required return. If an increased growth rate brings with it increased risk (thus raising the required return), then it is possible for the firm to remain at a constant value, or even have a lower intrinsic value. It should be noted that the two-stage model can be used for firms that are undergoing recovery or reorganization and expect a slower growth rate (g_L) for a period of time before returning to their steady state growth rate. We now turn our attention to capital market theory and the capital asset pricing model.

Capital Market Theory and the Capital Asset Pricing Model

- Allows for an exploration of the performance of security prices, risk-return relationships and an appropriate index of risk
- The CAPM was first known as the SML (security market line)
- The CAPM is the primary model for capital market theory [CMT]
- CAPM is a general equilibrium model with pricing implications
- Capital market theory is *positive*
- With the CAPM one can identify "good investment candidates"

Capital market theory allows for an exploration of the performance of security prices, risk-return relationships, and an appropriate index of risk. Total risk, as measured by the standard deviation, is essentially composed of two components: systematic risk and diversifiable risk. In a theoretical framework, because systematic risk is the only type of risk for which investors are rewarded, using standard deviation for individual investments is using an "inappropriate" measure of risk. The standard deviation is the appropriate measure for well-diversified portfolios. Capital market theory asserts that systematic risk is the non-diversifiable market risk component of the total risk. The theory supposes that because the unsystematic risk of a portfolio or security can be diversified away it is not relevant. Therefore, for a security the expected return is related only to the systematic risk. The focus on a single risk factor (namely systematic, non-diversifiable or market risk) leads to the security market line [SML] that became the capital asset pricing model [CAPM] once pricing implications were identified.

A portfolio manager should consequently focus on the market risk of a security or portfolio in which they invest. The CAPM is a general equilibrium model with pricing implications, and is the primary model for capital market theory. We now turn our attention to the single index model and the development of the CAPM.

The Development of the Capital Asset Pricing Model

- Total risk is comprised of two major components:
  (1) systematic or non-diversifiable risk (market related component)
  (2) unsystematic or diversifiable risk (specific risk component)
- In a well-diversified portfolio unsystematic risk should approach zero, which in turn implies returns are based on only one risk factor – namely the market
- The SML/CAPM is a simple linear regression of a security or portfolio return (R_j) against market return (R_m) as the independent variable to generate the characteristic line (see figure below – left side)
- Beta (β) the slope of characteristic line, measures responsiveness of the security or portfolio to market $(\Delta R_j/\Delta R_m)$
- Intercept of regression line (W) measures return of security or portfolio when market return is zero

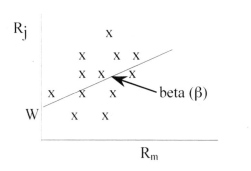

Characteristic Line   Security Market Line

- The slope of the characteristic line is the risk index (β) of the SML/CAPM
- After calculating β for many securities one could plot expected return and beta to derive the Security Market Line [SML] (see figure above, right side). The SML is better known as the CAPM and is represented by the following equation:

  $R_s = R_f + \beta_s(R_m - R_f)$

  where R_s is the return of a security or portfolio,
  R_f is the risk-free rate (also known as the price of time),
  β_s is the index of systematic risk, and
  R_m is the market return.
- Measuring risk and return with the CAPM
  - return is combination of two components
    - specific return component represented by the intercept, or when beta is zero (R_f)
    - market return component represented by product of beta and market return above the specific return $[\beta_s(R_m - R_f)]$
  - risk is represented by beta or beta can be considered the "price of risk"
  - in equilibrium all securities and portfolios should lie on the CAPM (theory concept)
  - securities not on the CAPM have pricing implications

The CAPM can be described as a model of stock returns that decomposes influences on returns into a systematic factor, as measured by the return on a broad market index, and firm specific factors. The model is constructed by plotting the security (or portfolio) return against the return on the market (Characteristic Line). Using simple linear regression we are able to measure the responsiveness of the security (or portfolio) to the market. Beta (β) is the slope of the regression line and serves as an index of systematic risk. Then we can create a plot of returns for various securities against systematic risk, and obtain the SML, better known as the CAPM. In equilibrium, all securities and portfolios lie on the SML; however, in the pragmatic world this is subject to question and raised pricing implications. Recognizing this pricing implication lead to the development of the capital asset pricing model.

Capital Asset Pricing Model [CAPM]

- CAPM specifies relationship between expected return and risk for all investments
- Expected return of a security in excess of the risk-free rate is proportional to systematic risk associated with the investment
- Measurement of risk is the systemic risk – Beta (β)
- Risk-return relationship (see figure below)
  - in equilibrium all investments should plot "on" the CAPM
  - $\beta > 1$, aggressive securities [A*] expected to earn above average returns
  - $\beta < 1$, defensive securities [D*] expected to earn below average returns
  - $\beta = 1$, market return or average return

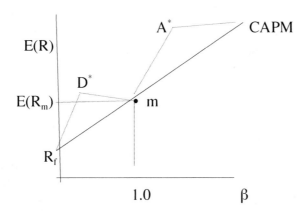

Securities having a beta greater than one are considered aggressive and would plot (see figure above) on the upper portion of the CAPM (A*). Those securities having betas less than one would be classified as defensive and plot on the lower portion of the CAPM (D*).

- Undervalued and overvalued securities
  - assuming that the risk estimate, beta, is correct, if a security does not plot on the CAPM there are pricing implications (see figure below)
    - stocks plotting above the line presumably are undervalued
    - stocks plotting below the line presumably are overvalued
  - practical implications include
    - identifying undervalued or overvalued stocks
      - 'U' is an undervalued security
      - 'O' is an overvalued security
    - the distance off the line is know as alpha [α]

- above the line is a positive alpha stock [+α]
- below the line is a negative alpha stock [-α]
• a portfolio of positive alpha stocks (above the CAPM line) should provide superior performance

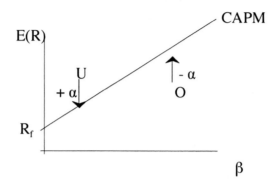

The equation of the CAPM can be described as $R_s = R_f + \beta_s(R_m - R_f)$, where R_s is the security (or portfolio) return, R_f is the risk-free rate (also known as the price of time), β_s is the index of systematic risk, and R_m is the market return. In equilibrium, all securities should plot on the CAPM. In reality though, few securities actually lie on the CAPM; hence, questions about the risk-return relationship arise. Assuming that risk estimate, β, is correct, stocks plotting off the line indicate mispricing in the market due to: 1) transaction costs, 2) taxes, and/or 3) imperfect information. To address this situation, the concept of alpha [α], which measures the difference in return for that security when compared to the return as described by the CAPM, was introduced. α measures the excess or deficiency of return. On the graph above, securities with positive α lie above the CAPM and are undervalued (U), while securities with negative α lie below it and are overvalued (O). If the security is undervalued, U, the price needs to increase so the return would decrease and the security would then plot on the line. On the other hand, if the security is overvalued, O, the price needs to fall in order for the security to plot on the line. Securities plotting above the line are considered candidates for a "long investment" in a portfolio while securities below the line are considered candidates for a "short sale" in a portfolio setting. While this is a theoretical model and behavioral aspects are not included it is an excellent model for investing and building portfolios. In fact, it gives rise to three possible strategies for creating portfolios:

1. buy securities with positive α, which represent a return greater than the expected return for the risk undertaken
2. short securities with negative α, which represent a return lower than the expected return for the risk undertaken
3. combine strategies 1 and 2

The development of the CAPM requires a series of assumptions. One needs to be aware of these assumptions when applying the model in pragmatic settings. Even though assumptions are needed, which simplify the pragmatic world, the CAPM provides a solid foundation for investing and developing portfolios in the pragmatic world. Let us now briefly turn our attention to the assumptions and implications.

Assumptions and Implications
- Assumptions include:
  - investors are risk-averse
  - investors maximize expected utility
  - investors choose portfolios on the basis of expected mean and variance of return
  - investors have a single period time horizon (same for all investors)
  - unrestricted borrowing and lending at R_f
  - investor expectations regarding means, variances, and covariances of security returns are homogenous (homogeneous expectations)
  - no taxes
  - no market imperfections, including no fees or transaction costs
- Implications: CAPM provides framework for expected risk-return relations in individual securities and portfolios

Capital market theory considers all investments: individual securities, asset classes, and portfolios. It is important to recognize the assumptions underlying CAPM, which provides a solid foundation for analyzing individual investments. A major implication is that the CAPM provides a positive theory for developing investment strategies and selecting securities to build portfolios. As always, it is necessary to recognize that finance models do not provide answers, rather they provide information so one can make better decisions.

The Market Line Technique
- Empirical counter part of the CAPM
- Provides:
  - a way of simultaneously considering risk and return
  - an explicit link between theory of valuation and valuation models and the more formal models of relationships between risk and return
  - a way to estimate required return, r, by solving the CAPM equation:

$$\text{Required return } (r) = r_f + \beta[E(r_m) - r_f]$$

- Uses of the market line include:
  - evaluate the overall attractiveness of market
  - assess the relationship between risk and return in equity market
  - evaluate the relative attractiveness of individual stocks
- Evaluation of individual securities
  - relative attractiveness of individual stocks
  - construct a portfolio of stocks that plot above the CAPM line (positive alpha securities)
  - however, the investor needs to recognize that the positive alpha could be actual mispricing or an error in risk and/or return estimates
  - the investor needs to remember the assumptions behind the model and that the results only provide useable information

An illustration of valuation using the CAPM methodology follows:

Stock price (31 December 2012)	$53.00
2013 estimated earnings	$ 4.25
2013 estimated book value	$ 25.00
Expected dividend	$ 0.40
Beta	1.10
Risk-free return	5.0%
High grade corporate bond yield	8.0%
Risk premium – stocks over bonds	4.0%

The expected return on the stock market is the bond yield plus the risk of premium of stocks over bonds: $E(r_m) = 8\% + 4\% = 12\%$

Next calculate ROE in order to find g. ROE is the estimated EPS divided by estimated book value:

ROE = EPS/Estimated book value = 4.25/25 = 17%
Dividend payout = .40/4.25 = .094

b = 1 - .094 = .906
g = b x ROE = .906 x 17% = 15.4% per year

The next calculations are to determine implied total return and the required return, and then to compare them to determine is the security is a possible investment candidate:

Implied total return = dividend yield + g
= .40/53 + .154 = .0075 + .154
= .162 or 16.2% per year

Required return = $r_f + \beta(E(r_m) - r_f) = 5\% + 1.1(12\% - 5\%) = 12.7\%$ per year

The implied total return exceeds the required return using the CAPM. This suggests that its stock is undervalued, has a positive alpha of 3.5 ($\alpha = 16.2 - 12.7 = 3.5$), and is an attractive investment. However, before investing one needs to consider portfolio implications.

Extra-Market Factor
- Consider that returns are not only based on the market, but that risk is multifaceted
- Return on a stock is a function of its sensitivity to two factors:
  - market factor
  - liquidity factor (log of the market capitalization of the company)
- Two factor stock valuation
  - recognize the relative attractiveness of individual stocks
  - factor pricing relationship

- extra factor can be based on many different elements (e.g., liquidity, industry, sector, et cetera)
- Expected return with liquidity (L) as the extra market factor:

$$E(r) = [r_f + \beta(E(r_m) - r_f)] + \beta_L E(R_L)$$

Using CAPM concepts and expanding to include an "extra-market" factor to estimate the required return links capital market theory to DDMs and other equity valuation models. In the equation above, the first portion is just the CAPM model and the second term represents an extra market factor that impacts the return of the security – in this case it is liquidity but it could also be an industry, sector, or some other relevant factor. The factor beta is calculated in a similar fashion as the beta of the CAPM. Basically, the slope of the regression line between return on the security and factor being used in the model. Using these techniques helps to evaluate and estimate the risk return relationship needed for solid estimates of value.

Summary
- Models from DDM to the CAPM are introduced, and one needs to be aware of the assumptions used to develop the models
- Recognizing assumptions allows the investor to use an appropriate model or models
- Practical problems of using valuation models to develop explicit returns for common stocks exist but can be addressed so models provide useful information
- Forecasting future flows and estimating risk are the keys to generating useful results from the models
- Importance of developing inputs that are well founded cannot be ignored
- The model and factors to incorporate need to be considered and should be appropriate for the security being valued
- Using more than one model provides additional useful information for the portfolio manager and investor
- Templates for constant growth and non-constant growth models are presented at the end of Chapter 5

This chapter presents the more traditional equity valuation models (e.g., DDM) and shows how they can be combined with capital market theory (the CAPM). Combining valuation methods can provide additional information. The best model(s) to use is dependent on assumptions, as well as the person employing them, and how they interpret and use the information. Generally speaking, the model should be appropriate for the firm being analyzed, and using more than one model can produce useful information. Inputs to the model drive the result, so accurate inputs are essential.

The constant growth DDM might be a better tool at valuing the stock market as a whole rather than an individual stock because DDM makes the assumption that growth is at an average rate. Individual companies' growth rates are more likely to vary from their estimates more than those for the markets as a whole. This is because in a large portfolio the deviations tend to cancel themselves out. Likewise, the dividend forecasts are likely to be better for the market as a whole than for individual companies. The same logic also applies to sectors of the market (e.g., consumer durables, financials, technology, energy, et cetera) or industries (e.g., mining, construction, manufacturing, retail trade, et cetera) or other extra market groupings (e.g., liquid, energy, cyclical, et cetera). Overall, with better input, the constant growth DDM provides a better output for the estimation of a fair value for the stock market as a whole or a sub-sector thereof. However, assuming solid inputs, the DDM provides useful information for individual firms, especially those in the stable phase of their life cycle. For new or high growth companies, the two-stage model will provide better information. The key is to make use of the information in a consistent manner, learn and slowly adjust your buy and sell criteria.

Information gleaned from the CAPM allow an investor to better understand financial markets and provide a solid foundation to build on and reference. CAPM provides a method to identify positive alpha securities as candidates for investing. Beta works better for well-diversified portfolios – similar in concept to the way DDM works better for the overall market or sector. Beta is also useful for individual securities as long as one does not get carried away with the accuracy of beta and try to use it as a "ratio number." The CAPM provides useful information for an investor.

CHAPTER 4
THOUGHT QUESTIONS

1. Discuss the underlying theory of equity valuation models and how these models have been applied to solve practical problems of stock valuation.

2. Discuss the CAPM and how the market line is constructed in practice and illustrate three major uses of the market line.

Questions and Problems:

1. The common stock of WHJ Corporation pays out 40% of its earnings as dividends, which are expected to be $3 at year-end. The return on retained earnings is 15%, and the required return on stock is 14%. Determine the P/E ratio.
2. A firm is earning $2 per share and pays out $0.80 in dividends. The required return is 16%, and the projected growth rate in dividends is 9%. Because of government actions inflation increases from 5% to 7%. Determine the change in stock price assuming (a) no ability to adjust for the increased inflation, and (b) a 75% adjustment to the change in inflation.
3. Determine the price for a company paying a $1 dividend that is expected to grow at a rate of 30% per annum for the next five years and then grow at a rate of 10% beyond that period. Assume a 16% required return for the stock.
4. Discuss the concept of "multiplier" models and why they are popular in the pragmatic world. Relate your answer to behavioral aspects.

5. What are the two major components of risk in the development of the capital asset pricing model [CAPM]. Under this theory what risk drives the return of the security? Do you agree with this concept? Why or why not?
6. Betsy estimated the following ex ante security market line:

$$R_s = 6\% + \beta_s \, (5\%)$$

   a. what is the estimated price of risk?
   b. what is the ex ante alpha for a stock with a beta of 1.1 and an expected return of 13%?
   c. would the stock be considered a defensive or an aggressive stock?
   d. what is the estimated return of the market (R_m)?
7. Discuss the simplifying assumptions that underlie the discounted cash dividends valuation models. Compare those assumptions to the assumptions used for the development of the CAPM. What problems, if any, may arise from using such simplifications?
8. What extra market factors do you think should possibility be included in a valuation model? How is the extra market factor beta calculated?

Chapter 5 Equity Valuation Models:
Modifications and Applications

CHAPTER OVERVIEW

We continue the discussion of valuing equity securities in this chapter. Desirable characteristics in valuation models that relate to practical applications are reviewed. Generalized approaches that have been developed to solve practical problems are discussed along with their strengths and deficiencies in applications. DDM based models can be used to develop better insights into understanding the riskiness of equities and to assess changes in the underlying risk. Throughout the chapter, both theory and pragmatic world considerations are discussed and related to investment management. As always, one should keep in the behavioral aspects when analyzing securities.

Introduction
- Continues the discussion of equity valuation models and builds on the DDM and capital market theory
- Valuation is important because of its perspective on risk, which is the prime focus of investing
- Developing return inputs is critical in investments and for adding value through stock selection, industry rotation, sector rotation, or tactical asset allocation
- Excel provides models and data can be obtained from Internet sources such as Value line and Morning Star

Equity valuation models provide information for investors so they can make better decisions. The models provide perspective on risk and value of individual securities. We need to keep in mind that in this section of the book we review valuation models that can be used to help identify candidates worthy of investment. However, before purchasing a security, one should evaluate the security from a portfolio perspective – does it help in diversification? Let us now turn our attention to criteria for model usefulness along with expansion and simplification of models that were introduced previously.

Valuation Models
- Provide a benchmark so investors can make comparisons
- Provide a systematic basis for objective evaluation of process and a means of improving the process over time
- Enhance analytical effort, making processing more consistent and allowing greater coordination of research effort
- Criteria to qualify as useful in practice
    - analytically valid (well developed and connected to notions of value)
    - simple and intuitively appealing
    - pragmatic world application – provide useful information to make better investment decisions

- not theoretically elegant and obtuse
- global in application, and across a wide universe of securities
- Degree of success of various techniques depends greatly on the quality of input to the models and the interpretation of the output
- Models deal with the future and therefore **do not** provide answers, they only provide information for the investor/portfolio manager to make more informed investment decisions

Valuation models are used to provide a benchmark for comparison, to provide a basis for objective evaluation, and to enhance the analytical effort to make the process more efficient. Thus, the important characteristics of a valuation model should be that they are analytically valid, simple and intuitive, yet applicable in the pragmatic world. The better the model, the more widely it can be applied, not just in different markets but also across different types of securities.

Theoretically elegant models can provide a sound basis for a better understanding of security valuation. While they simplify market and investors actions (with sometimes non-pragmatic assumptions) they nonetheless provide clear insights into actual valuation. However, it is advisable to note that the additional time it takes to build and run the model should be worth the marginal information made available. If the extra time and details involved in the use of the model does not yield any better information, than you are better off using the simplified version of the model and not the more "advanced" or "sophisticated" version(s) of the model. It is important to note that models cannot predict with complete certainty the true value of the security. A model can only point you in the right direction. Elegant and simple models do just that; they provide solutions that point in the right direction while being relatively simple and straightforward to understand.

A model should also be uncomplicated to use and should produce results that are easy for the end-user (average investor) to comprehend. For practical applications, the models need to produce results/information that is understood by all, not just financial gurus and/or finance professors. The information should translate into a clear path of action. Ideally, models should be a quick, easy, and objective process that produces a clear measure of the risk-return question. Additionally, the models should provide a systematic basis for objective evaluation of process and a means of improving the process over time.

Evolution of Systematic Security Valuation
- Graham and Dodd
  - pioneered the development of systematic methods of security valuation in the 1930s
  - relies on the examination of accounting statements in establishing an "intrinsic value" for the security which is then compared to the current market price
  - invest if a "margin of safety" exists (conservative orientation)
  - stood the test of time
  - concepts associated with Graham and Dodd philosophy
    o school of "value investing"
    o contrarian investing

      o   academic and qualitative research
- easily understood, broad degree of useful application
- weakness, inadequacy of accounting statements
- lacks usefulness across a complete universe of companies

The Graham and Dodd valuation method is an intuitively appealing and easily understood approach; although, it relies heavily on accounting data to reflect the value of an enterprise. It has found widespread applications, so it has a useful pragmatic world application. The major benefit of Graham and Dodd was the establishment of systematic methods. The weakness of Graham and Dodd is that the "answer" is dependent on the method used and it may not include all relevant factors. For example, if one uses the P/E ratio as a measure of worth it does not directly include various growth prospects. Current users of the Graham and Dodd philosophy of investing include Warren Buffet, Bill Miller, and many other portfolio managers. The margin of safety implies there is more upside potential than downside and the downside should be limited. If a two to one ratio of upside to downside is not available continue to look for investment candidates. The Graham Dodd approach does not work across the complete universe of companies.

- The dividend discount model [DDM]
    - based on discounting a stream of cash flows that can be compared to a cash outlay or price
    - it seems incontestable as a basis for valuation
    - explicit rate of return, which can be used as a basis of comparison: stocks and other investments
    - applicable across a wide universe of common stocks (best if in maturity stage)
    - implementation can be complex, and generating quality inputs is difficult
    - risk must be recognized; return should not be sole investment criterion
    - market line technique
        o uses dividend discount model as component, but also incorporates risk
        o integrates valuation methodology and capital market theory into a practical tool
        o criterion = alpha value, a risk-adjusted excess return above or below the line
        o alpha should not be sole criteria, instead one needs to recognize risk, that beta is not constant over time, and the theoretical assumptions behind the model

DDMs at some point invoke the assumptions of constant growth because it fits well with the life-cycle approach of a firm or industry. As a firm matures, it is likely to reach some stable and constant rate of growth from that time forward. The trick is to forecast when in the future constant growth will begin, or if the firm is already in the mature stage. At times, firms in the mature stage move into another growth phase due to new markets, new products, and/or new technology; and hence, the analyst needs to choose the correct model to employ. Assuming constants in the future is done as a matter of practicality, it would be virtually impossible to project varying cash flows (dividends) into perpetuity with any reasonable degree of accuracy. Yet forecasting for several, if not many, years in the future is precisely what must be done because stocks/companies have an ongoing or infinite life, thus the assumption is reasonable.

Three-Stage DDM Application

- Offers a "practical" means of implementing the DDM method of stock valuation when the simplifying assumptions do not hold
- Builds on the two-stage model introduced in Chapter 3 by recognizing changing growth over a period of time instead of all at once
- First stage [V_1]: year-by-year forecast of earnings of high growth period [time 0 to a], preferably incorporating an economic cycle
- Second stage [V_2]: transition period (time a to b) to reflect a natural tapering down of growth for a rapidly growing company to a more steady state growth rate
- Third stage [V_3]: maturity phase [time b to $+ \propto$] where companies are assumed to reach steady state of growth in line with overall economy or average of a broad market index, sector or industry
- In sum, the model has the following format:

$$P = V_1 + V_2 + V_3$$

$$P = \sum_{t=1}^{a} \frac{D(1+g_h)^t}{(1+r)^t} + \frac{\sum_{t=1}^{b} \frac{D_{(a+t)}}{(1+r)^t}}{(1+r)^a} + \frac{\frac{D_b(1+g_s)}{(r-g_s)}}{(1+r)^b}$$

- The graph below is a pictorial representation of the three-stage growth model with the tapered decrease from high growth (g_h) to steady state growth (g_s) during time 'a' to time 'b' (time of transition is 'a-b')

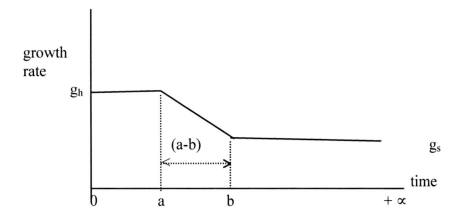

- Model is comprehensive, albeit with complexity, which reflects theoretical value
- Allows comparison, applies across a wide universe of stocks, including new and high growth companies
- Reflects life-cycle nature of firms
- Deficiencies of using the model range from complexity to large number of quality inputs far out into the future, which requires expertise
- Three stage model captures more and is used for practical applications
- Assumptions and forecasts are critical to reliability of results

When using the three-stage growth model, the analyst needs to estimate the growth rate and duration for stage 1 (the growth or pioneering phase). Next, the analyst needs to identify the period of time and characteristics therein for a firm to reposition from high growth to a the constant grow rate (length of and growth rates in transition phase). The last step is to estimate the constant growth rate itself and the discount rate. Generally, it is assumed that the discount rate is constant and reflects the overall risk of the firm. Typically, the two-stage and three-state models assume an initial higher growth rate; however, they also work for firms with a lower growth rate moving up to a steady state growth. Firms in this situation are moving from an adverse situation to a more "normal" situation – the adverse situation could be due to various reasons ranging from government regulation or policy to some sort of legal action or competition.

With the two-stage model Testsoup, Inc. went from a 25% supernormal growth rate to 8% in year 5, a step function. For the three-stage model the decline from 25% to 8% will take place over 4 years, or a = 5 and b = 9. For the first five years growth = g_h = 25%, and for the next four years growth will decrease by 4.25% each year so g_6 = 21.75%, g_7 = 16.50%, g_8 = 12.25% and g_9 = 8% the steady state growth rate.

Value of the high growth dividend stream:

t	g	Dividend	Present Value. R=12%
1	25%	$1.25	$1.12
2	25%	$1.56	$1.25
3	25%	$1.95	$1.39
4	25%	$2.44	$1.55
5	25%	$3.05	$1.73

or $V_1 = \$7.04$

Value of the transition period:

t	G	Dividend	Present Value. R=12%
6	21.75%	$3.68	$1.87
7	16.50%	$4.29	$1.94
8	12.25%	$4.82	$1.95
9	8.00%	$5.20	$1.88
h			or $V_2 = \$7.63$

Next we need to determine the value of the firm with a steady growth at t = 9:
$P_9 = D_9(1 + g_s)/(r-g_s) = 5.20(1 + .08)/(0.12 - 0.08) = \$140.52$
The present value is = $[140.52/(1 + .12)^9] = \$50.67 = V_3$

Adding the present values of the high growth stage to transition period to the steady state value we determine the estimate price for Testsoup:
$P_0 = V_1 + V_2 + V_3 = \$7.04 + \$7.63 + \$50.67 = \$65.34$

Having the decline occur over a four year period adds $ 11.25 to the estimated value of the company.

The three-stage model more accurately tracks a company's life cycle. Thus, the use of the three-stage model should provide a better estimate of the value of a company. An analyst derives the inputs for the models, whether he/she is doing the two- or three-stage model. Using a computer program such as an Excel model allows the more complex calculations of the three-stage model to be easily performed, and allows for sensitivity analysis. However, one needs to recognize that while the three-stage model is alleged to be "practical" it requires a lot of detailed and accurate forecasting over longer periods of time, which is not an easy task. Hence, one can ask how practical it really is in the pragmatic world. Fortunately, a lot of good data can be found on the Internet. The next model presented reduces the workload of the three-stage model while still maintaining the concepts and information gained.

H-Model
- Simplifies the basic three-stage DDM yet retains much of its power
- H-model
  - provides for a taper in the firms' above-average growth rate starting from t = 0
  - at H-years the growth rate is halfway between above-average rate and steady state growth rate
  - H is the midpoint of the tapered growth in the three-stage model, or the mid-point between a and b time period (see graph below)

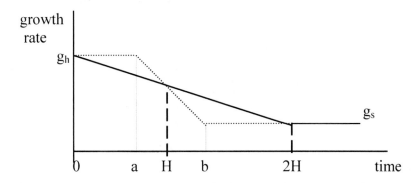

  - at 2H-years growth rate levels off at expected long-run steady state growth rate
  - the three-stage model reduces to the following:

$$P = \frac{D(1 + g_s)}{r - g_s} + \frac{DH(g_h - g_s)}{r - g_s}$$

or

$$P = \frac{D}{r - g_s}\left[(1 + g_s) + H(g_h - g_s)\right]$$

- Provides a way of directly measuring value of above average growth by incorporating a term to reflect the premium due to growth prospects
  - The first term is the steady state or normalized growth of the firm from time equal zero to plus infinity and is similar to the DDM

- The second term represents the value added by having high or super growth for a finite period of time
- The H-model allows for a direct solution of the discount rate

$$r = \frac{D}{P}\left[(1 + g_s) + H(g_h - g_s)\right] + g_s$$

- Results: value typically falls between two-stage and full three-stage model
  - the shorter the transition period the closer to the two-stage
  - the longer transition the closer to the three-stage
  - when the transition period approaches around 10 years the result is very close to the three-stage model
- Able to identify value due to different growth opportunities
- Limitations include: it is only an approximation, and inputs are still difficult to estimate/forecast

The H-model is a variation of the three-stage DDM and it simplifies the model structure, yet retains much of its power for deriving a value/price estimate and the expected return. The H-model requires fewer inputs than the three-stage DDM and it makes other inputs easier to develop. Because of this, the H-model makes it simpler to perform sensitivity analysis by making it more straightforward to change the input values. Furthermore, the H-model allows for some analytical insights which are not readily apparent from the more complex DDMs. Both the H-model and the three-stage model generate "similar" results, which makes for a good comparison.

Because the H-model is a simplification of the three-stage DDM, it only approximates the return. The three-stage DDM offers a practical, even if somewhat complicated, model for implementing the full DDM approach to stock valuation. Furthermore, the three-stage process incorporates growth rates relative to the typical life cycle of a successful corporation. While the full model is more complex than the H-model, it is still understandable. Moreover, the full model provides a fairly accurate estimation of the theoretical stock price and provides comparison across a variety of company types. Development of the model inputs can be a complicated task; however, it allows for conducting sensitivity analysis on the various inputs.

The three-stage dividend model requires estimating the growth rate of a company for, say the first 5 years, then reducing this high growth rate over a period of, say 4 years, before reaching the mature growth rate. The H-model begins with the high growth rate of the three-stage model, but then immediately begins a linear taper to the mature growth rate such that at H years the growth rate is halfway between the initial above average growth rate (g_h) and the steady state growth rate (g_s).

Applying the H Model to Testsoup, Inc.: a stock growing at 25% for 5 years, then declining to an average rate of 8% over a four year period, discount rate is 12%, dividend equals $1. Because of the short transition period (4 years), one would expect the price to be closer to the two-stage model (P = $53.79) than the three-stage model (P = $65.34).

Estimated price using the H model, where H = (5) + (4/2) = 7:

$$\text{Price} = \frac{D}{r - g_s}\left[(1 + g_s) + H(g_h - g_s)\right]$$

P= [1 / (.12-.08)] * [(1.08) + 7(.25 - .08)] = $56.75

Indeed, as expected, the price is closer to the two-stage model. The price can be divided into two portions: (1) value attributed to standard growth and (2) value attributed to superior growth.

Standard Growth: $\dfrac{D(1 + g_s)}{r - g_s} = \dfrac{1(1 + .08)}{.12 - .08} = 27.00$ or $27

Superior Growth: $\dfrac{DH(g_h - g_s)}{r - g_s} = \dfrac{(1)(7)(.25 - .08)}{.12 - .08} = 29.75$ or $29.75

If the high growth period was only three years and the taper period was also three years then H = 3 + 3/2 = 4.5 years. Using an H of 4.5 the price is $46.125 and the standard growth value of $27 does not change but the superior growth value decreases to $19.125. This shows how the H-model allows for sensitivity analysis. Holding all else constant, the longer the time period of high growth or the taper period the greater the value of the security.

When using the various dividend valuation models (DDM, two-stage, three-stage and H) one needs to be consistent with inputs for comparable results. The end of the high growth period needs to be same for each model (e.g., say, 5 years), the high growth rate needs to be the same as does the steady state growth rate. The same is true for the required return and the dividend. After having a base to judge from the variables can be modified and results can be analyzed to determine the impact of the change. For example the required return, r, is 12% in the base case, but you decide that if the growth models are more appropriate then DDM to use it means that there is more risk so you use a r=13%. With a standard base you can then determine what the higher risk does to the estimated value. Doing an sensitivity analysis is normally a good idea when forecasting, or estimating various inputs into models.

The H-model is also useful for evaluating the overall market. The portfolio manager can use the S&P500 for an estimate of price, use the S&P500 dividend yield to estimate dividend, and then estimate high growth and steady state growth rates for the overall economy. The model is then solved for H:

$$H = \frac{(r - g_s)P - D(r + g_s)}{(g_h - g_s)}$$

If H is 56 years, it implies that the midpoint of the transition from high to steady state growth is 56 years in the future, or that for the next 112 years we will have above average growth. This type of result should give one pause to reflect on the input numbers, and if you feel they are reasonable then the market is overvalued. An alternative way of using the H-model is to estimate the growths, a reasonable H, and the dividend yield of the S&P500 and solve for price – or the predicted value of what the market should be given the inputs to the model. The portfolio manager can then determine if the market is under- or overvalued. For a sector one could use the SPDR of the sector, and for an industry one of the industry indices could be used. With the H-model, it is relatively simple to change one of the input variables and do a sensitivity analysis. As with all models, one must keep in mind the assumptions behind the model, the quality of the input, and that models only provide information not answers.

Yield, Growth, and Revaluation
- Growth prospects of firms change the value of the firm and are reflected in the P/E multiple: an upward change in P/E is presumed to reflect improved growth prospects (and vice versa)
- The model augments the DDM – it indicates that return in stock will be function of current dividend yield, the projected growth rate over the forecasting horizon, and a revaluation factor (RV)
- RV is a function of future P/E ratios
- Three yield model: $E(r) = D/P + g + RV_{(P/E)}$
- Need estimate of future P/E at end of growth rate period to estimate RV, quality inputs are difficult to obtain

The "three-yield" model is an extension of the simplified dividend discount model (DDM). The three-yield model, like the DDM, indicates that the return of a stock is a function of the current yield and the projected growth rate over the time horizon. However, in contrast to the simplified DDM (a two input model), the forecasted growth rate for the three-yield model is over a set time horizon rather than an indefinitely long period. In addition, the three-yield model requires a third input which is an estimate of the future P/E multiplier for the stock at the end of the growth period, a reevaluation factor (RV). When the expected P/E is higher the RV would be a positive number and if lower the RV would be negative. If there is no change in P/E, then the three-yield model and the simplified DDM show the same results. The RV can be calculated by taking a ratio of the expected $(P/E)_n$ divided by the current $(P/E)_0$, and then adjust the ratio by the natural log of the ratio divided by the transition period (n) for the change in P/E: $RV = (\ln((P/E)_n/(P/E)_0)/n)$. RV is then added or subtracted from the simplified DDM estimate of expected return. For example, assume a company is currently selling with a P/E of 25, a dividend yield of 1.5% and currently growing at 25% per annum. However the forecast is for the growth to decline to 8% in 5 years and then sell at 15 times earnings. The ratio of expected to current P/E is 15/25 = 0.6 and the natural log of 0.6 is -0.5108, which, divided by 5, becomes -0.1022, indicating a negative third yield of 10.22%. Using $E(r) = D/P + g + RV$ we have an expected investment return of approximately 16.3% per annum $[E(r) = 0.015 + 0.25 - 0.1022]$. Or, the return is 1.5% dividend plus 25% growth minus 10.22% revaluation discount. There is a discount because the P/E ratio decreased.

P/B Valuation Model
- Focuses on book values and explains pricing relative to book value [B]
- Investors are familiar with book value, and model depends on accounting data, quality of forecasting and inputs
- PB model: $E(r) = D/P + g_B + RV_{(P/B)}$

The PB model, similar to the three-yield model, adds a third term to the simplified DDM to reflect changes in valuation. In this model, the growth rate and the change in valuation component are related to the book value instead of the P/E ratio.

Disadvantages include:
- a) both models are dependent on the quality of accounting data – book value and earnings
- b) both models require difficult estimates: the P/B model requires a proper ROE estimate and the three-yield model requires a terminal P/E estimate

Advantages include:
- a) both models augment the DDM by adding a term to account for changes in future growth
- b) in the three-yield model, the growth rate is forecasted over a finite period rather than infinite
- c) for the P/B model, book value is generally a more stable benchmark than earnings

The Q Ratio
- Ratio of market value of the firm as reflected in the financial markets to the replacement value of the assets
- Asset-value orientation, associated with practitioners
- Alternative to income flow valuation (e.g., DDM), valid in times of restructuring, and can be related to DDM
- Investment warranted until the marginal return is equal to the discount rate, at which point, in theory, the Q ratio becomes one (Q = 1.0)
- Q above one could indicate overvaluation while values below one be a sign of undervaluation
- Provides standard for asset valuation, but difficult to determine replacement value
- An alternative is to use "equity q"
  - based on current market price to and book value
  - compare the equity q to the mean market price to book average instead of a theoretical value of 1.0
  - similar in concept to the relative valuation ratios
- In some foreign countries accounting regulations allow companies to adjust asset values and liabilities based on current market conditions and prices for them, which implies that the price to book ratio is similar to the Q ratio (assuming adjustments are done correctly and accurately)

The Q ratio is a measure that provides a useful perspective for discussing asset based valuation. It provides an alternative method to the income/earnings based valuation models. The Q ratio is the ratio of the market value of a firm as reflected in the financial markets to the replacement value of the assets. The Q ratio not only provides a link between the "real" economy and the financial markets, but also presents another perspective for evaluating growth opportunities. Furthermore, it can be used to represent a standard for asset valuation of individual common stocks. A Q ratio greater than one would indicate that a stock is overvalued, whereas a Q less than one would signify an undervalued security. If Q is equal to one then the stock would be considered to be selling at a fair value. Valuation is influenced by the particular characteristics of the security and the most difficult problem for assessing valuation to specific stocks is to appraise the replacement value of the company's assets. Because of this, it may be necessary to treat certain companies or industries on a case-by-case basis. Under some international accounting standards firms can value their assets at current value instead of the historical values that are used in GAAP accounting systems in the U.S. When companies accomplish that task with good information, the market-to-book ratio would be the Q ratio for the firm.

An alternative to the Q ratio is the "equity q" ratio which is based on the stock price and book value of the firm or price to book ratio, which is used for valuation in pragmatic settings. The equity q ratio is useful on a relative basis – e.g., the average q ratio for the market place is similar in role to q = 1.0. Firms with a equity q greater than the market q would be overvalued and a firm with a equity q less than market q would be a candidate for investment. Depending on circumstances a ratio less than the market, industry, or index could also indicate a deficiency of prospects for the company. Never base a recommendation or decision on only one number, get confirmation from further analysis.

Private Market Value
- Worth of a firm to a buyer interested in corporate control
- Two complementary methods
  - direct appraisals of assets, based on adjusted book value
  - capitalization of free cash flow, based on a multiple of the flows given an estimated risk of the firm
- As in all valuation models and gaining control one must be sure the end result is maximizing the long-term wealth of the owners, and not the managers (agency considerations), while treating all stakeholders objectively and fairly

The concept of private market value, or asset value, denotes the true worth of a corporation or at least the worth to a buyer interested in corporate control. It can be applied when an analyst feels that the corporate value does not reflect the underlying asset value. Two approaches allow its practical application: (1) the direct appraisal approach, and (2) the capitalization of free cash flow method. The appraisal method starts with stated book value, and it is then adjusted to reflect such things as goodwill, pension plan funding, deferred tax reserves, inflation, and LIFO inventory reserves. The free cash flow approach starts with earnings before depreciation interest and taxes, and it then adjusts for projected capital expenditures.

The private market value concept and its various methods are useful for appraising the worth of companies, because they help to establish a value where buyers can finance the purchase of the corporate assets. The financing process sets up a kind of "quasi-

80

arbitrage" mechanism for maintaining a floor value for the firm's assets. The free cash flow asset valuation method is commonly used to estimate a floor value for the company. The object is for the buyer to purchase the company, and then borrow enough funds to finance the purchase while using the free cash flow of the company to pay down the debt. The private market value could represent a floor value from which a premium or discount from the current price can be calculated. Also, one must be careful that corporate management has not lost their moral compass, especially for the acquiring firm.

Relative Value
- Approaches to valuing stocks relative attractiveness
    - relative P/E technique : relative P/E = (firm P/E)/(P/E of index)
    - relative P/B technique : relative P/B = (firm P/B)/(P/B of index)
    - DDM evaluation
    - cash flow asset valuation
- Consistency of results can confirm attractiveness
- Relative value of the stock market
    - compared to other investments
    - Fed Model – dividend yield compared to bond yield

The price earnings ratio is the price of the stock divided by the earnings per share. This multiple gives the investor an indication of how much they are paying for a company's earning power. The higher the P/E the more the investors are paying, but they also expect more earnings growth. During a period of increased growth, companies will tend to have better than average earnings which drives prices even higher so their P/E ratio normally increases. If the business cycle is winding down, earnings will tend to recede along with the price of the stock, which generally results in lower P/E ratios. Rapidly growing companies will have high P/E ratios while companies that are more mature with earning stability will have low relative P/E ratios. Typically, firms which are more sensitive (exposed to high business risk) to the business cycle will have a high degree of variability in their earnings and in their prices.

On the other hand, the relationship of the P/E ratio and the business cycle could tend to be inversely related in the short-term. As earnings are lower because of poor business conditions, the P/E ratio will increase. Improved business conditions will increase reported earnings and lower P/E ratios. These relationships assume the price of the stock is relatively constant, or moves less than the earnings. One also needs to be consistent regarding the earnings being used - are they trailing/historical or leading?

As noted previously, P/E ratios are calculated by taking the current market price of the firm divided by the current earnings (i.e., trailing 12 month earnings) per share of the firm. Problems involved in deciding which "earnings" to use are mostly due to generally accepted accounting principals [GAAP]. Some GAAP policies that affect earnings include such items as depreciation, inventory valuation, and revenue recognition. These items are at the discretion of the firm and are thus subject to manipulation (possible "window dressing" and perhaps outright fraud – this potential for abuse is now reduced due to the Sarbanes-Oxley Act). Because of variations in acceptable accounting practices, analysts may modify some of the numbers to calculate comparable earnings. Another problem centers around which year's earnings should be used to calculate the multiple. Some analysts use earnings from the prior year and some use forecasted earnings for the next year. In sum, basically, the decision on which earnings figure to use is subject to the nature of the firm and the industry. Obviously, many of the same difficulties apply to the P/B ratio because book value is also an accounting number. The key to using either P/E or P/B is consistency in the information and in the way the ratios are calculated. As with all ratios they need to be comparable: to either a standard, to each other, or over time.

A relative P/E is the P/E multiple of a firm relative to that of the market (or some other comparison P/E, e.g., sector or industry). It is calculated by dividing a company's P/E by that of the market. The resulting measure is interpreted as the relative valuation of the firm with respect to the market (i.e., is the stock selling at a premium or a discount to the market). The same applies to relative price-to-book ratios [P/B].

$$\text{Relative P/E} = \frac{\text{P/E of specific company}}{\text{P/E of S\&P500}}$$

$$\text{Relative P/B} = \frac{\text{P/B of specific company}}{\text{P/B of S\&P500}}$$

P/E ratios have varied during the years because growth prospects and economic conditions are forever changing. Because P/E is a measure of risk, as investors interpret more or less risk in the market place P/E multiples will vary accordingly over time. The long term market P/E has ranged from a low of around 6 to a high of about 40, and the average is 14 to 16.[1] If the relative ratio, as defined above, is 'much' greater or less than 1.0 the investor or analyst needs to determine why the difference exists and if it is appropriate. Before making any investment decisions one should also look at the relative ratio based on an industry or group standard because at times some groups have higher or lower ratios than the market as measured by the S&P500. If the difference in relative P/E cannot be explained, the security may be a candidate for investment (either a long purchase or a short sale).

For an indication of the overall stock market, one can use the Fed Model which is used to assess the relative value of the stock market. Is the stock market over- undervalued compared to the Treasuries? In this model, the dividend yield is compared to a 'long-term' Treasury, typically the 10-year or the 30-year bond. This model can be useful in tactical asset allocation decisions: e.g., over the next year should stocks to over- or underweighted as compared to bonds? However, it should not be the sole criteria used in making such allocation decisions since it does not take into account perceived risks.

Valuation, Risk Changes and Discount Rate
- Anticipating change in risk is potentially useful in distinguishing between stocks
- Change in the riskiness of a stock should have direct impact on discount rate or expected return of stock

---

[1] The numbers are not exact because it depends on time frame and which earnings are used.

- Increase in discount rate should lead to price decline, while a decrease should lead to a price increase (similar to bond valuation rule #1)
- Forecast risk changing by decomposing the risk premium (see below)
- Analyze the four factors of the risk premium
  1) Interest rate risk
     - duration for a stock is simply the inverse of the dividend yield
       o $d = P/D$
       o $d = 1/(r-g)$
     - bond duration characteristics also apply to equity duration
     - low dividend yields have long durations and are relatively more sensitive to discount rate changes; high growth stocks are generally characterized by relatively low dividend yields and would be more subject to discount rate changes
     - longer-duration stock shows greater variability with respect to discount rate changes than short-duration stock
     - use duration to compare stocks and bonds to evaluate relative riskiness and exposure to interest rate changes
  2) Purchasing power risk
     - stocks may have the ability to offset inflation with dividend increases (over longer periods)
     - adjustment period may lag, and the greater the adjustment the less the change in discount rate and value of stock
  3) Business risk and 4) Financial risk
     - varying degrees of business and financial risk within the equity markets
     - they have elements of both systematic and unsystematic risk
     - factors increasing business and financial risk include the following:
       o small size
       o position in industry
       o level of fixed operating cost
       o extensive operating leverage
       o sensitivity to business cycle
       o significant variability in earnings
       o heavy debt financing resulting in fixed financing costs (interest payments)
       o status of economy and how the industry and firm fit in with general economic conditions
     - if and only if CAPM is valid, able to use the CAPM as analytical framework

An evaluation of the risk factors allow the investment manager to anticipate changes in the market, extra market groupings, and movement of individual securities, especially high yielding ones. At times the FED tries not only to control inflation by interest rate policy but also to influence the stock market. For example, when Allan Greenspan talked about "irrational exuberance" in the mid- to late 1990s, and then the FED decided to undertake a series of interest rate hikes in the name of fighting "anticiflation." After the markets crashed in 2000 and before President Bush took office in January 2001, the FED had an emergency meeting and started the process of lowering the interest rate to help stimulate the economy. In 2008 after the housing bust and liquidity crisis there were many discussions that the FED should officially step in and influence financial markets when bubbles are evident instead of waiting for the markets to "correct" the situation and then help clean up the mess. For example, after the real estate bubble burst the FED provided additional liquidity and helped Goldman Sachs acquire Bear Sterns. The efforts continued into with quantitative easing in an effort to keep interest rates low and hope that the economy would respond positively. A second round of quantitative easing was introduced along with operation twist (issue short term Treasuries and then buy longer term Treasuries – lower overall cost of interest). While the interest rates remained low, the economy was still mixed at best, and the question of possible inflation in the future became more important (how can the national debt increase by 50% in just over three years, coupled with increasing prices of everyday essential items like food and gas, and the economy not have inflation?).

Summary
- Valuation is an essential component of investing
- Three-stage DDM is the "best" from a theoretical basis, but difficult to implement
- Simplified models make systematic valuation more feasible
- H-model is the "best" elegant model from a pragmatic point of view, and can be used for sensitivity analysis
- Equity valuation is multi-dimensional, and one should include differing approaches
- Models provide information so the investor, analyst, or portfolio manager can make more informed, better decisions

Equity valuation is more of a challenge than bond valuation since there are more unknowns and growth is difficult to forecast. However, the models presented in Section II (Chapters 3, 4 and 5) provide a solid framework to generate information regarding value and risk for both debt and equity securities. Moreover, the same basic considerations of cash flows, risk involved and time value is used for the pricing of all financial instruments.

The DDM set of models can be applied across a universe of common stocks of differing character. DDMs are theoretically well derived; nonetheless, they suffer from the fact that for the more complex models implementation is complex, and generating quality inputs is difficult. Even though the models are difficult they are used in pragmatic settings, especially the simplified versions. Capital market theory and the CAPM also provides useful information, and complement the DDM information.

However, let us recognize that sophisticated risk/value models cannot match human unpredictability ("irrational behavior"). For example, the dot.com high tech mania of the late 1990s where many participants moved from price/earnings multiples (P/E ratios) to P/F ratios – price to fantasy. When people say, "it is different this time," they are in an emotional state where it is difficult to envision a different market environment than the one that made them emotional in the first place. As Warren Buffet said, "Be fearful when others are greedy and greedy when others are fearful." Financial models provide information from a known base that allows cool heads and seasoned eyes to make intelligent decisions, especially when a financial crisis is brewing. As a complement to fundamental models, technical analysis can help measure emotions by examining supply and demand. Moreover, using portfolio strategies of holding securities and assets with low correlations can help reduce the impact of bursting bubbles.

CHAPTER 5
THOUGHT QUESTIONS

1. Identify the characteristics that are desirable in a valuation model and the sort of uses that are important for practical application. What is your opinion of theoretically elegant models that do not apply to the pragmatic world (be sure to indicate strengths and weaknesses of the models)?

2. Describe how the DDM-based valuation approach can be used to develop better insight into understanding the riskiness of equities. How can this understanding create potential investment opportunities for a portfolio manager?

Questions and Problems:

1. What are some desirable criteria for a valuation model?
2. Compare the H model to the three-stage dividend discount model. What are the similarities and differences?
3. Assume that a high tech company is expected to grow at a rate of 25% over the next 4 years and then decline over the next three years (years 5 – 7) to a growth rate of 10%. Determine the price of the stock that is currently paying a $1 dividend and has a discount rate of 17% by using
   a. the three-stage growth model
   b. the H-model
   c. explain the reasons for the difference
4. A stock is currently selling with a P/E of 25, a dividend yield of 1.5% and currently growing at 25% per annum but is expected to decline to 8% in 5 years and then sell at 15 times earnings. What is the expected return of the stock?
5. Identify some benchmarks that investors use. Why is it important to have a benchmark?
6. Scott's Dairy stock sells for $20 per share, and the most recent dividend was $1.00. An analyst using the three-stage growth model estimated that the high growth rate (g_h) of 10% will only last for two years before it declines to a constant, long-run normal growth rate (g_s) of 7% over a three-year transition period (b-a = 3).
   a. what is the expected growth rate in year 3; the first year of phase 2; the transition period?
   b. what are the expected dividends in years 5 and 6?
   c. if the analyst feels that 12% is an appropriate discount rate and given the risk characteristics of the what, what is the present value or all expected future dividends?

d. what is the expected return associated with this stock, given the current market price of $20 and the analyst's estimates of future dividends?
7. Using the H-model
   a. what is the present value of the expected dividends for Scott's Dairy in Question 6?
   b. what is the expected return?
   c. What is the alpha?
8. Regarding the P/E multiplier model:
   a. how are price-earnings ratio calculated?
   b. what are the problems involved in deciding which "earnings" to use in calculating this ratio?
   c. what are relative P/Es and how are they calculated and used?
   d. why have P/E ratios varied so much during the past 30 years?
   e. do the same concerns relate to other multiplier models?
9. Identify the four risk factors of the risk premium. Why is it important for an investor to evaluate these risk factors before investing?
10. You are given the following information about two technology firms and the S&P 500.

	Firm J	Firm K	S&P 500
P/E ratio	24.00	20.00	12.00
Average annual growth	18%	15%	7%
Dividend yield	2%	3%	5%

   a. compute the duration of each company stock relative to the S&P 500
   b. compute the duration of Firm A to Firm B
   c. given these duration, what must you decide in order to make an investment decision?

STOCK ANALYSIS

Constant Growth Dividend Valuation Model

Stock _____   Exchange _____   Current Position _____

_____

Valuation Model Equation

_____

Financial Variable Values:

D_0 = _____   r = _____   g = _____

Valuation Result (*intrinsic value*)= _____

Current Market Price = _____

Current Valuation Status of Stock: OVERVALUED   UNDERVALUED

_____

Analysis of Investment Potential:
(include sensitivity analysis)

Investment Action   BUY   SELL   NO ACTION

_____

Rationale for Investment Action:

STOCK ANALYSIS

Non-constant Growth Dividend Valuation Model

Stock _____   Exchange _____   Current Position _____

Valuation Model Equation

Financial Variable Values: D_0 = _____   r = _____

Growth Periods:

g=   g=   g=   g=   g (constant) = _____

n = ___ to ___   n = ___ to ___   n = ___ to ___   n = ___ to ___

Valuation Result (*intrinsic value*)= _____

Current Market Price = _____

Current Valuation Status of Stock: OVERVALUED   UNDERVALUED

Analysis of Investment Potential:
(include sensitivity analysis)

Investment Action   BUY   SELL   NO ACTION

Rationale for Investment Action:

88

Section III: Strategies and Applications

In Section II we presented valuation models that are built on the idea that value should reflect cash flows in the form of interest payments, dividends or earnings, growth potential, and risk. Section III builds on the valuation methods and examines disciplined strategies for selecting securities and asset allocation in portfolio management in a global setting. We start in Chapter 6 with a focus on the equity investment process and stock selection. Active and passive strategies are presented along with the idea that forecasting ability is the key determinant to determine the level of activity. Culling criteria, the need for buy and sell disciplines, the impact of losses, costs, and taxes are discussed before moving onto portfolio construction and optimization. The most important decision in investing is asset allocation and we present this concept in Chapter 7. Asset allocation is based on the risk profile (the tolerance for accepting risk) of the investor, and at each stage of the process the strengths and weaknesses of the investment team needs to be recognized. The next chapter builds on the first two and goes into equity-style management and how quantitative techniques can be used to identify styles. Styles are based on differing behavior of securities in the market place and can be blended into an appropriate strategy to meet the objectives of the portfolio.

In Chapter 9, we expand the asset class management to recognize global considerations. Investing on an international basis can improve the performance of a portfolio while reducing risk, since international markets are not perfectly correlated to domestic markets. Strategies and security selection follow the same basic philosophy and techniques as investing in your home country. Chapter 10 builds on the prior chapters and moves into managing bond assets in both a domestic and international context. The term structure of interest rates, better known as the yield curve, is introduced and shown how it can be used to help in the implementation of investment strategies. We also present features of bonds and discuss embedded options within some debt instruments. Swaps, an active bond investment strategy, are also reviewed.

Overall, Section III drills down into some of the more pragmatic applications of the valuation models presented earlier in the book. The strategies and applications presented are good for building foundations and/or models on which to judge actual events. However, one should not think they describe pragmatic settings. Changing market conditions and behavioral aspects make investing and portfolio management moving targets. Also, it is helpful to realize that precision in numbers can lead to false confidence or to a belief that one can actually determine value. Before moving onto the chapters of this section, let us leave you with the following thoughts: markets are driven not only by financial information but also by human emotion. Human emotion runs the gambit of fear and greed to mob psychology. Fear leads to overreaction to negative news (e.g., earnings less than expected), which drives prices to lower levels. Greed is the opposite and leads to overconfidence, which leads to inflated prices. When fear or greed grips individual investors, then the market at large, mob psychology, takes over and drives prices, respectively, even lower or higher. Unfortunately, overreacting is catching. Overreacting is one reason why investors like Graham and Dodd propose a "margin of safety" in investment decisions. One would like to think investors would learn; however, in the "heat" of the events the rallying cry is always: "It is different this time around."

Chapter 6: Disciplined Stock Selection and Investment Strategies

CHAPTER OVERVIEW

This chapter illustrates how strategies focused on disciplined valuation methods and systematic investing techniques can be implemented as a core component of an equity investment plan. We focus the discussion onto the equity investment process and specifically on stock selection. Active and passive strategies are discussed, along with a framework to compare stock selection strategies and establish objectives. We also present culling criteria, sell and buy disciplines, loss considerations, and how expenses impact the performance of an investment (e.g., mutual fund). Throughout the chapter the implementation of strategy, recognizing weakness and strengths, predictive capability, and the importance of analyzing the investment process is discussed. Investing, including long/short strategies, and performance are briefly presented and discussed. Even though the focus of the chapter is on domestic equity securities the tools, techniques, process, and strategies have universal application.

Introduction
- Equity investment is the focus of the discussion
- Approaches include active and passive strategies
- A framework for a discipline stock selection process allows for:
    - comparison to other strategies, including a sensitivity analysis
    - establishing specific objectives
    - designing the investment process
    - implementing the strategy, evaluating results, and modifying as needed
- A disciplined approach to investing is applicable for all scenarios and investment vehicles
- Security selection accounts for about five percent of returns while asset allocation accounts for approximately ninety-one percent of returns
- To recommend an individual security that you believe has "excess returns" to capture you need to be able to explicitly state what the market has overlooked regarding that security (either in a positive or negative sense)

Even though the focus of the discussions in this chapter relate to equity securities, it should be recognized that the ideas and concepts herein have universal application in the investment field. Research has shown that the majority of investment returns are attributed to asset allocation and only small portions to security selection and market timing. However, despite this evidence investors, including investment banks and brokerage firms, spend most of their resources and time on individual securities. Behavior considerations can help explain this phenomenon. After all, we feel we can do something better than others, and if we want to distinguish ourselves we cannot just mimic an index.

The need to be able to explicitly state what the market has overlooked before investing comes directly from Bill Miller, former portfolio manager of Legg Mason Management Value Trust. If you cannot identify why, or what the market missed, it implies that perhaps the market is correct. Doing a sensitivity analysis can help determine why or what the market has overlooked. As always, of course, one needs to be careful they do not assign attributes that are not there, and one also needs to be objective and willing to admit mistakes.

Active-Passive Strategies

- Develop a framework for investment strategies, consider both risk and return, from three components
  - Market sector component
    - active: called market timing, change risk in rising markets by shifting between cash and stocks or by raising or lowering the beta of the investments given their forecast
    - market timing is at best difficult to implement and generally does not add significantly to returns (less than two percent on average)
    - passive: maintain risk of the investments in line with target for achieving long-term investment objectives
  - Industry or broad market sector
    - active: called group rotation, strategy of under- or overweighing a group, sector or industry according to whether assessment is unfavorable or favorable
    - passive: maintains investment weights in line with weightings in market index, or the benchmark of the investment portfolio
  - Individual security
    - active: stock selection strategy of under- or overweighing stocks identified as unfavorable or favorable respectively
    - passive: hold many stocks (diversification benefit) in line with weightings in an index
- The strategy employed should build on strengths and minimize the weaknesses of the investment team
  - an active strategy entails underweighting or overweighting an asset class, a stock, group or industry with respect to its weight in the market index, according to whether the outlook for the asset class, group or stock has been assessed as favorable or unfavorable
  - with an active strategy the investor believes he/she has predictive capability
  - a passive strategy involves setting investment weights for the broad market sectors and major industries in line with their weightings in a market index (e.g., S&P 500)
  - the passive stance will at all times maintain the risk so it is in line with the target for long-term objectives
  - an ultimate passive strategy is to create or invest in an index fund or ETF
  - the passive investor believes they do not have "predictive capability."
- No strategy works all the time, or for all levels of risk
- Strategies need to be reviewed, lessons learned need to be noted, and revised as needed slowly overtime

One of the fundamental axioms of finance is that in order to achieve higher returns, one must undertake riskier projects or investments. We should also recognize that it is difficult to "beat the market," especially on a consistent basis. One can only outperform the benchmark if he/she has better information or knowledge regarding the risk-return relationship of an asset class, group, or individual security. Having better information implies superior forecasting ability, which adds value to the investment process. Additionally, the added value has to be greater than the costs of obtaining the information and implementing the strategy. Turnover, especially excessive turnover, drags down the performance of an investment. Strategies do not work all the time or for all investors. Instead success depends on the character and behavioral aspects of the investor and how he/she interprets and reacts to the information being used to develop and implement the strategy. Bill Miller had an exceptional run of outperforming the market for 15 years, but things started to 'unravel' in the sixteenth year and modifications were not implemented soon enough. Were Miller and his team overconfident after their unbelievable success, or did they just miss something that changed in the market place?

Passive strategies generally provide the investor with returns and risk characteristics which are very close to the market index or appropriate benchmark. Because of this, there is generally less volatility of returns than with the active strategies. A totally active investing strategy is more risky, but the possibility for achieving greater returns as well as greater losses would increase substantially over the passive strategy. Active investors invest based on their ability to forecast market movements for asset classes or the relative attractiveness of certain industry sectors, groups, or individual stocks. Sometimes they are correct and will be rewarded with superior returns, but at other times they may be wrong and suffer losses. The truly passive investor simply invests in a market index. Following a passive strategy implies the portfolio manager forecasts are the same as the markets consensus of the risk-return relationship.

Active strategies available to obtain above average return include market timing, sector rotation, or active stock selection. Market timing strategies seek to raise the risk of investments during rising markets and to decrease risk during market declines. Changing risk can be accomplished by changing the beta of the investments by moving to higher or lower beta stocks or by decreasing or lowering cash levels. In contrast to active market timing, investors could take a passive stance with respect to market timing by maintaining the risk of their investments in line with the target for achieving long-term objectives. Active sector rotation entails the underweighting or overweighing of a particular section of the market depending upon the outlook associated with that sector. Passive strategies with regard to the sector component of returns involve setting portfolio weights for the broad market sectors in line with their weightings in the benchmark. Active stock selection entails overweighting or underweighting a particular stock relative to their weighting in the market index or benchmark, again depending upon relative attractiveness of the stock. Following an active strategy increases the cost investing from gathering information to implementation. Passive strategies with respect to stock selection entail holding a large number of securities and weighing them according to their weight in the market index or benchmark. In essence, passive stock selection involves the creation of an index, or investing in an index fund or ETF.

To hedge or neutralize market timing risk, investors should maintain the asset allocation designed to achieve long-term investment risk/return objectives throughout all types of markets. Following a total passive strategy (e.g., index fund) will assure her/him of having little divergence from the "neutral" performance of the general market.

An investor who has little or no skill in evaluating the attractiveness of the market, groups or individual stocks should pursue a strategy of passive investing such as buying an index fund or ETFs that best fits their objective(s). Once again it should be noted that one should recognize their weaknesses and strengths when deciding on/developing investment strategies.

Predictive Ability
- It is necessary/advisable to measure or assess predictive capability
  - distinguish between components levels, from individual stocks to market
  - ability to combine sources of information
- Information coefficient [IC] method, one of the best methods to evaluate ability
  - correlation of outcomes with predictions
  - the higher the IC the better the predictive ability
- Fundamental law of active management
  - value added by a strategy will be proportional to the information ratio [IR] squared [IR^2]
  - IR is a function of the information coefficient and the breadth of the strategy [B]
  - $IR = IC\sqrt{B}$
  - the information coefficient is a measure of predictive ability and the breadth [B] is an indication of how many independent forecasts are made during the year

The value of an investor's forecasting ability is directly related to the accuracy of their forecasts. The higher the IC the more value added. Breadth is also important, because we need to recognize how often forecasts are being made. The "fundamental law of active management" states that the value added is proportional to the information ratio squared. Hence, if an investor has a high IC and forecasts fairly often they add more value to the investment process and should follow an active strategy. On the other hand, if the IC is close to zero passive strategies should be followed. Furthermore, it should be recognized that it is more difficult to make many equally good forecasts. Hence, it is better to make fewer good forecasts and keep a high IC than to make many forecasts and lower the IC.

The Investment Process and Composite Forecasting
- Critical elements include:
  - predictive capability!
  - systematic investing procedures and strategies
  - investment rebalancing will occur over time and costs of rebalancing must be controlled
  - recognizing strengths and minimizing weaknesses

- Risk and return are both involved
- Multiple sources of information are desirable
- No single source provides constant level of predictive capability
- Generate optimum investments (high return minimal risk) and implement with an eye on costs

Information used to make investment decisions is a key element, but often overlooked consideration. All sources are NOT equal, despite what they may advertise. Information is readily available on the Internet. The available information ranges from highly useful to a waste of time and from free to very expensive. The source of the information also needs to be considered. For example, is the research report from an analyst free from bias? Is the analyst working for an investment banking firm or brokerage that want to maintain or create a relationship with the company being analyzed? Sarbanes Oxley Act addressed this situation and now the analyst needs to disclose all possible conflicts and relations. One excellent source of quality information from an independent source is the Argus Research Company.[1] Appendix A provides a listing of some useful websites, many of these sites were suggested by former students.

- Composite forecasting involves assembling separate individual sources to form a multiple source/composite prediction to stabilize and increase predictive capability
  - each individual source must have a positive information coefficient
  - individual sources should be independent (cross-correlation of zero is ideal)
  - weight each source according to its predictive power
  - composition and weights will change over time
- Applied composite forecasting
  - develop a process to assess relative attractiveness
  - consider four valuation principals:
    (1) long-term fundamentals
    (2) short-term fundamentals
    (3) trading fundamentals
    (4) analyst judgment
  - rank companies within industry according to alpha(s) based on various sources of information and relative weights
  - verify high alpha securities and consider for inclusion into the investment portfolio

The primary benefit of composite forecasting is that is has the potential for stabilizing predictive capability (reducing fluctuations) and at the same time increasing the power of the predictions. The process works best when there are a number of unrelated sources which provide a different prospect on the same investment. The sources need to have "predictive content," which will enhance the overall forecast, and it is best when they exhibit zero cross-correlation. By collecting a number of opinions from various independent sources an investor has in a sense diversified the risk of depending on one source that may or may not be accurate. The investor then uses the different opinions and

---

[1] In the spirit of full disclosure it should be noted that Professor Reinhart had access to Argus Research.

94

his/her own judgment to formulate a forecast upon which to base his/her investing strategy. Having positive ICs and independent sources are vital to good results.

Investment diagnostics can help to provide useful insight into analyzing composite forecasting and the risk-return characteristics of an investments. Because diagnostics allow the investor to categorize the sources of risk and return into individual and identifiable components, it becomes much easier to manage your investments. By understanding the underlying factors which affect a portfolio's performance, the investor will be better able to adjust to changes that occur in the market place and over time gather the appropriate information from various sources in order to increase their forecasting ability. Investment diagnostics provide the investor with the tools necessary to monitor the general market risk and to evaluate the asset weighting exposure of the portfolio to industry sectors. In turn, a more informed investor should be able to achieve higher returns in the long-term, especially if they are able to correctly estimate future events based on the sources they are using. Furthermore, just because a matrix worked yesterday does not mean that it will work tomorrow. Financial markets, investor psychology, investor behavior, rules, and regulations are extremely fluid – one of the propelling reasons to get into finance and investing is because it is so dynamic, even if it can be highly frustrating as you learn.

Generating Return Forecasts and Distributions
* Obtain over- or undervaluation judgments on individual stocks from security analysis process (fundamental analysis)
* Express judgments as return forecasts for degree of risk undertaken
* Adjust return forecasts for the degree of predictive capability possessed by the analyst
* Avoid scale and bias in return forecasts, prevent these difficulties by employing a rating scheme
* A good company is not necessarily a good stock and vice versa
* Do not forget technical analysis and behavioral aspects

When generating return forecasts and distributions that differ from the markets estimation, as reflected in the current stock price, the analyst/investor needs to be able to identify why his/her numbers differ. Generally, the market consensus is "correct" unless mob psychology or emotions of fear or greed are driving prices – which happens more often then one would expect and can range from an individual security to the overall market. Therefore it is incumbent on the analyst to "justify" their forecast. A general rule of thumb for investing: "if the upside potential is not twice the downside risk look for another investment."

Technical analysis should be used along with fundamental analysis to make investment decisions. Technical analysis allows the investor to identify trends, either upward or downward. Using both should provide better returns than just using one of them. Recognizing that a good company is not necessarily a good stock is important. There have been many good companies that never move, perhaps because they lack a 'story' or they are out of favor for whatever reason. It is also possible to have a company that has a "great story line," is being pushed by some people and is a "good" stock. However, it less than a good company – of course, sooner or later the truth and reasonableness prevails and the bubble bursts. Technical analysis, as noted previously, can help take some of the psychological factors out of the decision making process. Additionally, one could use charts to place a stop loss order at some previous support level.

Strategies for Selecting Securities or Assets
- Based on combinations of active and passive strategies associated with each component of risk and return
- Strategy is based on
  - predictive capability
  - type and sources of information
- Possible strategies:
  - index fund: remain totally passive with respect to all three return components (market, sector/industry/group and individual stock)
  - semi-passive: remain passive on market and stock selection, but shift weights on the group/industry/sector components
  - disciplined stock selection: remain passive with respect to market and group components and active with respect to stock selection
  - totally active: active with respect to all three components – market, industry/sector, and stock selection

Strategies for investment selection and asset allocation range from index funds to individual security selection. The objective, which is based on risk tolerance, sets the foundation for any strategy. From there, forecasting ability and information allow us to develop strategies. Selection of over- or underweighting needs to be based on expectations of receiving excess returns. If not, the selection should be passive strategies in one form or another.

One source of information used in selection strategies is excess security-specific returns as measured by alpha. These excess returns are attributed to a specific security after market and industry returns are accounted for. Security-specific risk is measured by residual risk – the risk that is attributable to a specific security after market and group risk are accounted for. A relatively small residual risk offers greater confidence that the alpha will be realized over time. Alphas that fit this pattern allow for more active strategies.

Passive strategies typically have called for an index fund (mutual fund or ETF), which can range from an industry or group to a style or the market as a whole. One challenge with mutual funds is that they normally are only traded at the end of day. Previously, mutual funds were the only choice; however, today there are other choices such as Exchange Traded Funds [ETFs], which trade like stocks. Both mutual funds and ETFs offer low cost and diversification, but differences exist and can impact your bottom line. Hence, you need to explore each type and decide what is best for your investment strategy.

Investment or Culling Criteria
- Stock Screening
  - sequential – prioritize criteria, order of importance

- simultaneous – all at once
- may not lead to the same result
- desired output – ranking of stocks selected, based on "value" criteria
- Characteristics of a good culling screen include:
  - easy to use and understand
  - founded on sound financial principals
  - easy to replicate (especially as data/time changes) by others
  - reflect the objective based on asset allocation, for example
    - value $\Rightarrow$ low P/B ratio
    - growth $\Rightarrow$ high free cash flow
- Possible screens include the following:
  - margin or net profit margin greater than industry average or market average
  - size (i.e., less than \$5b, with, less than 50% institutional ownership)
  - earnings estimate – consensus
  - relative strength (stock price performance compared to the index performance)
  - P/B or B/P ratios
  - ROA, ROE ratios (e.g., ROE > 15%)
  - D/B ratio or LTD/B ratio, where D = debt and B = book value or equity
  - D/B <1, or compared to industry (i.e., less the industry average)
  - current ratio, cash ratio, change from last year
  - turnover ratios, change from prior year
  - P/E ratio, relative to a "group," not just a raw number (sequential screen, e.g., lowest 10% of a group or industry)
  - dividend yield, greater than benchmark index or industry
  - earning growth greater than index – current and/or forecast
  - P/E < industry average (see above, similar to P/E relative to a group)
  - price earnings to growth (PEG = (P/E)/ g): PEG < 1 or PEG < 1.5
  - (P/E)/dividend yield < 4.0
  - g > 0 but less than 50% (positive information, but avoid over optimistic forecasts or fraud)
  - insider information – the buyer to seller ratio
  - institutional ownership < 50%
  - free cash flow, e.g., P_o < future three year free cash flow estimates
  - change in free cash flow (hopefully increasing)
  - E $\geq$ 2D, where D = dividends
- Z-score – a more quantitative approach to culling for good investment candidates
  - z score is a statistical measure: the distance in standard deviations of a sample from the mean
  - employs normal curve concepts
  - able to add "standardized" numbers
  - $z = (x - E(x))/\sigma_x$ where x is a culling criterion, and E is the expectation function
  - a way to combine different measures, screens, or culling criteria
  - weights of factors, equal or based on importance
  - need to be sure to define correctly and have correct sign based on belief [e.g., is low P/E good (+) or negative (-)]
  - need to be consistent

- after criteria are converted to a z-score add them together (weighted average if factors do not have equal import) for an overall rank
- higher the z-score the better the candidate for possible investment
- Need to define terms (e.g., what is D? – dividend or debt?)
- Technical considerations (see Chapter 2)
  - timing of decisions, e.g., when to buy or when to sell to avoid a potential loss
  - point and figure diagrams
  - support levels and resistant levels
  - advance decline lines and levels over time
  - put/call ratio
  - mutual fund cash levels
  - moving averages
  - relative strength

The culling criteria presented above are a combination of fundamental information and they also build on technical analysis and relative strength concepts. The investment criteria also recognize market anomalies (i.e., insider information). Using the culling criteria provides only the first step in identifying securities for possible investment. The securities that are identified still need to be fully analyzed, especially for downside risk. It is necessary to define terms (e.g., what is D? debt or dividend?) and do not assume. Using culling how does one identify a "good" stock. Once possible strategy is:

> Low debt ratio(s)
> Plenty of cash flow
> Cash on hand
> Catalyst? Story? Or why???

Without a catalyst or story a 'good company' may not be a 'good stock.'

Buy and Sell Discipline
- In investing it is important to have information from both buy and sell disciplines
- Disciplines must be maintained and modified, as needed, slowly, and over time
- Disciplines are based on forecasting ability, available information, and skill set of investor, analyst and/or portfolio manager
- Disciplines will be based on type of strategy being followed: e.g., active or passive
- Return forecasts and distribution provide indication of purchase price and sell price
- Buy disciplines are generally easier to establish and implement
- Sell disciplines are more difficult to establish and implement
  - psychological factors – pain from selling loser
  - difficult to find information on sell disciplines
- Buy disciplines can be based on investment and culling criteria presented above
- Sell criteria include the following:
  - company operational issues such as legal problems and/or a change of top management, especially the CEO
  - maturation of the growth cycle
    - slowing growth rates
    - declining return on capital
    - increased payout ratios

- position too large for the portfolio (portfolio needs rebalancing)
- objectives or risk tolerance has changed
- need for cash
- if $E \leq D$ sell
- made a mistake, limit the loss with a stop or 'stop loss' order (see below)
- tax management strategies
    - tax loss bond swap (see Chapter 10)
    - tax loss replacement securities [higher risk than a bond swap]
    - tax loss harvesting throughout the year [year end is the worst time to tax harvest]
- increasing tax efficiency will add to the bottom line
    - minimizing tax payments can materially enhance returns
    - compounding higher after-tax returns can raise long-term results

Disciplines for both buy and sell should focus on investing and not trading. This implies an expectation of longer holding periods. Before selling, one should do an evaluation of the security and see if it meets the buy criteria. If it does then one should just trim the position and not necessarily sell it all outright. After a sale, it is necessary to redeploy the funds; hence, it is best to keep a bullpen of potential buys. Building a correct portfolio to begin with will help keep turnover low and costs to a minimum. In rising markets, money managers may benefit from a more moderate sell discipline, while in down markets a strong sell discipline may be better. Bottom line, sell discipline should be viewed from a perspective of market conditions – e.g., rising or decreasing.

Losses and Mistakes
- When investing and managing portfolios losses are bound to occur sooner or later
- It is important to recognize mistakes or errors of judgment and have disciplined strategies to handle them (see sell criteria above)
  - identify the lessons learned from the loss
  - modify, as and if needed, the buy and/or sell criteria
- A portfolio focused on protecting principal and maximizing return should not hesitate to take losses in positions that are not benefiting the portfolio
- Tax benefits can result from recognizing a loss (e.g., offset recognized capital gains)
- A common error is to hold onto losers in the belief that they will come back

Loss	Gain To Get Even
0	0.0%
-5%	5.3%
-10%	11.1%
-15%	17.6%
-20%	25.0%
-25%	33.3%
-30%	42.9%
-35%	53.8%
-40%	66.7%
-50%	100.0%

- Regardless of the type, level or style of strategy the key is to avoid losses because it is more difficult to generate a return to just breakeven: for example, if the loss is 20% it takes a 25% return to just breakeven, never mind make a profit (see the above chart)

As discussed in Chapter 2, behavioral aspects, investors typically do not recognize losses and sell winners early. Recognizing a loss provides a tax benefit that can be used to enhance the overall return of investments. Moreover, holding onto losers and selling winners eventually leads to the investor holding a group of losers. As noted previously, creating a sell discipline is more difficult than establishing a buy discipline. This is perhaps true because of basic human emotions. Finance literature has lots of information regarding buy strategies and relatively little on sell strategies. Plus, it is well known that most analysts recommendations are for buy or hold and only a few suggest sell. Constructing a sell control is a challenge faced by the professionals as well as individual investors. Setting a stop or stop loss (e.g., 20% less than purchase price) on the purchase of a security is one way to implement a sell discipline. Once a security is down, say 15%, one should take a close look and see if it is still advisable to hold onto the security.

Do not "fall in love" with your investment decision – even if you think it is a correct decision. It is better to sell, wait for the market to drive the price down, and then use technical indicators to determine when it might be a good time to repurchase the security. Averaging price on the way down is a strategy with mixed reviews: (1) if the security continues down and does not recover you have magnified your losses; (2) it is difficult to time the market; hence, if you just sell and the market makes a quick recovery you may not have the opportunity to get back in before the price is high once again. Having a sell discipline in place can help reduce losses. To repeat, one sell discipline is to set a "stop loss" or "stop" sale price when the security is first purchased – e.g., 20% below the purchase price, to recover from a 20% loss one needs a 25% gain. A gain of 25% is not easy to achieve! Another sell discipline is to use technical analysis and set a stop just below a support level.

To err is human, therefore after a loss it is advisable to reflect and identify the lesson(s) learned so the same mistake is avoided in the future. The problem could be in either the buy or sell discipline, or the time it takes to implement the decision, or perhaps the market moved in a totally unexpected direction. A careful analysis of the situation may lead to slight changes in either or both disciplines. In any event, disciplines should be modified slowly and not in giant steps as lessons are learned. It is also possible that it was just a poor decision and no modifications are needed.

Transaction Costs and Taxes
- Compare costs with return opportunities (cost versus potential pickup in added return)
- A rule of thumb, estimated cost is two percent for round trip transactions; however, with the Internet, costs can be a lot lower
- Represent a hurdle rate that return spread must surpass in order to justify trade
- Organization with high IC is justified in developing more trades than organization with a low IC
- Keeping costs low improves results

- Compounding higher amounts due to lower costs, including lower taxes, can significantly improve terminal values and retirement benefits
- Taxes are a major cost
- In theoretical models taxes are generally assumed away
  - taxes differ from person to person, from country to country, and municipality to municipality
  - taxes are 'impossible' to meaningfully model in any reasonable way
  - taxes compound the mathematics

The difference of growth in two investments of $1,000 in separate portfolios with costs of 0.31% and 1.96%, respectively, is significant. If we assume a nominal return of 8% annually for each portfolio before expenses, over a 30 year time frame the ending value for the low expense portfolio is $9,231 and for the higher expense portfolio only $5,809. The Securities and Exchange Commission has a calculator on their website (www.sec.gov) to determine the impact of costs on the performance of a mutual fund.

Expenses, such as fees and turnover costs, impact the returns on an investment. For example, a 45 year old investor planning for retirement in twenty years expects a 10.5% annual return on either investment HF or LF. HF imposes a fee of 1.40% while LF has a fee of only 0.40%. The investor faces a 31% income tax rate and a 20% capital gains tax rate. An initial investment of $100,000 in fund HF generates approximately $294,119 after tax earnings over the 20 year period and would have an after-tax value of $394,119. On the other hand, fund LF generates approximately $355,677 after tax earnings and would have an after-tax value of $455,677 – approximately, 15.6% higher than the higher fee fund. Continuing the example, upon reaching retirement at 66 the investor wishes to withdraw the money over a period of twenty years in equal annual payments. The annual after-tax income derived from fund HF would be $27,974 – not a bad retirement income from an initial investment of $100,000. However, the annual after-tax income derived for the LF fund would be around 28.3% higher at $35,898 per annum. This straightforward example shows that the lower the expenses the higher the net return to the investor.

Turnover can also affect the performance of investments. It can be both positive and negative for an account. If the action is to lock in gains and then invest in other profitable investments the turnover is positive. Likewise, if losses are recognized to reduce taxes the turnover has positive aspects. Churning accounts to hopefully catch the next up movement is generally highly negative for an investment. Buy and sell disciplines can help keep down costs. Normally, for the same type of investment risk higher turnover results in higher expenses and lower returns.

Compounding of returns and tax impact investment returns. Compounding refers to the earning of returns on returns already received. One mathematical relationship is the "magic rule of 72," which relates to compounding and doubling the value of an investment. By way of illustration, if one earns 15% per year, it will take approximately five years to double the investment (72 divided by 15 is approximately five). On the other hand, if one earns 9%, it will take around eight years to double (72 divided by nine equals eight). Dividing 72 by the rate of return equals the approximate number of years to double your money. Similarly, dividing 72 by the number of years in the time horizon provides the approximate return needed to double the investment. A good way to illustrate the use of this rule in the pragmatic world is to examine plausible investment scenarios. For instance, if Sarah is approaching 30 years of age and wishes to retire at 66 as a millionaire and she figures she can earn 10% on her investments per year, how much will she need to invest and at what age? Working backwards and recognizing the investment doubles every 7.2 years, implies that just before turning 59 (58.8) one would need $500,000. In similar fashion, at 52 one needs $250,000; at 44, one needs $125, 000; at 37, $62,500; and at 30 only $31,250. If on the other hand one only earns 7.2%, it takes 10 years to double the money. Starting at age 30 with $31,250 one would have $62,500 at 40; $125,000 at 50; $250,000 at 60; $500,000 at 70; and finally $1,000,000 at age 80 – 14 years longer.

The tax impact on investments is often overlooked, either for simplification or because each individual faces a different tax picture. However, it is safe to say that it is better to accumulate wealth in a tax-free environment. If you assume a tax rate of 28% (federal, state, plus city and/or county) a 10% before tax return would only be 7.2% after tax. As we learned in the compounding example above, a decrease of 2.8% magnified the time to accumulate one million dollars by about forty percent (36 years at 10% versus 50 years at 7.2%). Implications of these scenarios for an investor are that costs should be kept to a minimum and investing in tax-deferred or tax-free accounts is preferable.

Portfolio Construction, Optimization and Performance (see Chapter 13 for more details)
- Construction
    - general fund (e.g., mutual fund): develop a well-defined objective and carry out construction process in a controlled and disciplined fashion
    - basic construction objectives for general fund whose benchmark is the market (e.g., the S&P 500)
        1) risk in line with S&P 500
        2) highly diversified with respect to group/industry risk
        3) individual stocks with high predictive content
    - if the portfolio is for an individual the objective should be based on investors risk tolerance (averseness to risk), and construction should consider the benchmark and asset classes used
- Statistical measures of diversification include:
    - the number of securities
    - the covariance of securities
    - the correlation between securities
    - the weighting of industries, sectors and stocks of the portfolio relative to the market/index weighting.
- Portfolio optimization
    - implementing the portfolio construction process in a disciplined manner
    - follow traditional types of constraints
        o industry guidelines, minimum number of securities, et cetera
        o effective when objectives defined and process delineated

- o simple and least costly to operate
- Optimization procedures are geared to obtain high return at minimal risk
- Evaluate the portfolio and performance, revise as need
- Managing the process over time
    - constantly repeat procedures presented above
    - setting an optimum rebalancing cycle is critical
    - necessary to consider benefits versus costs of rebalancing
    - high costs can damper the returns on any portfolio

Constructing and optimizing a portfolio involves many tasks. As discussed previously, the first task is to develop an appropriate objective based on the risk level desired or the risk tolerance if it is an individual and not a general fund. Optimization requires following a disciplined process, as discussed in various sections of this textbook. Rebalancing a portfolio carries a cost in the form of commissions, transaction costs, and perhaps the price impact from large trades. The cost of the transaction, which can range from a minimal amount to greater than 3% for a round trip, represents the minimum incremental benefit that must be derived from the rebalancing. Transaction costs represent a hurdle rate which must be overcome to justify rebalancing. Furthermore, as discussed above, excessive transactions costs could reduce a portfolio's return. In the next chapter, we discuss the reallocation of assets.

Other considerations are changing prices of the securities and cash flow from the investments. At times, a portfolio has to be rebalanced due to increases or decreases in the value of a particular security or asset class. For example, if your guidelines are to have a security be no more than three percent of the portfolio, and you have a highly successful investment go to five percent of the portfolio's value rebalancing becomes necessary. The investor needs to sell off part of the investment – either in a rebalancing strategy or to generate cash needed for liquidity requirements. Cash inflows, after the securities are selected, are another one of the challenges that investors face. Cash flows can be used for liquidity needs or they could be re-invested. One possible re-investment solution is making use of dividend re-investment plans [DRIP]. DRIPs are offered by many dividend paying firms and offer a low cost alternative to acquire additional shares. Many firms do not charge a fee, and some even offer a discount to the market share price. Moreover, at times, the discount can even be applied to extra money the investor sends in to purchase shares directly from the company. Generally, DRIPs should only be used if you have a well-diversified portfolio and are a long-term investor, a minimum of 3 to 5 years. As compared to the mid- and late 1990s, dividend paying stocks were once again in vogue during the early- to mid 2000s, especially after favorable tax laws were passed under President Bush in 2001 and 2002. After many aspects of the tax cuts were renewed in December 2010, plus a poor economy, dividend stocks were still in vogue. Unfortunately, the renewed tax cuts are set to expire in 2013 and tax policy (especially cuts or increases) is always a political issue. With the divide between the political parties, the expiring tax cuts will add uncertainty (risk) to the market place and the advisability of having dividend paying stocks may be a casualty.

- Monitor return estimating process
    - monitor IC's of separate sources (maintain predictive ability)
    - monitor combining process, avoid redundancy between sources
    - monitor how sources correlate to each other
- Monitor transaction costs over time since costs reduce performance
- Performance of strategy over time
    - strategies using long-term fundamentals should be compared to S&P 500
    - performance advantage directly in line with predictive content [IC score]
    - consistent application of strategy over time translates into significantly greater terminal wealth, especially if the IR is high
- Losses need to be recognized and used to enhance returns – from tax considerations to putting the funds into better performing securities/assets

The basic elements necessary to execute an active strategy of stock selection include:
1) investor must have some sort of predictive capability with respect to stocks
2) there must be some kind of systematic portfolio construction procedure
3) a monitoring and rebalancing process is necessary, which considers the magnitude of transaction costs

When constructing a portfolio, the investor should keep in mind the major components of equity returns and associated risk and keep them in relative balance to each other, especially for passive strategies.

Return	Risk
• overall market effect	• market risk
• affiliation to the industry or broad market sector	• group risk or extra market covariance
• unique characteristics of the individual security	• specific or residual risk

Risk factors that impact across subclasses of securities and create correlation in addition to that of the general market are considered to cause extra-market correlation. The extra-market risk arises from the inter-relationship across groups (industry or broad market sector) of securities. Failure to account for these extra-market sources of correlation can lead to errors in estimating risk for individual securities as well as problems in portfolios.

Beta measures the risk of a portfolio relative to a market benchmark. Cash adds stability and thus reduces volatility of a portfolio since its return has very low variability. Thus, adding cash will generally reduce a portfolio's beta and subtracting cash will increase the beta since the beta of cash is zero or near zero if funds are in money market instruments such as Treasuries.

The investment process should contain methods for appraising returns as well as risk for individual stocks. These assessments are then combined together in some type of portfolio optimization model to generate the portfolio that best incorporates risk/return objectives. After this process is performed, it must continually be re-evaluated and the portfolio re-balanced when conditions warrant.

Long/Short Strategies and Risk

- Growing more important in use in pragmatic settings
- Designed to take advantage of the full array of information
- Construct portfolio by going long on stocks with high positive alphas and selling short stocks with large negative alphas
- Combined position can be neutral with respect to market risk if properly constructed (long-short market-neutral strategy)
- Establish the portfolio position in line with market risk and diversification guidelines
- Possible to achieve long-short market-enhanced return
- Long/short risk
  - incremental return, regardless of strategy, derives from effectiveness of identifying negative and positive alphas
  - risk related to alpha return
    - o known as tracking error
    - o measures how much performance of portfolio will vary relative to an index over time
- Investment possibilities vary on the predictive capability and on the accuracy of the information

A long-short market neutral strategy is to construct an investment by going long on stocks with high positive alphas and selling short stocks with negative alphas. With proper weighting of long and short positions, the investment is neutral with respect to market risk. The key to this strategy is in following the same guidelines when selecting both long and short stocks. Also, a sufficient number of stocks in both long and short positions are necessary to reduce the specific risk component to a low level.

The long-short market neutral investment has three component positions which entail risk. These positions include securities purchased long, ones that are sold short, and the proceeds from short sales that are invested in a money market account. The return on the money market is generally considered to be "riskless[1]," but the returns for short and long positions (measured by alpha) are risky. The risk related to the alpha return is residual or specific stock related. Plus, an additional component of risk results from the estimated correlation between the long and short alpha. The degree of correlation (1 to -1) will have an impact upon the return for the investment. The component risk would be the stocks alpha and its correlation to other stocks in the portfolio. Market movements will produce either a positive or negative return in the typical long only investment, while for the long-short neutral investment return is partially dependent upon the correlation between the two offsetting positions.

---

[1] During the liquidity crisis in 2008 some money market funds 'lost' value and were not redeemable for several years, or until they recovered the lost value.

Example:

"Long portfolio:" $\beta = 1.0$, standard error = 4%, alpha = 2%

"Second portfolio:" $\beta = 1.0$, standard error = 3%, alpha = -1%

Assume: (1) combined long-short portfolio is long the "long portfolio," and short the "second portfolio," (2) since both have $\beta = 1$ the estimated correlation = 1.0, and (3) the long-short portfolio has a $\beta = 1.0$

$$E(alpha) = (.02) - (-.01) = .03 = 3\%$$
$$E(risk) = .03 + .04 = .07 = 7\%$$

Return Patterns: Long and Short Portfolio Positions

- Combined portfolio earns constant return regardless of direction of market in market-neutral strategy
- Enhanced market strategy shows higher returns
- Return consists of three components
  - alpha return from long portfolio
  - alpha return from short portfolio
  - earnings on proceeds of short sales
- Alpha return can enhance investment return
- Futures can be employed to enhance return, risk is also increased

If stock X had an expected alpha of 4%, while stock Y had an expected alpha of -2%, the expected excess return on an equally weighted investment of the two stocks would be .5(4) + .5(-2) = 1%. To improve the portfolio, an investor could put all funds into stock X (expected excess return of 4%), or a more risky approach would call for investing all funds in X, shorting stock Y, and having all proceeds go into Treasuries with a 0.1% return. This approach would have an expected excess return of 1(4) + (-1(-2)) + 1(.1) = 6.1%. Clearly, the risk objectives of the investment must be considered when deciding between equal weighting (the least risky), the concentrated weighting (intermediate risk), and the short-long weighting (the most risky).

Summary

- Important to analyze investment process
  - develop buy and sell disciplines
  - avoid large losses!!!
  - recognize impact and importance of expenses and taxes
- Emphasize areas of strength
- Downplay areas of weakness
- Potential for adding value with relatively limited risk
- Important to recognize the objective of the investor, and his/her risk tolerance as strategies are developed and implemented in pragmatic settings

To construct an investment process/strategy, it is important to develop an investment policy which describes the level of risk that the investor is willing to undertake, the types and instruments of investment, the benchmark of performance and time horizon of the investment. The risk profile of the investor is the most important aspect of investing. Assessing where the individual is in his/her life cycle would indicate to a large extent the amount of risk that he/she is willing to undertake. This is a critical base of investment management as it directs the future course of actions. The investor then needs to decide on:

    a. Asset allocation – percent invested in equities, debt, money market, ETFs, mutual funds, derivatives, et cetera

    b. Asset class weights used in construction of a portfolio – percent invested in growth or value stocks, treasuries, corporate or junk bonds, et cetera

    c. Security selection – once the weights of asset classes are determined, individual securities (from individual stocks and bonds to ETFs and mutual funds) are selected keeping in mind at all times the risk objective of the investor.

Over time, the investor needs to monitor the performance of the various components of the investment as well as monitor the market for new opportunities to increase returns without increasing the risk level of the portfolio. The investor needs to maintain a discipline at all times and should never let emotions dictate actions with respect to investing. Before an investment is made buy and sell disciplines are needed, especially sell disciplines so one does not have a portfolio of losers. Moreover, having a good forecasting ability (high IC and IR) is advisable, especially for active strategies. The buy sell disciplines allow the investor to know when to liquidate certain securities that are not performing well or when they reach the target sell price.

CHAPTER 6
THOUGHT QUESTIONS

1. Develop a framework for equity investing using active and passive strategies. What critical elements are involved, and what is the role of forecasting?

2. Portfolio construction should follow a well-defined objective and carry out the construction process in a controlled and disciplined fashion. Identify some construction objectives, and discuss how to optimize the investment and manage the process over time.

Questions:

1. Identify characteristics of passive and active strategies, and the differences thereof.
2. What is the main determinant of whether an investor should use active or passive strategies? Does the level (e.g., market, groups, individual securities) of investment make a difference? How does one measure forecasting ability?
3. Describe the benefits of composite forecasting.
4. What are some desirable characteristics of a culling screen, and identify some screens that meet the characteristics? Which ones would you consider using and why?
5. Identify some buy and sell disciplines, what are the differences between them, and why are they important to have.

6. How does behavioral aspects relate to losses and mistakes? What steps can an investor undertake to avoid/minimize losses?
7. Discuss the important of transaction costs and taxes when investing?
8. Identify tasks necessary to construct and optimize investment strategies and portfolios.
9. In a long-short market neutral portfolio , what are the components of risk and how does forecasting ability play a role?
10. What drives the return in a long-short strategy?

Chapter 7: Managing the Asset Class Mix

CHAPTER OVERVIEW

In this chapter, we describe different ways of determining the long-range strategic asset allocation of the investment plan. Ways for managing the asset mix through time with tactical asset allocation methods and other rebalancing alternatives are also presented. Risk and return considerations are discussed and it is imperative that the investor keeps in mind that the risk of the investment is based on the investor's objective and risk profile. Additionally, each stage of the process should recognize the strengths and weaknesses of the investment team.

Introduction
- Asset allocation encompasses the selection and proper blending of asset classes, and managing the mix over time
- Target asset mix is based on the risk-return objective, with a focus on longer-range goals, and should have an acceptable range around the target percentage
- Empirical studies show that 91.5% of a portfolio's return is based on asset allocation
- Managing assets overtime
  - tactical allocation, shorter-term orientation where mix is changed to meet opportunities and to recognize losses if and when they occur
  - buy and hold policy – a passive and more conservative strategy
  - dynamic rebalancing – an active and more aggressive strategy

The fundamental characteristics of asset classes and the "normal relationship" between and among them can be useful in devising an asset allocation because this knowledge enables the investment/portfolio to be matched with the level of risk consistent with the objective of the investment. Knowing the fundamental characteristics allows the investor to forecast better, which in turn allows for more active strategies in asset allocation. Active management should lead to higher returns for the same or lower risk. Moreover, the investor needs to be aware of the behavioral aspects of investing and changes in the market place.

Strategic Asset Allocation
- Process of putting assets together in an investment/portfolio to maximize return for a level of risk consistent with the objective, which is based on the risk tolerance of the investor
- Four key elements
  (1) determine eligible asset classes
  (2) determine expected risk and return for each class over the planning horizon
  (3) use optimization techniques to find investment/portfolio mixes providing highest return for each level of risk
  (4) choose investment/portfolio that meets objective
- Forecasting is used to determine expected risk and return
  - extrapolate the past into the future (see III below)
  - scenario approach (see IV below)

Strategic asset allocation is the process of putting assets together in a portfolio to maximize return for a level of risk consistent with the objectives of the investor. First, the investor needs to determine the assets that are eligible for investing. Second, it is necessary to determine expected risk and return for these eligible assets over the holding period or planning horizon that best fits the objective(s). Third, techniques of optimization should be used to find investment mixes providing the highest return for each level of risk. Finally, choose the investment/portfolio that provides the maximum return at the appropriate risk level based on the investor's tolerance for risk. For example: see the graph below for a pictorial representation of investments using two major asset classes based on the risk return relationship over the past 30 years. Investor A with a lower risk profile would hold a portfolio of 40% stocks and 60% bonds, while investor D with a higher risk tolerance would hold 75% stock and 25% bonds. Note: risk is total risk.

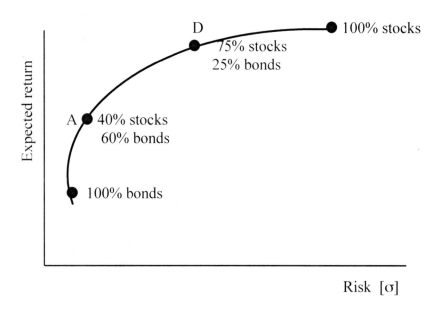

In regard to forecasting, the historical approach, used by the majority of investors, is used to develop input data for asset allocation and generally implies an infinite time horizon. On the other end of the scale, the scenario approach requires a more explicit statement of the forecast period. It is more costly and difficult then just extrapolating the past using a statistical technique like regression analysis. The scenario approach normally requires greater analytical effort and forecasting skill. However, looking at history can identify future scenarios and the ways these might impact asset class behavior. Using both approaches normally improves the information used to make investment decisions. These forecasting methods are discussed in the following two sections of this chapter.

Using the Past to Forecast the Future
- Reproduce returns and risks associated with asset classes
- Assume standard deviations and correlations among assets realized in past persist in the future – match economic conditions

110

- The level of interest rates is a primary determinant of the relationship among asset classes and expected return levels
- It is advisable to adjust for current levels of inflation, because real return is the primary concern
- Ordinary least square regression analysis is the typical tool of choice in this approach to forecasting
- Information can be gained by subdividing historical data
  - it is possible to gain further insight by subdividing into natural periods
  - performance of asset classes can diverge considerably (e.g., economic conditions change) over time
  - an examination of the various sectors/industries, styles of investment or company size will show that the performance and relationships vary over time
  - the key is to identity components that are most relevant for the future, best to use both technical and fundamental information in this determination

The historical risk-return profiles over time periods indicate that stocks generally have higher returns along with the greatest risk, while Treasury bills have had the lowest risk and return. During different time periods the degree of difference between performances has varied. However, over any rolling time period of ten or more years stocks always have done better than investment quality corporate bonds, which in turn performed better than Treasuries. It is also important to determine if behavioral factors impacted returns during differing time periods; for example, the dot.com era of the late 1990s and early 2000 is a recent example of irrationality in the marketplace where stock prices were driven by something other than cash flows. During this time frame investors were using the P/F ratio instead of the P/E ratio, or using "price to fantasy" based on the number of hits to the web site instead of ratios relating to cash flows. Besides looking at the past the investor needs to recognize the current and expected future conditions, e.g., is it expected that greed or fear will prevail in the upcoming time period, or will the "normal, more rational" investment climate prevail. It is also necessary to anticipate the "political climate" and how that effects government policies and regulations which, in turn, impacts businesses and the economy.

When employing a historical approach to forecasting one ordinarily assumes that the standard deviations and correlations among assets realized over the past persist into the future. However, subdividing historical data is helpful in making a forecast in that it gives the analyst perspective in identifying that component of history that is most relevant for the future. It allows the forecaster to improve the information instead of just using long-term averages, and if predictive ability exists the results should be enhanced. Additionally, projected returns should be adjusted for current and projected levels of inflation, mob psychological factors (if any), and the expected component of history that is most relevant for the forecasting period (e.g., good or poor economic times). Many forecasters accommodate differing inflation levels when making a forecast by calculating real return after inflation is taken into account.

Historical events and data help us understand how markets work. Even though "history repeats itself," the investor should not base their forecasts of the future solely based on history. History is important to consider in forecasting because it shows how markets, economies and individuals reacted in the past to certain events that unfolded. History gives an insight into general attributes of asset classes – how they performed given a certain economic environment. If we look at historical periods where market conditions have been similar to what is expected in the near future, we are then able to better understand the probable behavior of markets and asset classes. However, besides the need to temper historical data with a realistic adjustment for current factors such as inflation and behavioral aspects the forecaster should also factor in elements such as the effects of globalization, politics, and trends in terrorism that have emerged in recent times. History does not provide answers, nor can it. Overall history can provide a good basis for understanding probable scenarios that help analysts and investors make better and more informed decisions.

Scenario Forecasting
- Requires greater analytical effort and forecasting skill
- Provides greater flexibility in dealing with the changing environment and derives more effective forecasts
- Explicit statement of workable forecast period needed – 3 to 5 years
- Steps to implement the forecast
    - identify possible range of economic environments, including expected real growth and inflation
    - for each scenario develop implications for interest rates, stock prices, and holding period returns for each asset class
    - establish probabilities of each scenario–the number of possible scenarios differs based on expected economic conditions and the forecaster
    - arrive at a consensus forecast after several iterations

Market history may be useful in setting probabilities for differing market scenarios because it provides a common base on which to compare. Also, history has shown a tendency to repeat itself, and in the longer-term it averages out. The scenario approach can be used as a benchmark for comparing current consensus expectations for market return by looking at how the expectations would be affected in different scenarios.

Scenario forecasting typically builds on the past to some degree, but it should also be asking questions about what the future may hold (e.g., what is the likelihood of inflation, a depression, economic prosperity, a terror attack, a bird flu epidemic, et cetera). This allows for the identification of common elements, allows one to react quickly when events do occur, and provides the investor with solid information to make good decisions. Scenario forecasting can allow one to include elements that are difficult to formalize, including behavioral aspects. Different combinations and permutations of plausible situations and challenges that relate to economic and behavioral factors are analyzed and a most likely scenario is formalized and used for planning purposes. Typically, this is an iterative process and involves several, if not many, participants.

- Capital-market approach to scenario forecasting
    - returns for traditional asset classes are developed

- scenarios are generally consistent with an expected risk-return relation between asset classes (while similar to historical approach, differences occur based or expected economic conditions and the forecaster)

The components to a scenario method of forecasting are as follows: First, identify the possible range of economic environments that could exist. Second, develop for each scenario the implications for interest rates, stock prices, and holding period returns for each asset class. The final component is determining the probability associated with the occurrences of each scenario. A Monte Carlo simulation can help in this analysis.

Some comparisons between the scenario, historical, and capital-market approaches to forecasting include:
- historical implies an infinite time horizon, while scenario requires an explicit time period (say 1 to 5 years)
- scenario requires a greater analytic effort
- knowing history can help improve scenario forecasting
- capital-market approaches, while based on theory and similar to historical, move towards the scenario approach

Before moving on let us look at an example of forecasting and asset allocation. The following is an example of how the asset allocation can change to provide a better risk-return tradeoff for a moderately conservative investor. Because the performance numbers are based on historical numbers, one should anticipate that actual performance will vary except for the "guaranteed asset class." The guaranteed asset is a lower risk choice that is typically offered by an insurance company. The insurance company provides a certain rate of return, which is normally lower than most of the other asset classes, because the insurance company assumes all the risk. Furthermore, the guarantee is only as good as the insurance company, the guarantee is not backed by the government.

Asset Class	Current Asset Mix	Proposed Asset Mix	Percent Change
Guaranteed	14.9%	19.3%	+4.4%
Equity	54.4%	42.1%	-12.3%
Real Estate	0.5%	2.8%	+2.3%
Fixed Income	1.5%	33.0%	+31.5%
Cash/Money Market	28.7%	2.8%	-25.9%
Total	100.00%	100.00%	0.0%

Performance	Current	Proposed
Projected Annual Rate of Return	6.90%	6.85%
Standard Deviation	12.43%	9.66%
Return per unit of risk	0.56	0.71

The investor's projected return is reduced by 0.05% while the standard deviation is reduced by 2.77%. In pragmatic settings, a forecast of 6.9% versus 6.85% is basically the same, and to achieve the same return for a projected reduction in volatility of 22% shows the power of asset allocation and why periodic monitoring of a portfolio is required.

Furthermore the return per unit of risk summaries the benefits of each strategy, and the proposed asset mix has the superior ratio (0.71 versus 0.56).

The next step in this process would be to run a Monte Carlo simulation, of say 500 to 1000 trials. Simulating a number of possible outcomes based on expected economic conditions rather than only using the average return year after year helps to provide further insight. After doing a simulation, one can then state that the likelihood of the proposed allocation achieving a predetermined goal: i.e., based on a simulation of 600 trials – in 556 trials 95% or more of the goal was achieved; in 34 trials 70 to 95% of the goal was achieved; and in 10 trials less than 70% of the goal was achieved. For a more complete picture, the same type of simulation would be done for the current portfolio and this may increase the motivation to move to the proposed allocation, or it may provide contradictory information which causes the analyst to step back and rethink the situation and arrive at an optimum allocation.

Determining the Optimum Asset Allocation
- Following modern portfolio theory this is a two-step process
  - first, develop portfolios of assets that provide optimum risk-return combinations
  - second, choose a portfolio that meets the objective
- Because asset allocation is the primary driver of investment/portfolio performance asset allocation is the crucial step of successful investing

As noted previously, academic studies indicate that over ninety percent of a portfolios return is based on asset allocation. A straightforward sample of this two-step process was presented earlier in this chapter. Techniques and strategies all build on a successful original target allocation (i.e., investor A had 40% stock and 60% bonds) that can then be modified based on forecasting ability. It is generally advisable to have an acceptable range for each asset class in the target allocation. If the target allocation for stocks is 40%, an acceptable range could be 30% to 50%. If one does not have an acceptable range around the target allocation, it implies that the portfolio needs to be rebalanced on a daily basis, which would drive up costs tremendously. If you manage investments for someone else, a second reason for having a range is that all too often we operate in a litigious society.

Market Behavior, Timing, and Tactical Asset Allocation [TAA]
- Performance of S&P 500, asset classes, and other indexes vary over time
- Performance of the sectors within the index vary over time
- Process of forecasting shorter-term return movements and varying the asset mix accordingly is tactical asset allocation
- Changing behavior of market is relevant to implementing a tactical a TAA strategy
  - especially when it is cyclical in nature
  - length of changes impacts TAA performance and the ability to implement the strategy
  - After the event takes place, the investment is generally returned to its long-term or strategic allocation
  - Without special information or forecasting ability TAA does not work

- TAA presumes predictive capability and incremental returns greater than costs
- Assessing Predictive Ability
  - use information coefficient (IC) method presented in Chapter 6
  - generating inputs, comparing differing time periods, and making relative judgments is difficult
- Adjustment can be based on a formal analytical framework
- Engaging in market timing assumes some trade-off between risk and return
  - expected incremental return greater than cost to shift asset allocation
  - Sharpe ratio = (expected return - risk-free rate)/(standard deviation of return)
  - adjust risk of portfolio to keep Sharpe ratio constant
  - compare to Sharpe ratio of benchmark
- The key is to avoid large losses [see Chapter 6]

TAA is the attempt to identify and classify pricing discrepancies and then change the long-term investment mix to hopefully capture an opportunity. By its nature TAA has a shorter-term orientation and has the potential for adding value over time but also presents significant risks. Strategic asset allocation is the process of putting assets together in a portfolio in such a way as to maximize return at a level of risk consistent with the investor's objective over a longer time period. TAA involves forecasting shorter-term return movements and varying the asset mix accordingly. For many investors TAA is not a preferred strategy over strategic asset allocation due to a lack of understanding the market place and poor forecasting ability.

Cyclical market behavior can be long-term in nature while at other times it is short term. For example, the energy sector in the 1990s varied around the middle to lower portion of the sectors and then in 2004 was the top performer. The consumer staples sector was the top sector in 2002 with a loss of 6.3% and then second from the bottom in 2003 with a positive return of 9.2%. Information technology's average performance ranks among the top sectors, but individual years have ranged from -41% to +78.4%. The same type of variability is also true for global asset classes and style performance. EAFE Index funds were on the top in 1993 and 1994 before falling to the bottom in 1995 – 1997. EAFE then varied from high to low until 2004 when it once again was on top, where it stayed for three years before going slightly lower. Small stocks were the best asset class in 2003, but then varied downward to the worse in 2007, just to return to the best in 2010. Long-term government bonds were the worst asset class in 2006 and 2009, but were the best in 2008. International stocks were the best from 2004 -2007 only to fall to the worst asset class in 2008. In 2009, international stocks went back to the top to fall to second from the bottom in 2010. Being able to identify and forecast cycles is imperative if one plans to implement this type of strategy.

Studies have shown that market timing is difficult at best and adds only a little to the overall return of the portfolio (approximately 1.8% of a portfolios return is attributed to market timing). In order to justify managing market sensitivities the expected benefits need to outweigh the additional costs by enough to make the moves worthwhile. Obviously predictive capability is essential to take advantage of this type of strategy. Keeping track of the Sharpe Ratio is one way to measure how successful the market timing strategy is, especially when the ratio is compared to the Sharpe Ratio for the benchmark. The key behind this type of adjustment to the strategic composition of the portfolio is to avoid large losses. In Chapter 6, we showed that to just breakeven the percentage return has to be a greater percent than the percentage loss (starting from a smaller base).

Bullish percent indicators for the overall market and sectors can be useful for market timing and asset allocations. As noted in Chapter 2, if the indicator is over 70% the market is overbought and one should consider defensive strategies, while when under 30% one could be more aggressive as the market is oversold. The same concept is applicable to sectors or other groupings.

Forecasting the Market
- Success of forecasting depends on the skill of forecaster interpreting the data
- Technique of forecasting depends on preference of forecaster
- Valuation indicators
  - using the market line: compare current market returns with those of other periods to develop a perspective
  - develop a risk-premium valuation indicator by comparing current absolute returns between alternative investments
  - compare returns to inflation and assess real return levels
- Market implied returns
  - scenario framework provides perspective in evaluating current attractiveness of the market
  - revise probability of scenario based on the latest information
- Economic and technical indicators
  - relationship between economic variables and stock returns
  - economic indicators (e.g., rate of change of corporate profits, growth in the real money supply, et cetera) can be used to anticipate shorter-term changes, albeit with difficulty since it is not an "easy" task to understand all the relationships
  - the use of technical indicators, based on empirically derived relationships (many exist), improves the results
- Technical analysis (see Chapter 2) provides useful information to help forecast the market
- Composite stock market forecasting
  - individual predictors can be combined
    - each has some predictive power (positive ICs)
    - low degree of intercorrelation between predictors enhances the process
  - for example, using expected real return for stocks and an index of business conditions
  - indicators should be combined in line with the relative predictive power of the indicator, or a weighted composite provides the most useful information

Economic and technical indicators can both be used to assess the attractiveness of the market. Economic indicators have theoretical support and can be used to anticipate changes in shorter-term basic factors (e.g., growth of real money supply). Technical indicators are mainly based on empirically derived relationships (e.g., simple relation of recent returns to past returns on the market). Standard technical analysis (e.g., current level crossing a moving average) also provides useful information regarding the future at the macro level as well as for sectors of the economy. The risk premium approach to forecasting the market direction involves comparing the current absolute returns with the return on alternative investments, such as bonds and T-bills, to develop a relative attractiveness measure.

Multiple inputs are generally helpful in forecasting the attractiveness of the market because no one single source is always accurate. In order for a combination of inputs to be productive in forecasting the market, there must be predictive power for each of the inputs. Combining works best when the individual predictors show a low degree of interdependence among themselves.

Asset Mix Management
- Each approach to deciding on the appropriate asset mix has its own distinctive character, costs, and benefits
- Asset allocation is the most important driver of portfolio returns ($\approx 91.5\%$)
- No one approach is clearly superior, rather results depend on:
  - market environment
  - risk profile of investor
  - the ability of the investment team
- Choosing an approach that fits longer-term investing style usually works the best
- Buy-and-hold strategies
  - do not undertake rebalancing overtime
  - minimum transaction costs and management fees
  - avoids risk of poor forecast; however, no reaction to a changing environment increases risk
  - relative weightings within the portfolio change as market prices change
- Constant-mix strategy
  - active and requires periodic rebalancing
  - need to compare cost to expected benefit of rebalancing
  - maintain constant proportionate representation of assets (e.g. 60/35/5 stock-bond-money market mix)
  - market timing [tactical asset allocation] is a variant because it attempts to adjust for relative changes in asset values
  - results vary compared to buy-and-hold, they depend on market environment and forecasting ability
- Portfolio insurance
  - provides participation in high return periods of the stock market, while at the same time limits the extent of downside risk
  - inherently the most dynamic and requires the greatest degree of rebalancing
  - significant practical problems exist in effectively executing this type of approach
  - constant-proportion portfolio insurance is one way to undertake this strategy
- Strategy considerations
  - compare asset mix approaches to determine which one works best

- action required, payoff pattern, favored market environment and degree of liquidity are delineated
- one strategy will not work for all periods; however, it is not advisable to chase strategy based on the current period; instead, strategy should be based on maximizing strengths, minimizing weaknesses, forecasts, and following a well defined discipline
- any change in strategy should be done after analysis and slowly; normally it is better to tinker with current strategy to improve performance than undertake a radical change such as moving from buy and hold to constant-mix all at once

- Asset/liability optimization
  - investment plans have obligations that need to be founded by assets of the plan
  - liabilities should be considered as well when developing an investment mix
  - taxes are also another separate and very important consideration in the optimization of an investment or portfolio
  - process for asset/liability optimization
    - general process for allocation is similar to asset-only case, but the recommended mix can differ depending on the character of the liabilities
    - risk of asset classes can change given the character of the liabilities
    - match expected cash inflows and outflows

The best strategy to use depends on market conditions, from volatile markets to bull and bear markets, with and without volatility. Additionally, the strategy implemented should be matched to forecasting ability. Managing investments over time involves the process of putting assets together to maximize return for a level of risk consistent with the objective of the investor. Three major strategies for managing assets in a portfolio over time include:

(1) tactical asset allocation [TAA]
(2) buy and hold
(3) dynamic rebalancing (portfolio insurance)

TAA has the potential for adding value over time as the asset mix is changed to meet the forecast (assuming predictive content). Furthermore, it is a strategy that involves taking an incremental risk in order to achieve an incremental return. In a highly volatile market, TAA would not do well because it is doubtful that the trend could easily be predicted. Buy and hold would also not do well in a highly volatile market because of its linear relationship with the market. The best performer in highly volatile markets would be portfolio insurance because the portfolio would be protected from the large market fluctuations.

In a stable but trendless market, portfolio insurance would not do well because of the cost of the insurance. TAA would also not do well because of the associated transaction costs and the lack of a trend. The best performer in a market without a trend would be the buy and hold strategy because of the minimal costs associated with this strategy.

In a bull market with volatility, portfolio insurance would do the worst because of the reduction of returns due to the insurance. Buy and hold would be second best because the value of the portfolio would increase over time. However, the best performer would be TAA because of allocating the portfolio's assets most effectively to capture the high returns of the bull market.

In a bear market with volatility, buy and hold would do the worst since you are doing nothing to realize a positive return and the market is going down. TAA falls in the middle in this type of market because you would be moving out of the worst performers. The best performer would be portfolio insurance because you would be protecting the value of the portfolio as the market is declining.

In a bull market with low volatility, the portfolio insurance would do the worst because you are lowering your returns. TAA would do better because you would realize gains but you would have high transactions costs. The best performer would be buy and hold because you would realize the increase in portfolio value associated with the bull market.

At times the goal is not just reducing risk for an expected level of return. Instead, portfolio objectives need to recognize obligations or liabilities, such as health insurance and pension plans. The nature of the liabilities will determine the best allocation of assets. The key is to match expected returns with "known' outflows. Regardless of the asset mix and management thereof, a key element is forecasting ability, and as noted above no one approach is clearly superior.

Summary
- Investment models provide a framework for determining asset allocation that best meets longer-term goals
- An analytical framework that considers the time horizon and forecasting ability is needed for successful asset allocation
- The composition of assets in a portfolio is critical because the allocation of assets determines the performance of the investment
- Forecasting ability is a major consideration and helps drive the investment strategy

Asset allocation is the most important consideration in managing investments since studies have shown that over 90 percent of the portfolio return can be attributed to the allocation of assets. The allocation of assets is based on the objective of the investor, which in turn is based on the risk profile of the investor – or simply put, the allocation is based on risk considerations because an investor manages risk and returns follow. After the initial determination of asset allocation, the strategies followed to shift the weighting of them over time is based primarily on the forecasting ability of the investor and the information available. Buy and sell disciplines are also important.

CHAPTER 7
THOUGHT QUESTIONS

1. Discuss asset allocation from an investor's point of view, including the process of putting assets together and managing the mix over time. Which strategy would you use to manage assets over time, and why would you prefer the strategy?

2. What lessons can be learned from the past to help forecast the future? Derive a general forecast for the next three years from public sources (media, Internet, et cetera), and then make your own forecast, indicate which asset management strategy you would use. Why?

Questions:

1. Identify the key elements of asset allocation.
2. Discuss how the fundamental characteristics of asset classes can be useful in devising an investment strategy, and how forecasting and behavioral aspects impact the strategy.
3. Provide a general description of the historical and scenario approaches to forecasting.
4. Discuss how forecasting impacts asset allocation.
5. What is the major driver of investment/portfolio performance?
6. What is tactical asset allocation [TAA]?
7. How can technical analysis be used to help forecast the market?
8. Discuss three strategies on asset mix management and what determines performance.
9. Assume the following market environments: (a) highly volatility, (b) stable but trendless, (c) bull market with volatility, (d) bear market with volatility, and (e) bull market with low volatility. Describe how each of the three strategies would fare in each of the market environments listed above.

Ice Fishing

	Ice	*Investing*
Set a goal	*beyond viewable horizon*	*beyond viewable horizon*
Forecast	*location of fish*	*hopeful possible return*
Research and knowledge	*believe hole will yield fish*	*believe a positive return in future*
Luck	*little doubt*	*do not overlook or underrate*

Use available tools and information to make the
best possible decisions,
outcomes are uncertain.

Chapter 8: Equity Investment:
Styles and Strategies

CHAPTER OVERVIEW

In this chapter, building on the prior two chapters, we continue the focus on equity investments and describe equity-style management and how quantitative techniques can be used to identify relevant styles. These styles can be blended into the overall equity strategy. Two of the most popular ways of investing according to style differentiations are: (1) investing according to size of company and (2) investing according to growth or value characteristics of stocks. Styles are based on the differing behavior of grouping of stocks in the market place. We also discuss how executing style-based strategies calls for relevant groupings, appropriate classification of stocks, active/passive strategies, and balancing risk against potential returns. As always, the overall risk of the investment/portfolio, regardless of the style, should be based on the objectives.

Introduction
- Styles of investing
  - investment strategies
    - growth
    - value
  - differentiation according to size – assets or capitalization of the company
    - small-cap
    - mid-cap
    - large-cap
  - there is no single unique definition for market cap sizes
- Rotators attempt to shift focus into style that promises best performance
- Styles are based on the differing behavior of groupings of stocks in the market place
- Groupings represent subcomponents of a broader stock market which allow differing strategies based on expected group behavior
- Concepts relate well to investment models
- Differing groups have implications for investment strategies and investor behavior

Styles and strategies for equity securities are varied, and no single strategy results in consistently better performance. Bill Miller basically followed a value style and outperformed the S&P500 for 15 years; however, for the next several years the performance of the Value Trust fund was less than stellar. Managing by size also has up and downs in the performance. In many ways, the concept of styles is just recognizing that risk is multifaceted and it relates well to investment models (e.g., including an extra group risk factor). Because implications for each style vary over time one strategy is to divide a portfolio into style allocations, e.g., 40% growth, 40% value, and 20% dividend yield. Of course a buy and sell discipline needs to be developed and implemented for each style of investing. Also, styles have a lot of overlap and should not be considered mutually exclusive. For example, growth companies are generally smaller in size, while value companies tend to be larger.

Size Classification and Strategies
- Justification is based on differing liquid characteristics and empirical evidence
- Small stocks have: less liquidity, greater expected return than large stocks, and more volatility (supported by empirical evidence)
- Performance varies significantly within a group, especially for small stocks
- Performance is dependent on market environment
- Benchmarks exist to monitor performance
    - large firms: S&P 500 Index, Russell 1000 Value Index, Wilshire Large Growth Index, among many
    - smaller firms: Russell 2000 Index, Wilshire Small Cap 1750 Index, S&P Mid-Cap Index, among many
- blending small-capitalization strategy with a large-capitalization strategy has potential for improving risk-return characteristics of overall investment program
    - low correlation between sizes
    - above-average returns on small-cap investing
    - enhance returns by applying discipline valuation procedures to small-cap stocks
- risk-return profile of strategies is dependent on market environment and expectations of future
- overall risk of portfolio should be in line with objectives of the investor

An examination of the performance of relative size over several years leads to several observations. When large-cap stocks were doing well (e.g., mid to late 1990s) small-cap stocks were not doing as well. In the early to mid 2000s small-caps did better and large-caps did not do as well. It should be noted that it is also possible to classify stocks by combing size and growth or value: e.g., large value, small growth, et cetera. Small cap growth outperformed small cap value in 2009 and 2010. Emerging markets did the best from 2003 to 2007. As expected during difficult years such as 2002 and 2008 bonds did very well. An active strategy of shifting between styles, size, or sectors of investing should only be undertaken if there is some degree of success in forecasting trends. If there is little or no forecasting ability then a passive strategy of weights similar to an index that matches the investors risk tolerance would be appropriate.

Annual returns of key indices demonstrate the variability in performance. After being among the worse performers in 2000 and 2002 the Russell 2000 Growth index was nearly the top performer in 2003, just to fall to the middle in 2004. The Russell 2000 Value index was at the bottom in the late 1990s and then shot to the top in the new millennium. In the mid- to late 1990s the S&P 500 Index was near the top, and from 2000 to 2006 it was in the mid- to lower half of relative returns of key indices.[1] As the preceding demonstrates, diversification is necessary to achieve steady returns over the years. This also points out the uncertainty inherent in the financial markets. The rankings in the tables provided by Callan Associates, Inc. and others change every year. Additionally, the above demonstrates why it is important to diversify across styles, size and sectors/regions.

---

[1] See http://www.callan.com/research/ for charts of returns for various indices.

Growth, Value and Dividend Stock Groupings
- Fundamental characteristics usually differ significantly in growth and value groupings
- Traditional objectives of funds describe (1) growth and (2) income/growth which is also known as value
- Broadly characterized as:
  - growth, expected to grow at superior rate
  - value, growing in line with economy
- Value investing is in line with Graham and Dodd or Warren Buffet
- Measure growth expectation by: ROE*b = sustainable growth, where b = retention rate
- Groupings of growth and value are distinguished by retention rates, profitability rates, price to book ratios, P/E ratios, and dividend yield
- Growth/value performance indexes
  - needed for proper evaluation of performance of investors/managers
  - underlying fundamental attribute used to classify stocks and develop index (e.g., rate of growth, P/E or P/B or PEG)
  - index provides benchmark for gauging performance
  - both growth and value "indexes" can be derived from the S&P 500
- Dividend is not a typical asset grouping
  - expected dividend yield significantly higher than market or index average
  - long history of paying dividends and a reasonable risk level
  - has overlap with value grouping
  - provides a safety net, especially in down markets
- Characteristics of groups are not mutually exclusive

Growth and value styles are two primary ways of investing in equity securities. Firms with higher expected growth coupled with low or no dividends are considered growth stocks. Firms with higher dividends and lower growth prospects are considered value firms. As noted previously, neither strategy is superior for all periods. During the mid to late 1990s growth was the area to be in; however, with the collapse of the dot.com bubble growth stocks were 'slaughtered' and value stocks were the heroes.

Dividend stocks are often overlooked in strategies and classification or groups. With poor economic growth 2008 – 2012, high unemployment, low yields on debt instruments, and uncertainty about future prospects dividend paying stocks attracted attention. When identifying a high yield dividend stock one needs to be careful because in some cases high yield stocks are securities that should be avoided. For example, a firm that pays a dividend but has a low stock price because of poor business prospects or negative performance will have a high yield – obviously not a good selection for a long position. In fact, some firms have been known to borrow money in order to pay a dividend as they are trying to avoid bankruptcy. Hence, one needs to be sure the risk is in line with the market or index and that the firm has a history of paying dividends. Dividend stocks have a yield significantly higher than the average yield, and represent a safe haven for investors in that they provide a cushion if markets are not performing well. On the other hand, in boom conditions dividend stocks generally do not perform as well because they still only provide dividend income and not growth. Over the longer term, having some dividend stocks will help the portfolio outperform its benchmark.

It should be kept in mind that characteristics to define groups can vary over time, and are not deterministic. One should not look at just one characteristic and determine a group for a firm or an industry. For example, in 2012 the S&P 500 telecom industry group had a (P/E) ratio of 16.0, the highest among the S&P 500 industry groupings. Normally a high (P/E) signifies a growth classification and expectations of low dividends. However, while carrying a (P/E) = 16 the telecom group also had a dividend yield of 5.5% (the highest yield among the S&P 500 industry groupings). Typically high yields are an indication of value, and with a yield of 5.5% it would classify as a dividend grouping. We should note this above is the average for the S&P 500 industry group and each stock would have to be evaluated separately and classified according to their individual characteristics.

Price Action Groups
- Another way of classifying stocks into groups is to analyze differing price behavior
- Statistical techniques, such as discriminate analysis or cluster analysis, can be used to separate stocks into groups
  - groupings are homogeneous
  - stocks within each group show a strong pricing co-movement and tend to act independently of other groupings
- Four groupings which have been identified and shown useful for investment strategies (with implications for both active and passive strategies) are:
  1) growth
  2) cyclical
  3) stable
  4) energy

Distinguishing characteristics of the four subgroupings include the following:
1. Growth - earnings of these companies are expected to show a faster rate of secular expansion than the average company.
2. Cyclical - these companies have an above-average exposure to the economic cycle. Earnings would be expected to be down more than the average in a recession and up more than the average during the expansion phase of the business cycle.
3. Stable - these companies have a below-average exposure on the economic cycle. Earnings would be expected to be down less than the average in a recession and up less than average during the expansion phase of the business cycle. Earnings of these companies are the most adversely impacted by inflation but fare relatively the best in periods of decelerating inflation, or disinflation.
4. Energy - these companies supply energy to both producers and consumers. The earnings of these companies are affected by the economic cycle but more importantly by trends in the relative price of energy.

The market behavior of these stocks qualifies them as homogeneous because stocks within each group show a strong co-movement, and at the same time tend to act independently of other stock groupings. They are indicative of extra-market risk and return relationship discussed previously and can be used in a multi-index model.

Portfolio Construction: Passive and Active Strategies
- Passive strategy
    - compare fund weights of style, size or price action to some market average (e.g., S&P 500) or index that has risk relevant to the objective of the portfolio
    - determine if the portfolio is diversified relative to average or if concentrated in a particular area that results in different risks and performance expectations
    - weighting should be in line with the index and a passive strategy avoids overweighting a wrong group or concentrating in the group doing better than the average (period dependent results)

- Active strategy or group rotation
    - pursue policy of shifting fund weightings among groups based on outlook for the groups, know as group rotation, if able to forecast
    - returns to investment strategies need to be examined (e.g., group rotation versus buy and hold) to see if benefits outweigh the costs
    - substantial opportunity for improving portfolio performance exists; however, one needs some predictive ability to be successful
    - without forecasting ability one should follow a passive strategy in order to avoid losses that could be incurred with poor predictions

Rotation strategies apply to size classification, styles, price action and combinations thereof. As an investor follows an active rotation strategy they need to keep in mind the overall risk tolerance and the objectives of the portfolio. All too often individual investors chase the latest, hottest style and catch it on the downside instead of the upside. Casual empiricism shows that size classifications follow a three to six year cycle – hence, if large value has performed well over several years investing in small value might be prudent instead of trying to catch the large value bandwagon. Using technical analysis might help one judge the timing of active rotation strategies. One also needs to keep in mind the costs associated with an active rotation strategy, and expected benefits should exceed the cost.

Forecasting Growth Stock Performance
- Relative swings between growth and value stocks present opportunities for investors
- However, normally if an investor is good in growth stocks they will not be as good with value stocks, and vice versa
- Analyze different factors to judge direction of performance growth versus value, and cyclical, stable, and energy stocks
- Interest rate impact
    - common stocks display a long duration
    - classify growth versus non-growth by duration, with growth having longer duration due to lower dividend yield
    - interest rate changes should have major impact on growth stocks and their P/E ratios which provides an additional benefit if interest decreases
    - dividend stocks will have lower durations on a relative basis to growth stocks
- Yield Curve

- relative performance of growth versus value stocks correlate well with interest rates or decline in corporate earnings
- slope of yield curve may be an implicit forecast of earnings changes given slope signals information about future economic conditions (e.g., strength of economy)
- growth, value, and dividend performance depend on the slope of the yield curve
- Relative P/Es
  - appraise growth stocks as compared to overall market based on relative P/E (e.g., firm P/E compared to market or index P/E)
  - growth group tends to go to extremes in valuation; hence, valuation can be helpful in appraising relative attractiveness of the growth group

Interest rates are a major factor in investment selection and performance. Interest rates have behavioral implications especially when inflation is included. Because wages typically lag inflation, when higher levels of inflation occur people tend not to purchase as much because their money does not go as far. Inflation is a useful predictor of stock prices because there is generally an inverse relationship between inflation (as measured by the CPI excluding volatile food and energy prices) and average P/E ratios of the S&P 500. Hence, when inflation increases or is expected to increase, the P/E ratio decreases as do stock prices, at least in the short term. As a reminder, just because the relationship held in the past does not mean it will hold in the future, and the future is what counts.

Fundamental Characteristics of Non-Growth Groupings
- Analyzing a companies' source(s) of profit with fundamental characteristics can help discriminate among the groupings
- Characteristics include general level of prices (e.g., inflation), service/product of the company, stage of processing, backorders, et cetera
- Relative performance of non-growth groupings
  - stable stocks compared to the wholesale price index divided by the consumer price index ratio (WPI/CPI) have low correlations
  - cyclical stocks compared to the WPI/CPI ratio have higher correlations
  - energy stocks relative to the price of energy (which is an important component in both WPI and CPI) is highly correlated
  - given differing group reactions to changes in price levels (WPI and CPI) and on its components investors have the opportunity (if they have forecasting ability) to change the weightings of the various groupings within the portfolio with the expectations of improving returns

Fundamental characteristics can be used to help group securities and develop portfolios based on the objectives thereof. As noted previously, inflation is a major concern of the financial markets and even the expectations of inflation can drive consumer behavior, investment decisions, and performance of securities. Inflation is also used to help group stocks because of how different stocks behave to various levels of inflation. Assuming a capability for predicting inflation and/or groups moves, the extent the investor should act on the forecast can be based on techniques of active-passive investment management. A possible procedure: generate forecasts of relative attractiveness of groups; convert into explicit forecast of non-market return; and consider riskiness of each group to determine optimum investment strategy.

Economic Value Analysis [EVA] Style of investing
- Focus is on fundamentals of wealth creation
- Economic versus accounting earnings
- Return on equity greater than 'cost of capital'

The EVA style of investing emphasizes the fundamentals of wealth creation in the profiling of a company and its stock. Its focus is on the ability of the firm to generate economic earnings rather than 'merely' accounting earnings. EVA measures the returns above the weighted average cost of capital, or the net present value and wealth creation. This approach is in contrast to the typical traditional approach that focuses on accounting information and ratios like the P/E or P/B or fundamentals like cash flow. Implementing EVA is more difficult because the analyst really needs to know accounting and footnotes need to be delved into and taken apart to see how they impact earnings. However, at times a simplistic approach is used by comparing ROE to the required return (as measured by a weighted cost of capital), and if ROE is larger one concludes that wealth is being created and the security is a candidate for investment. Before investing an investor should determine if it provides diversification benefits.

Optimum Weighting
- To determine optimum weighting consider market and non-market risks of the groups along with the return opportunities
- Important to consider both risk and return
- Changing weightings changes risk of the investment/portfolio

Passive strategies remove a certain risk element of forecasting and reduce the cost of managing investments, but they also give up the opportunity to outperform the index. On the other hand, opportunities that are available from a strategy of underweighting or overweighting the major stock groups or styles are that it is possible to take advantage of a return opportunity while avoiding a potential loss. This occurs because the major stock groups or styles do not all move in the same way during different economic times. Rather they react differently to different economic conditions. If one has predictive capability and costs are controlled, it is possible to improve investment performance by under- or overweighting the different groups/styles. Employing this type of strategy adds nonmarket risk to the portfolio, which in turn could move the investment risk level and expose the portfolio to a different level of market risk.

Summary
- In devising a strategy for investing in domestic equity markets the investor needs to recognize subgroupings within the market place
- Each subgrouping and investment style needs to be evaluated on its own level
- Executing style-based strategies calls for relevant groupings, appropriate classification of stocks, active/passive strategies, and balancing risk against potential return

- As strategies are implemented the investor needs to be cognizant of the overall risk of the portfolio and how it relates to the objectives
- A portfolio manager or investor should not be chasing returns, manage risk not returns

Along with asset allocation the investor needs to be mindful of groups, styles and other sub-groupings of securities in the market place. Groups are based on factors such as size, industry, sector, et cetera. Styles are based on differing behavior of grouping of stocks in the market place. When determining asset allocation you need to be aware of these characteristics since saying an investment should be two-thirds in stocks is a far cry from specifying the groupings of stocks that should comprise the two-third portion of the portfolio.

CHAPTER 8
THOUGHT QUESTION

1. Discuss how styles can be blended into an overall strategy for equity investing, and identify reasons, benefits and costs of doing so. Would you blend them? Briefly explain why or why not.

2. Explain how styles of investing (investment strategies based on differing behavior of groups in the marketplace) relate to passive and active strategies.

Questions:

1. Indicate some variables that can be used to distinguish groups and how the variables are different in the groups (e.g., level of P/E ratio in growth versus non growth groups – high is growth, low in value).
2. What benchmarks can be used for groupings based on size? Based on growth and value? Why are benchmarks important?
3. Assume a forecast of a period of declining real growth with an increase in the general rate of inflation, as well as an increase in the rate of wholesale and energy prices. Which groups would be benefited, relatively, and which would be affected less favorably. Also indicate a strategy for such an environment.
4. How does a dividend stock grouping vary from growth and value stock groupings?
5. Identify three price action groups and indicate distinguishing characteristics of each group.
6. Describe how rotators use groupings in active strategies, and indicate grouping they can use.
7. Describe economic value analysis [EVA], what it emphasizes in profiling a stock and how it differs from the typical approach that focuses on "accounting information."

Chapter 9: Global Investing

CHAPTER OVERVIEW

In this chapter, we expand asset class possibilities into a global context and also describe strategies that can be used to manage the international equity component of an investment. The size and characteristics of the market and potential benefits to be derived from an international investment program are significant. Currency risk and its importance is discussed and a framework for analyzing currency rate differentials is established. Additionally, passive and active strategies are described for investing in international markets. These strategies follow the same basic philosophy and techniques as for domestic investing. Technology and Internet advances have made it a smaller world and one in which it is relatively easy to invest globally and gain diversification benefits. j

Introduction

- Expanding the assets classes to include international securities, which generally show a lower degree of correlation with domestic assets, is beneficial to the portfolio
- Low correlation between global assets expands the investment opportunities; however, it should be recognized that the correlation is increasing as more and more investors invest overseas, and the Internet becomes commonplace in the lives of investors
- Global investing, while beneficial, differs in that the security is normally denominated in different currencies
- Foreign exchange risk exists due to currencies whose relative values fluctuate
- Behavioral aspects also impact global considerations – basic investor behavior is similar worldwide, even if it varies somewhat based on cultural norms

International investing is normally beneficial for diversification because: 1) it expands the investment universe, 2) foreign securities typically have lower correlations with the U.S. securities than U.S. securities among themselves, and 3) it can increase the returns of investments while decreasing or maintaining the same level of risk. All of these factors serve to reinforce the benefits of diversifying. On an international level, benefits of diversification are even more evident than between asset classes within a country because of the low correlation between global markets. The MSCI EAFE Index (Morgan Stanley Capital International – Europe, Australasia, and Far East) is the pre-eminent benchmark in the U.S. for investing in stocks globally. It comprises 'developed markets' from around the world, 21 in total, excluding the U.S. and Canada.

The correlation across international equities while getting higher over time should continue to remain relatively low since many of the factors that affect stock values such as tax laws, monetary policy, and the general political climate are peculiar to the individual domestic economy. Furthermore, even factors that affect the world economy, including events such as the sudden increase in oil prices or wars, are likely to impact individual economies differently. The advent of the European Union and the introduction of the

Euro reduced the differences between European countries/markets. However, with the debt crisis in Greece and other Euro countries differences started to increase as well as risk. The Internet is increasing the correlations at a faster pace than previously. Likewise, events like the terrorist attacks on 11 September have a tendency to impact markets in such a way that correlations increase – especially immediately after the event.

The inclusion of foreign securities might be beneficial even if expected returns are lower for these securities because of the risk-reduction power. Since foreign securities help to lower total investment risk, the investor can accept a lower level of return, as long as the return is not so low as to offset the risk reduction benefits.

Global Equity Markets
- Global markets are constantly under change
  - United States is the most significant single market
  - close to one-half of the global market is outside the USA
  - relative size of U.S. market is declining over time
  - three major geographic regions
    1) North America
    2) Pacific Rim
    3) Europe
  - within groupings, individual countries tend to be more highly correlated than with countries outside the region
  - omitting any of the three groupings would degrade diversification
  - many securities, both U.S. and foreign, are listed on exchanges around the world
  - foreign companies listed on U.S. exchanges are known as ADRs, American Depository Receipts, and are denominated in U.S. dollars
  - securities are traded twenty-four hours a day (one reason why opening prices may not match the closing price of the day before)
  - as technology advances global markets are becoming more efficient, still there is a long way to go for many markets (especially ones in less developed countries)
- Risk-return character of global equity market
  - currency changes impact the performance of international equity investing
  - conversion to or from U.S. dollars can result in an added gain or loss on returns earned in the foreign market
  - two major periods
    1) 1995 - 2001 dollar strength, loss on return
    2) 2001 – present (2013) dollar weakness, gain on return
  - similar patterns were observed with the strong dollar in the early 1980s and the weak dollar during the late 1980s to mid 1990s
  - currency exchanges can impact realized returns significantly over shorter intervals, but over the longer term will average out; however, risk is increased
- The Internet has made global investing easier
  - currency conversion calculators are readily available
  - for example, http://www.oanda.com/convert/classic
  - information regarding everything from companies to countries is available

International equities are an asset class that can add diversification and excess returns to a portfolio. In 2003 the MSCI EAFE Index gained 39% compared to the S&P500 performance of 29%. Of the 39%, approximately 15% was due to currency exchange rate changes. Moreover, it should be recognized that there is a rising correlation between U.S. equities and international equities. Nevertheless, some predictions are that international equities could outperform their U.S. counterparts over the next several years. The primary reasons for this forecast are lower valuations and higher dividends found in most asset classes. Of course, exchange rate considerations also need to be considered. Additionally, it should be recognized that emerging markets still represent higher risk.

The returns generated in a local currency might differ from the U.S. dollar return because of changes in the U.S. dollar exchange rate with that local currency (exchange rate risk). If the dollar appreciates with respect to that currency, returns to the U.S. investor will be lower in dollar terms than in local currency terms. Similarly, if the dollar declines in value, returns to the U.S. investor will be greater than those expressed in terms of the local currency.

The flow of funds in an international investment is shown in the chart below, and then two examples, which ignore fees and transaction costs, are presented.

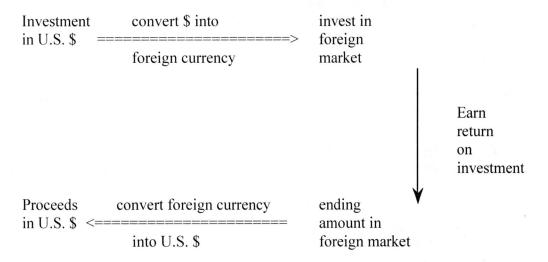

The performance (r) of the investment is:

r = ((Proceeds – Investment)/Investment)*100, all in U.S. dollars

For example, on 9 June 2006 a $1 investment converted into Euros (assume an exchange rate of 1.27 $/€) would equal around €0.79, which then realized a gain of 15% on an investment in Germany for an ending Euro amount of about €0.91 on June 9th 2007. The ending Euro amount converted back to U.S. dollars (assume an exchange rate of 1.34 $/€) equals about $1.22. The overall performance of the investment is +22% [((1.22 - 1)/1)*100]. Breaking down the performance shows a positive 15% return from the investment in Germany, and an additional 7% from the change in the exchange rate. The majority of the return is based on the investment (15%); however, in this example with the

131

dollar becoming weaker a very good investment in Germany generates an outstanding return.

The first example shows what happens to an investment when the home currency gets weaker. Let us now look at an example where the home currency got stronger. Using the same time frame as the first example and placing ourselves in Australia, from a down under point of view, an investment of $1A into the U.S. on June 9, 2006 (assuming an exchange rate of 1.35AUD/USD) would equal around $.74US. The investment realized a gain of 10% for an ending USD amount of about $0.81 on 9 June 2007. The ending USD amount converted back to Australian dollars (assume an exchange rate of 1.19 AUD/USD) equals about $0.96A. The performance of the investment is - 4% [(.96 – 1)/1]. Breaking down the performance shows a positive 10% return from the investment in the United States, but the exchange rate swamps the positive return because of a 14% strengthening of the AUD for a net - 4% performance.

Investing globally adds another dimension, which increases variability to the possible outcomes. Hence, risk increases because of the introduction of exchange rate risk and other risks such as political risk. Positive investment returns can turn to negative performance just as easily as positive returns can be enhanced. In fact negative investment returns can be turned into net positive returns after accounting for the exchange rate (i.e., negative return on a foreign investment along with a weakening home currency).

From a behavioral aspect, the strength of your currency impacts attitudes and investment practice. If your source of income is based in a weak currency you have a tendency to avoid global investments since you are not getting enough for your money. On the other hand if you enjoy a strong currency you are more likely to invest globally because you then you get more for your money. From a U.S. perspective, paying 86 cents for a Euro in 2001 is more pleasant than paying $1.58 for the same unit of currency in 2008 or $1.30 in 2012. However, if you did invest in the Euro in 2001 when the dollar was strong and then converted back when the dollar is weaker you would have received a nice return. The examples above show both sides of this coin and the impact of changing exchange rates. Your expectations of change are the true driving force for global investing. If you think your currency is going to become stronger, you will avoid investing. On the other hand if you think it will become weaker, you expect positive gains above and beyond the investment return.

Financial markets of the future will most likely look vastly different than they are today – a seismic shift in many ways. By 2050 China will most likely be the largest market with the U.S. being number two. After the U.S. many predict India, Brazil, Japan, Indonesia, Mexico, Germany, United Kingdom and Russia, respectively, to complete the top 10 markets. You will note a significant shift of wealth and importance in the economic structure. The actual structure of the world will depend on many factors, including the dubious science of the so-called global warming, the "Green Religion" that is an outgrowth of alleged global warming,[1] terrorist activities, the financial power of the Middle East, and the impact of the baby boomers retiring. An investor needs to be aware of these forecasts and possibilities, along with actual changes as they occur, so they can implement appropriate strategies to keep risk in line with expected returns.

Advantages of Global Investing
- Favorable effects on diversification, higher expected return for same level of risk, or same expected level of return for lower risk
- Foreign markets provide a wider array of assets with relatively low correlation
- Potential of international diversification likely to persist into the future
- Market volatility and cross-correlation
    - correlations tend to increase when markets are most volatile, for example when tragedy or disaster strikes that had the potential to impact all markets
    - uniformity of October 1987 and September 2001 strongly imply a triggering variable that swamped usual influences of country-specific events
- Returns for international investing
    - lower returns from international are acceptable due to diversification (risk reduction) benefit
    - minimum acceptable return would be one that provided the same risk-return trade-off as a solely domestic investment
    - systematic risk or extra market risk are the relevant components
    - minimum acceptable returns were easily exceeded in the past, but it may not be safe to assume this will be the case in the future

The diagram below shows the benefits of investing globally. The EF moves to E'F' which has less risk for the same return, or more return for the same risk when investments are in a portfolio. Many foreign markets are not considered as efficient as the

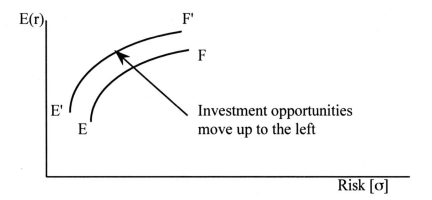

U.S. market, especially those in less developed countries. For the investor there may be barriers to international transactions such as exchange contracts, double taxation, and restrictions on ownership. Moreover, there are difficulties in obtaining information, differences in reporting practices, transaction costs, plus some foreign markets are

---

[1] They have switched to "climate change" because they finally realized that the earth has been in a warming trend for thousands of years and that variations occur. 'Many" global warmers not long ago were saying the earth was moving towards another ice age because of human activity.

generally less liquid than the U.S. market. Nonetheless, the Internet makes information gathering easier and there is a movement to standardize accounting practices. In the U.S. GAAP (generally accepted accounting principals) is used for financial statements and internationally IRFS (international financial reporting standards) is used. At the beginning many thought that the best of both systems would be used to create a universally accepting accounting system. Somewhere along the lines that concept was lost. GAAP is too onerous for international firms, and the Sarbanes-Oxly requirements made it even more so. IRFS has brevity; however, perhaps, it also provides too much discretion. Nonetheless, the International Accounting Standards Board [IASB] and the U.S. Financial Accounting Standards Board [FASB] continue to discuss common standards and framework in which to work. When they arrive at a common solution to financial/accounting statements and transparency requirements global investing should become less risky

Even if each national market were efficient, the markets might remain segmented due to such factors as psychological barriers, legal restrictions, political risk, and currency exchange risks. The degree of benefit of global investing is decreasing as the world becomes "smaller" and as more investors invest internationally. A decrease in potential benefits implies that the global market place is becoming more efficient and total risk is decreasing.

Currency Risk

- Assess the source and degree of exchange risk
  - spot market, currencies are exchanged immediately at the prevailing rate of exchange
  - forward market, traders buy and sell currency for delivery at a fixed future date, but at a price that is set currently
  - forward rates can be higher or lower than current exchange rates
  - forward rates are based on expectations about future spot rates, relative strength of the currencies, and the demand for them

The spot market is where currencies are exchanged immediately at the prevailing rate of exchange. The forward foreign exchange market is where traders buy and sell currency for delivery at a fixed future date but at a price that is set currently. A premium is when the forward exchange rate is greater than the spot rate. A discount is just the opposite: the spot rate is greater than the forward rate. Various factors such as political actions, inflation, interest rate levels, strength of the economy, growth rate of the economy, employment statistics, war, and natural disasters impact the expected future rates.

If the forward rate was not equal to the expected change in the spot rate, arbitrage opportunities would be available. If traders expected spot rates to be higher than the forward rate, they would not be willing to sell the foreign currency. They would buy the forward rate until it equaled the expected future spot rate, putting the rates in equilibrium. In Chapter 12, futures are introduced as an investment vehicle.

- Fundamental determinants of exchange rates
  - a four way interrelationship among expected inflation, differences in interest rates, expected changes in exchange rates, and forward rates exists:
    1. difference between forward and spot rate equals expected change in spot rate
    2. expected change in spot rate equals expected difference in inflation rates
    3. expected difference in inflation rates equals difference in interest rates
    4. difference in interest rates equals difference between forward and spot rate
  - relationships are consistent, and if three are established the fourth is then determined
  - purchasing power parity [PPP] theorem (relationship number 2 above)
    - o identical goods should trade at the same price
    - o over longer periods offers a fairly good description of exchange rate behavior
    - o in shorter periods, of say 3 - 12 months, exchange rate changes may be unrelated to commodity price changes
  - Fisher Effect (relationship number 3 above)
    - o investors are interested in real rather than nominal returns
    - o inflation would account for differences in nominal rates across countries
    - o impediments, such as governmental actions, can prevent this from occurring for extended periods
  - interest rate parity theorem (relationship number 4 above)
    - o differences in interest rates should be equal to differences between forward and spot rates
    - o based on arbitrage principals
    - o keeps risk free [R_f] securities in a particular relationship to each other
    - o net returns $= \dfrac{R_f*(\text{Forward price*})}{(\text{Current price*})}$

      where * represents any foreign country/market
    - o if net return is not equal to U.S. R_f, then arbitrage possibilities are available
    - o $R_F = R_f* \dfrac{FP*}{CP*}$ in U.S. dollars

      if R_f = right hand side, no arbitrage possibilities exist

      if R_f < right hand side, arbitrage possibilities exist, invest in U.S. dollars

      if R_f > right hand side, arbitrage possibilities exist, invest in foreign currency
  - the forward rate is an unbiased estimate of future spot rates (provides a good standard for assessing forecasting expertise)

According to the Purchasing Power Parity [PPP] theorem, the expected change in spot rates should be related to the expected difference in the inflation rates in the two countries. PPP is based on the law of one price, which states that a good should sell at the same price no matter where it is sold. If this were not so, there would be tremendous arbitrage opportunities available to investors. For example, goods that can be bought more cheaply abroad will be imported, thus forcing down the price of the domestic product. PPP states that if there are pricing differences between two goods, then it must be because of differential inflation, and thus differential inflation must be incorporated into the exchange rate between the two countries. Short-term PPP may not hold, but over the long-term it generally will.

Differences in interest rates should be related to differences in inflation rates. This relationship is derived from the Fisher effect, which indicates that investors are interested in real rather than nominal returns. If this is so, then prices of securities or interest rates should adjust to provide the expected real return. This would in turn occur across different countries allowing for a tendency toward an equalization of real returns or real interest rates between countries. Differences in inflation rates would then account for the difference in nominal interest rates across countries.

Interest rate parity indicates that the differences in interest rates between two countries be equal to the difference between forward and spot rates. This is a very strong relationship that is based on arbitrage. The difference between forward and spot prices must be equal to the difference in interest rates, or else investors will be able to profit without bearing any risk. This is accomplished by borrowing in the currency where interest rates are low, investing the proceeds in the money market where interest rates are high, and removing the exchange risk by covering in the forward market. The actions of investors attempting to take advantage of a possible interest rate/forward discount (premium) disequilibrium will force the interest rate differential between two countries to equal the difference between spot and forward prices.

The forward rate can be used as the consensus expectation for the change in the spot. Past deviations in the currency can approximate the variance in the exchange rate. From these pieces of information, the analyst can forecast the expected future exchange rate. As with any forecast it is just that – a forecast – and it can be accurate or not.

- Managing Currency Risks
  - pragmatic-world factors such as taxes, exchange controls, transaction costs, and others distort equilibrium
  - exchange rates diverge in the short-run and create substantial fluctuations that need to be considered in designing active and passive strategies
    - o hedge by borrowing or entering into forward currency contracts
    - o diversify across many foreign markets, which reduces costs
  - weighting countries based on forecast increases costs, risks, and expected return

In the 1960s, the gold standard tied most foreign currencies to the U.S. dollar. Thus, returns stated in local currency and U.S. dollars were very similar. However, the gold standard was masking real changes in each country's currency relative to the U.S. dollar. Under President Nixon the gold standard was removed in the early 1970s, and the U.S. dollar declined significantly relative to other currencies, making local currency returns and U.S. dollar stated returns very different. Also, the correlation coefficients among the markets were high in the 1970s, and relatively low in the 1960s.

Exchange rates create risk in global investing because "only" in the long run is there a tendency towards equilibrium. Exchange rates can diverge in the short-run and can exhibit substantial unexpected fluctuations that investment managers need to consider in designing and implementing strategies. Exchange rates between two countries can change due to such factors as government risk, inflation, depression, recession, financial risk, terrorist activities, and natural disasters.

A Passive Strategy
- Use the MSCI EAFE Index or create an index representative of the world market and invest accordingly
- Foreign country markets
    - may be dominated by only a few companies – if so, there is a greater degree of mispricing
    - market efficiency ranges in countries: less developed countries have less market efficiencies than developed countries, and even among each group there are variations
- Constructing an index
    - focus on major country markets that tend to dominate world markets
    - excludes some countries as well as emerging-type countries
    - within countries use stratified sampling across industries and major companies
    - should be in line with the objectives of the portfolio, or the objective of the portion invested in international securities

One might execute a passive strategy of international investing by creating a global index fund or an ETF. However, there is not one index that all investors agree upon as truly representative of the total world market. The total world market index would be different from MSCI EAFE Index – remember, MSCI EAFE does not include the U.S. (largest market in the world) nor Canada. To effectively execute a passive strategy, there are three basic approaches. The first one is to focus only on the major country markets of the world. The second is to create a world index by combining MSCI EAFE and, say, the S&P500 into a world index and invest according to the weights in the index. The third one is to select securities of major companies across industries through stratification. While all three strategies leave out certain areas of the world market, they can be most effective and cost efficient in diversifying globally. Following a passive strategy, similar to domestic investing strategies discussed previously, implies a lack forecasting ability.

An Active Strategy
- develop explicit forecasts of the market return, includes both currency and equity portions
- adjust forecasts for predictive capability
- consider risk along with forecast return and generate an optimum portfolio
- return forecast (currency, equity and total) for several major international markets

The essential elements of developing an active strategy for global investing are to develop a return forecast for a particular market, estimate currency changes over the investment horizon, and adjust each forecast for predictive capability. All three elements are important to a successful active global investing strategy. The results of this analysis would be to weight attractive markets high in the portfolio and to underweight unattractive markets up to and including not having them in the portfolio. The decision to employ an active strategy assumes that some predictive capability exists. A final element would be to generate an optimal portfolio, which incorporates risk as well as the forecasted returns.

An active strategy of global investing presumes a predictive capability, whereas a passive strategy assumes that it is difficult if not impossible to predict market outcomes. Both; however, recognize the diversification benefit of investing in foreign securities that reduce the portfolio's risk below what otherwise would be possible for a domestic only portfolio. With an active or passive strategy one has to identify a benchmark index so performance can be judged in a fair and accurate manner.

Optimum Global Portfolio
- Consider risk and return
    - currency/exchange rate risk
    - political risk
    - social/cultural risk
- Compare current portfolio to optimum, both risk and return
- Stock selection strategies: global markets
    - extend same philosophy and techniques as used for domestic market
    - Japanese stock market, at times, appears especially promising, and represents about 50% of the non-U.S. equity market (2007)
    - the introduction of the Euro, and consolidation of markets represents potential opportunities which did not exist previously, e.g., common currency but vastly different markets (i.e., the French CAC versus the German DAX)
    - in applying disciplined stock selection to other markets, it is necessary to properly address the differences that exist
- Valuation
    - apply the same type of multidimensional valuation approach as used in the valuation of U.S. securities
    - the following valuation dimensions are effective in global investing
        o long-term fundamentals
        o short-term fundamentals
        o fundamental analytical approaches
        o methods to assess market dynamics
        o factors related to economic dynamics
    - expected excess returns, positive alpha value
    - alpha dispersion in foreign markets is greater than the U.S. markets
- Portfolio Construction
    - focus on high-ranked (alpha) stocks
    - consider risk
        o market risk
        o macro risk
        o currency risk
        o industry risk
        o unique risk, including political and social risks

- develop investments that have favorable return prospects and a controlled risk profile that is in agreement with the objectives
- have the beta of the portfolio/investments in line with objective of the investor

After exchange rate risk political risk is another key aspect, and it obviously impacts exchange rate risk. Aon Limited, London provides political risk rankings which can be used to help assess political risk [go to www.aon.com/politicalrisk for the latest information]. However, forecasting the political risk map is difficult due to the turbulent times we live in. Generally, in the global investing political risk levels remain relatively high. Higher risk situations are less developed countries in Latin America, Africa and Asia. In addition to the less developed countries, higher risk countries include the PIIGS set – Portugal, Ireland, Italy, Greece and Spain. Greece is the most problematic followed by Ireland. The other members of the ECU and the IMF are helping these countries, but challenges occur because the countries need to demonstrate fiscal responsibility – which is a political challenge after living in excess. Safer countries are the more developed ones such as Australia or Japan, or ones in North America and Europe. Safer is best thought of in relative terms, for example, with the debt and budget problems in the United States, compounded by political challenges, is the USA not far behind Greece? The Internet and other media outlets are a good way to keep up with events, and as a general rule – if in doubt do not invest, or reduce your exposure if you are invested.

Making use of the MSCI EAFE index can help in diversification because of a correlation of less than plus one with a domestic index. Then again, making use of emerging markets and small-cap stocks can add even more value because of even lower correlations to U.S. indices and even the MSCI EAFE index. Hence, following a strategy of using MSCI EAFE indices along with emerging market and small-cap stocks can generate higher returns with less risk than just using MSCI EAFE indices.

Investing internationally should follow the same strategies as for domestic investing. For example, diversify over different sectors, groups, or industries. Outsourcing is becoming more of a reality for both U.S. and European companies. They are finding China, India, and other countries attractive due to low-wage, high skill workers. As this trend continues one should consider the risks of the high paid domestic workers and the lack of domestic production. Of course, over time the workers in countries like India and China are demanding higher wages.

Investing in countries like China and India have potentially high returns. Still, the investor must remember that there is significant risk involved above and beyond the normal high risk. Behavioral implications, possible government actions, and the social culture of the local investors must also be considered. Using a Western standard could lead to misleading estimates of risk. It is important, even as the investing world becomes more global, to recognize local factors. Looking at only global influences in a particular industry or sector may miss some of the unique industry and style risks for a specific market that will impact the return of a particular security. World markets are not fully integrated at this point in time. Investors and analysts need to consider both the global and specific influences when evaluating a particular company.

Summary
- Global investing expands the set of opportunities
- Offers potential for generating a portfolio with a higher return per unit of risk
- Potential obstacles include
  - formal barriers such as exchange contracts, possible double taxation, and restrictions on ownership of securities
  - informal barriers such as difficulty of obtaining information, transaction costs, and less liquid markets
  - remote in most countries, yet it needs to be recognized that there is an extreme risk of government confiscation or expropriation of assets, especially assets that have foreign ownership (e.g., Venezuela)
- As technology and the Internet advance the world becomes "smaller," information is easier to obtain and investors invest globally the diversification benefits will be reduced

The degree of activity in the global market will not only depend on the forecasting ability, but also on how stable the overall world situation is in reference to economics, war (including terrorists, and 'civil' wars), and general attitude of people and governments. In many ways we are fast approaching a true 24-hour a day market, and as we move in that direction there are implications for investors, especially those who pursue an active strategy.

You are in essence an international investor whether you want to be or not. Look at the clothes you wear – where are they from? What type of car do you drive? If you have a quality pen where was it made? your watch? the home appliances? your cell phone? the wine you drink? and it goes on for all aspects of life and material goods. Many large firms are international players so in some ways investing in an IBM or GE you are exposed to international aspects; however, adding foreign securities to your investment mix adds diversification benefits!

One challenge that still exists is the differences in financial information between countries. As noted previously, there is a move towards a global standard and there has been steady progress towards the goal. As stated by the International Financial Reporting Standards Foundation [IFRS] and the International Accounting Standards Board [IASB], the goal "is to develop, in the public interest, a single set of high-quality, understandable, enforceable and globally accepted financial reporting states based upon clearly articulated principles." Having a common solution to financial/accounting statements and transparency requirements should make global investing less risky. It should be noted that the major economies of the world, including the USA, have agreed to converge with or adopt IFRS in the near future – but implementing is different and more difficult to achieve than to agree. To find out the latest status one can go to the Internet: www.IASB.org.

CHAPTER 9
THOUGHT QUESTIONS

1. Briefly discuss the four fundamental determinants of exchange rates, and how they help insure international efficient markets. How can they be used in portfolio management?

2. Briefly compare international investing with domestic investing. Include expected benefits and costs. What is your opinion about investing internationally and the impact of the Internet on global investing.

Questions and Problems:

1. Identify the major global equity markets and compare the relative sizes of those markets.
2. Why might the return generated in local currency differ from the returned earned in dollars for a U.S. investor investing internationally?
3. How has the Internet impacted global investing?
4. What behavioral aspects are involved with global investing? Does the strength of your currency impact your investment decisions? Explain, why or why not?
5. Identify several advantages of global investing.
6. Explain how you might go about executing a passive strategy of global investing? An active strategy? What determines if you follow a passive or active strategy?
7. In general, are foreign securities markets as efficient as U.S. markets? Explain why or why not, citing evidence.
8. Identify additional risks an investor faces when they invest globally. Do behavioral considerations play a role in global investing? Explain why or why not, and cite a factor and/or sin.
9. How does correlation play a role in global investing?
10. Identify the fundamental determinants of exchange rates.
11. Describe the interest rate parity theorem and indicate arbitrage possibilities.
12. Assume that the exchange rate of Euros to dollars was $0.79 at the beginning of the year and $0.91 at the end of the year. Over the same period the return on German stocks was 15%. What would the net return be for a U.S. investor over the year? Identify the components of the return.

Chapter 10: Yield Curve and Bond Strategies

CHAPTER OVERVIEW

This chapter describes strategies for managing the bond asset class, both in a domestic and an international context. As with equity securities, while managing risk, investors endeavor to increase returns or enhance the value of the portfolio. One of the basic analytical structures investors use is the term structure of interest rate, better known as the yield curve. In this chapter, we describe how to explain the yield curve, how to analyze investments with respect to the yield curve, and the use of active strategies. We also discuss using the binomial model to value the embedded call option present in some corporate bonds. An analytical approach to evaluating swaps is then discussed, and several types of swaps are presented. International bond markets are described along with the benefit and risks involved when investing in them. Potential returns need to be balanced against the increased risks and costs of implementing the strategies. Behavioral aspects also apply to debt investing.

Introduction
- Bond investments follow many of the same concepts as equity investments
- Securitization of debt instruments or the slicing and dicing of debt obligations are not considered an option or feature of a bond
    - shifting of risk to the investor
    - not well understood in the market place
    - behavioral aspects, from issuers to investors, are involved
- Investors endeavor to increase returns via:
    - forecasting interest rate changes
    - valuing embedded options
    - investing in lower quality bonds
    - identifying mispriced bonds and switching (swaps)
    - investing in foreign bonds
- Bond features can be considered an 'embedded option,' for example:
    - call option
    - put option
    - convertible feature
    - alternative delivery feature
    - adjustable interest rates
- Call options
    - popular feature in many corporate bonds
    - transfer risk of lower interest rates to the investor
    - allows for the ability to refinance when interest rates are lower
- Yield curves provide a convenient framework for a standard of comparison and for implementing strategies

This chapter builds on the valuation and risk analysis presented in Chapter 3. Creating a bond portfolio follows the same principals of diversification as stocks. Bonds should be diversified by industry, group, or sector risk, as well as within a group. It should be noted that bonds are not safer than stock is all cases. If low quality bonds are purchased (i.e., ratings of BB/Ba or lower) risk is high. A recent example in Spring 2007 demonstrates this risk – namely, the sub-prime market in the USA. The sub-prime market was mandated by the Federal Government, especially during the Clinton Administration in the 1990s, and was based on the belief that "everyone has the right to own a house, regardless whether or not they could pay for it." The loan originators (e.g., commercial banks, savings and loans, et cetera) shielded themselves from the high risk by securitizing the loans and selling them to investors and financial institutions. In 1995 the Clinton administration instructed government sponsored entities [GSE] to have 50% of their portfolios in subprime mortgages. The best known GSEs are Ginnie Mae and Freddie Mac. These government policies helped lead to the real estate bubble. The Federal government eventually had to take over Ginnie Mae and Freddie Mac.

Should anyone be surprised when loans to risky borrowers with bad credit start to have higher default rates if the economy turns slightly negative or if interest rates increase? Unfortunately, based on the media reports, some people including many reporters, financial advisors, and bankers were caught by surprise in 2007. One should not be overly surprised that reporters were caught unaware since they are not normally trained in finance. Regretfully, the same cannot be said for many in the investment business – from financial advisors and mutual fund managers to CEOs and investment bankers. This surprise might be attributed to behavioral characteristics like shortcut investing where people perhaps thought: "secured by mortgage, therefore the investment must be safe." Another reason might be that a large number of people, including professionals, were really not aware of the risk involved with many of the new issues of debt instruments where risk was being transferred to the investor. An indication of the surprise in the professional ranks was the lack of liquidity in the market place once the subprime crisis started to unfold. If professionals were aware they would have known the risks and priced them accordingly. Why were so many people so eager to purchase these securitized high-risk loans? Perhaps a surplus of liquidity in the market place, 'good' interest rates and greed were the driving forces. One interesting behavioral aspect of this crisis is that people were willing to default on their home loan instead of their car loan or credit card loan. Are you surprised? After the collapse of the real estate bubble would you want to keep making payments on an asset whose value is significantly less than the loan that the asset secures? Or would you want continue payments on items you consider more essential? After all, having a car to commute to work is more important than if you live in a house or an apartment. In any event, as discussed previously, if you are trying to increase returns you are undertaking more risk. There is no such thing as a "free lunch," even if it is mandated by the Federal Government. In fact, as time goes on this is becoming more apparent.

Bond features from call options to convertibility change the risk-return profile of the bond. Call options are one of the more popular features included in many corporate bonds since it transfers the risk of lower interest rates to the investor, or it allows the corporation the ability to refinance and lock in lower rates. Municipals bonds with advanced refunding possibilities, especially if the bonds to be paid are selected randomly, face similar risk. As a reminder, bonds are purchased based on their yield and not their price - prices are quoted as a percent of par or face value. Therefore, the investor needs to know the appropriate yield: yield to call versus yield to maturity and which one is more appropriate. www.investinginbonds.com is an excellent source of yield on many debt instruments. Let us now turn our attention to yield curve principals before moving onto bond strategies.

The Term Structure of Interest Rates (or Yield Curve)
- Relationship between yield to maturity and time to maturity for a given risk class at a given point in time
- U.S. Treasuries are used to derive term structure of interest rates, which is also called the yield curve
- Level of curve determined by general level of interest rates
- Shape of curve largely determined by what investors expect interest rates to be in the future and the economic cycle
- Over the history of the U.S. three basic shapes of the curve include:
  1) ascending or upward sloping: investors expect rates in the future to be higher, trough of the economic cycle
  2) descending or downward sloping: investors expect rates in the future to decline, peak of the economic cycle
  3) flat: investors expect rate to be the same in the future, midpoint of the cycle
- Term structure typically has an upward slope that can be attributed to risk aversion of investors and their expectations about rates, or the longer the time horizon the greater the risk
- The ascending yield curve is considered "normal" (see graph below)
- If the curve is not upward sloping there are economic implications, and the change in the curve from normal to flat or descending is a leading indicator of the economy
- Three theories to explain the shape of the yield curve include:
  1) liquidity preference theorem
  2) expectations hypothesis
  3) market segmentation hypothesis
- The yield curve structure is part of the risk factors in assessing the risk of investments

A typical yield curve is presented below:

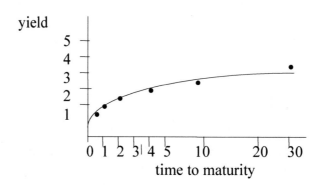

The term structure of interest rates (or the yield curve, as it is more popularly known) is a static function that relates the term to maturity to the yield to maturity for a sample of bonds in a given risk class at a given point of time. It represents a cross section of yields for a category of bonds that are comparable in all respects but maturity. Specifically, the quality of the issues (risk) should be constant. Ideally, if using corporate bonds to create the curve, you should have issues with similar coupons and call features within a single industry category. The yield curve is generally constructed using government debt issues – a single issuer with multiple maturities make Treasures the ideal instruments to construct the yield curve. Yields of other bonds can then be compared to the Treasures.[1]

It is generally presumed that investors require a premium return to invest in long-term rather than short-term bonds to compensate for the sacrifice in liquidity. Additionally, long-term bonds have greater capital risk. Their price varies the most, as compared to shorter-term bonds, with a given interest rate change. Due to lesser liquidity long-term bonds need to pay a premium. This is part of the reason why the ascending curve is considered the normal shape of the yield curve.

The theory of liquidity preference deems that long-term securities should provide higher returns than shorter issues to compensate for investors sacrificing liquidity. The liquidity premium compensates long-term investors for the added uncertainty surrounding rate changes and less stable prices. Moreover, longer-term bonds generally have a higher duration.

- Yield curve and forward rates
  - expectations hypothesis
    - long-term rates are an unbiased average of future short-term rates
    - the theory that best explains the changing shape of the yield curve
    - yield difference between long-term bonds and short-term bonds can be used to determine what investors expect future short-term rates to be
  - segmentation hypothesis
    - the supply and demand for each maturity set the clearing price (yield)
    - investors have maturity needs, and confine their bond investments to specific maturity segments
  - introduction of zero coupon treasury bonds (e.g., STRIPS, CATS, TIGRs,) in the 1980's allowed for a better estimation of the "true" risk-free yield curve, and future short-term rates

The expectations theory of term structure postulates that the shape of the yield curve results from interest rate expectations of market participants. It is the theory that best explains the shape and most of the changes in the shape of the yield curve. Specifically, expectations theory says that any long-term interest rate simply represents the geometric mean of current and future 1-year interest rates expected to prevail over the maturity of

---

[1] The yield curve in 2012 has extremely low interest rates due to the Federal Reserve intervening in the market place in an attempt to increase growth so the U.S. economy moves from recession/slow growth to a more robust and strongly growing situation. Interventions include quantitative easing and operation twist.

the issue. This does not imply that future interest rates will be the same each year. It relates well to market efficiency because as expectations change (i.e., when new information becomes available) the expectations theory explains rapid adjustments to the shape of the yield curve.

Generally, expectations tend to change in line with the economy as it progresses through the economic cycle. The liquidity premium hypothesis states that the yield curve tends to be upward sloping most of the time as investors must be paid a premium to compensate for the greater liquidity risk associated with longer-term bonds. The segmented market hypothesis states that investors have different maturity needs that lead them to confine their security selections to specific maturity segments. The supply and demand of each maturity date sets the clearing price (yield).

Before moving onto how future rates can be derived form the yield curve let us briefly examine each of the theories to explain the shape of the curve. Liquidity preference hypothesis: an upward sloping curve is explained by the need to compensate for greater liquidity risk. Thus bonds of different maturities can have higher yields even if expected short-term rates are equal to current short-term rates. An upward sloping yield can be consistent even with expectations of falling short-term rates if liquidity premiums are high enough. If; however, the yield curve is downward sloping and liquidity premiums are assumed to be positive, then we can conclude that future short-term rates are expected to be lower than the current short-term rate.

Segmentation hypothesis: the hypothesis would explain a sloping yield curve by the imbalance between supply and demand for bonds of different maturities. An upward sloping yield curve is evident of supply pressure in the long-term market and the demand pressure in the short-term market. According to the segmentation hypothesis, expectations of future rates have little to do with the shape of the yield curve.

Expectations hypothesis: An upward sloping curve is explained by future short-term rates being higher than the current rate. A downward-sloping yield curve implies expected future short-rates are lower than the current short-term rate. Thus, the bonds of different maturities have different yields if expectations of future short-term rates are different from the current short-term rates. If rates are expected to be the same in the future, you have a flat yield curve. As a result the changing shape of the yield curve provides a forecast of the future economy. For example, if the shape changes from ascending to flat and then descending it is a forecast for a slowing economy and perhaps a recession. On the other hand, moving from an inverted curve to a normal upward slopping curve would be a forecast for better economic times in the future. These implications are based on the assumption that the FED is not manipulating the market (i.e., quantitative easing).

Separate Trading of Registered Interest and Principal Securities (STRIPS) were introduced by the Treasury in 1985. STRIPS facilitate the calculation and estimation of the forward rates for bonds by essentially creating zero-coupon bonds with a wide spectrum of maturities. Each of the periodic interest payments is "stripped" away from the principal payments, and then the interest and principal payments are sold separately.

By "creating" zero-coupon bonds, the market is able to observe the forward rates of bonds more easily (see below). Practical problems while fewer with the introduction and widespread acceptance of STRIPS still include items such as taxes, liquidity premiums, embedded options, transaction costs, and other market imperfections. Rates can only be inferred, not measured.

Using the yield curve for zero coupon bonds the implied forward rates can be calculated by using standard present value and compounding techniques:
- the yield curve supplies the annual rates, e.g., 1 year, 2years, 3years, and so on
  - the one year rate is $= {_0}f_1$
  - the two year rate is $= {_0}f_2$
  - the three year rate is $= {_0}f_3$
  - and so on
- the implied one year rate from period 1 to period 2 $({_1}f_2)$
  - ${_0}f_2 = [(1 + {_0}f_1)(1 + {_1}f_2)]^{1/2} - 1$
  - ${_1}f_2 = [(1 + {_0}f_2)^2/(1 + {_0}f_1)] - 1$
- the implied one year rate from period 2 to period 3 $({_2}f_3)$
  - ${_0}f_3 = [(1 + {_0}f_1)(1 + {_1}f_2)(1 + {_2}f_3)]^{1/3} - 1$
  - ${_2}f_3 = [(1 + {_0}f_3)^3/(1 + {_0}f_1)(1 + {_1}f_2)] - 1 = [(1 + {_0}f_3)^3/(1 + {_0}f_2)^2] - 1$
- the pattern established above continues for all future one year implied rates
- the rates are inferred, not measured
- items such as taxes, liquidity, embedded options, and transactions costs are not included in the calculations

If prices are known instead of the annual rates one can calculate the rates from the prices, using present value techniques. For example:

$P_0 = P_1/({_0}f_1)$, so ${_0}f_1 = (P_1/P_0) - 1$;
$P_0 = P_2/({_0}f_2)^2$, so ${_0}f_2 = (P_2/P_0)^{1/2} - 1$; et cetera

After the annual rates are determined the implied forward rates can be estimated by using the process outlined above.

- Term-structure models
  - a critical task for investors is to determine the way the investment will respond to a change in the yield curve:
    1) assess systematic factors that are most important in the responsiveness of the bond or bond portfolio to changes in the level and structure of interest rates
    2) measure the sensitivity of the bond to these factors
  - a two-factor model best explains the process that generates bond returns: duration and volatility (the spread between short-term and long-term rates)
    - duration factor: most important factor, indicates level to which curve will shift, and is an indicator of exposure to interest- rate movements
    - volatility factor: the spread is driven by the volatility of interest rates, and captures the changes in the structure of rates across the maturity spectrum
    - price change of a bond is a function of these two factors

Factor models explain the process of generating bond returns. This is useful in understanding what determines the return of a particular bond or bond portfolio. Duration is the most important factor as it indicates the level to which a yield curve shift (assumed parallel) will affect the return. Another major factor is the spread between short and long term rates captured in the term structure of interest rates. This factor is generally driven by changes in the volatility of interest rates.

Bond Investments
- A bond portfolio exposure to duration and volatility factors is simply a weighted average of the individual bonds
- Compare portfolio average to those of an index to
  - position bond investments according to the objective of the portfolio
  - take advantage of perceived trends in interest rates
  - take advantage of volatility of interest rates
- An active bond strategy
  - forecast the level and shape of the yield curve
  - calculate expected returns (yield and capital gain or loss)
- Scenario forecasting
  - explicitly takes into account interest-rate risk
  - derive several scenarios, then use a weighted average to arrive at a consensus forecast to develop expected return and standard deviation for each bond
  - evaluate the uncertainty of the expected return in a risk-reward framework to determine the portfolio that provides the best balance between risk and return

The shape and change in shape over time for the yield curve can be attributable to investor expectations. These expectations are, in turn, changed by the general economic trends persisting over time. In applying active bond strategies, the investor must forecast the level and the shape of the yield curve at the end of a particular forecasting horizon. Given this forecast, the investor can calculate the returns attributable to the bonds in the portfolio owing to the yield curve change. It would be useful for the investor to forecast several different possible yield curve scenarios and calculate the resulting returns. The scenarios could then be weighted with an expected probability of occurrence, and thus expected return and standard deviation of the bond or bond portfolio could be generated. From these calculations, the investor could then alter the investments to provide the best risk/return combination based on the yield curve forecast. A risk-reward analysis could be undertaken to identify the best portfolio.

A study by Fabozzi, Martelli and Priaulet indicates that using a multifactor model of default spread, equity volatility, and short-term and forward rates it is possible to predict changes in the slope of the yield curve and to a lesser extent the changes in its curvature. Using trading strategies based on this model it is possible to produce statistically and economically significant performance.

As with equity securities, to follow an active strategy requires forecasting ability. One strategy is "riding the yield curve," which is dependent on the shape of the curve at maturity. If the shape is 'normal' (ascending) then as the debt instrument starts to approach maturity the yield should decrease. As yields decrease prices increase; hence, there is a possibility that an investor could capture capital gains by following this strategy and selling the bonds before maturity. Of course, one also needs to include the additional transaction costs that are involved with this strategy along with any tax consequences.

A more passive bond strategy would be to build a laddered portfolio, which is considered a relatively safe strategy. Building a bond ladder means purchasing bonds scheduled to come due in successive years. For example a five-year ladder would have approximately 20% of the bonds with a one-year maturity, 20% with a two-year maturity, and so on out to five years. Each maturity in the ladder should contain several different bonds for diversification; but, smaller size portfolios might only contain one bond for a particular year. After a step matures the proceeds are then invested in five-year maturity bonds. The shorter the ladder the lower the risk, and generally it would have lower returns. However, when the yield curve is flat or inverted this would not be the case.

Convertible, Call and Put Provisions in Bonds
- Convertible bonds allow the investor to convert the debt instrument into equity, at the option of the investor
- Many corporate bonds are issued with a call provision (ability for the issuer to redeem the bond prior to maturity)
- Call provision allows the firm to force conversion into equity if the stock value of the bond is greater than a straight bond
- Call premium: difference between call price and par value
- Call provision valuable to corporation, but disadvantageous to investor
- Callable bond – investor buys a bond and simultaneously sells back to the issuer a call option
- Callable bonds offer a higher coupon rate or sell at discount to noncallable bonds
  - price discount equals the premium for a call option
  - the embedded call option creates a degree of uncertainty and reduces potential return if interest rates fall
- Put bonds are relatively new and this provision allows the investor to redeem the bond prior to maturity and receive full face value
- Put provision valuable to the investor, but disadvantageous to the issuer
- Put bond investor buys a bond and simultaneously buys a put option from the issuer
- Put bonds offer a lower coupon rate or sell at a premium to standard bonds
  - price premium equals the cost for a put option
  - the embedded put option creates a degree of uncertainty and increases potential return if interest rates rise
- Yield curves for differing bond types, higher risk for callable bonds and put bonds should not be part of a yield curve unless the curve is for higher risk debt instruments

Bonds issued with either call or put options are based on expectations of future interest rates or the likelihood of conversion. If the equity value of a convertible bond is greater than a comparable straight bond the issuer may want to force conversion if the investors are not converting. Benefits of conversion for the issuer is that it reduces financial leverage, decreases outgoing cash flow before taxes, and increases financial flexibility. The investor normally benefits because they now have shares of stock, and if they do not want the shares they can sell them in the market place and recognize the capital gain. Of course, upon conversion the investor no longer receives the interest payment, and that could be a detriment for some investors. Nonetheless, the investor after selling the stock could invest the after tax proceeds from the sale into a new debt instrument and generate interest income.

Bonds with call provisions have been around for years while the put option is one of the innovations that occurred with bonds during the 1980s. If the issuer thinks interest rates will decline they want to have the option to call the bonds and reissue the debt with a lower interest rate. Due to the transfer of risk to the investor, the stated interest rate of the bond will increase or the bond will sell at a discount. On the other hand, if expectations are for higher interest rates an issuer may have to offer a put option to induce the investor to buy the bond in an environment where prices will decrease if interest rates do increase. The put option allows the investor to sell the bond back to the company under certain conditions for a stated price, typically the face value of the bond. In essence this shifts the risk of higher interest rates to the issuer of the bond. Because of the transfer of risk to the issuer, the put option reduces the stated interest rate on the bond or the bond sells at a premium. Put bonds will generally act the opposite of a bond with a call feature.

Valuing Embedded Options
- Bonds can be viewed as a package of cash flows (coupons and principal payments) plus a package of options/features on those cash flows (embedded options)
    - long a callable bond = long on option-free bond + short a call option on the bond
    - long a convertible bond = long on option-free bond + short a convertible option of the bond
    - long a put bond = long on option-free bond - long a put option on the bond
- Developing value of an embedded option entails the valuation of a bond with an embedded option and a comparable bond without an option, the difference becomes the estimated value of embedded option
    - value of call option = value of option-free bond - value of callable bond
    - value of put option = value of put bond - value of option-free bond
- To calculate values of option-free bond and callable bond or a put bond, need to recognize impact of duration and volatility factors using the binomial process
- Binomial model is used by some practitioners
- Binomial model provides a way of analytically portraying different interest rate paths, given an assumed level of interest rate volatility

An example of an embedded option in a bond is when a company issues a bond that has a call option on the bond, which allows the company to call away that bond at a specific time for a specific price (normally at greater than the face value). In essence the investor has sold to the company a call option. This is similar to listed options on a stock or the market index in that the same factors that affect a callable bond also affect a stock or index option: interest rates, exercise price, time to maturity, and volatility. The volatility of interest rates plays a major role in the valuation of bonds with embedded options, because the higher the volatility the greater the chance of the underlying bond changing its value. As variance increases so does the chance that the bond will be called.

The valuation on an embedded option in a bond is generally calculated by use of the binomial option model. Conversely, the Black-Schools model for option valuation is generally the method by which professionals determine the value for call options on a stock or index. Options are discussed in Chapter 11 in the derivative section of the book. Valuation of an embedded option differs from a listed option in that the embedded option is typically issued with debt and does not become "callable" or "putable" until a few years into the term of the debt. Once the bond becomes callable or putable, it typically remains callable or putable until the maturity date of the bond. A publicly traded stock or index option is immediately tradable and typically has a maturity of less than one year. Longer-term options on stocks are called LEAPS [Long-term Equity AnticiPation Securities] and typically have maturities of two to five years. Time value and volatility are critical components in determining an option's value; therefore, different approaches must be used in valuing an embedded option versus a listed freely traded option.

The general procedure for valuing an embedded bond option is to develop a value for both the bond with an embedded option and a comparable bond without an option. The difference between these two becomes the estimated value of the embedded option. In order to generate comparative values for option free and option embedded bonds, one must: 1) project cash flows for each bond, and 2) discount these back to present value at an appropriate interest rate. The standard practice for discounting these cash flows is to use a risk-free rate as estimated from the term structure of interest rates.

A binomial model values the embedded option based on specific scenarios of interest rate changes. The value of an interest rate dependent security is determined by market-wide assumptions about future interest rate behavior. The model typically assumes that the market is efficient and riskless arbitrage is prohibited. Using the binomial method entails forecasting different scenarios (create a binomial tree), estimating the probability thereof, and then determining the option price at then end of each node. The option value is then the present value of the ending node prices.

Moreover, if the price of the underlying stock declines the returns to bond, stock, call, and put change. Obviously, the return to the stock decreases, unless the stock was sold short in which case the return would increase. The return to a bond without an embedded option probably remains unchanged unless the price decline is due to increased default risk or increased interest rate risk. The return for a bond with an embedded option would decrease as does a call option. The return for a put would increase.

Changing Volatility and Bond Value
- Changing volatility of callable bonds (e.g., a 25-year corporate bond) compared to Treasuries (a 10-year Treasury)
- Callable bond behaves like:
  - a short-term bond as interest rates decline (expectations of call increases)
  - a long-term bond as interest rates rise (due to its long maturity and the likelihood of a call decreases)
- A put bond behaves the opposite of a callable bond

If there is an anticipated decline in interest rate volatility, the expected impact on returns for callable corporates vis-à-vis governments is that the return premium for the corporates will be lower. This is true because the value of the corporate with an embedded option decreases when there is a decline in interest rate volatility. Just as any option's value decreases when there is a decrease in volatility with all other factors remaining the same.

For a change in interest rates across the yield curve, bond investment values have an inverse relationship to interest rate change, and the amount of value change depends on such factors as maturity, size of coupons, and call/put features. As discussed in Chapter 3, these characteristics are best summed up in the duration measure. The higher the duration the greater the price change and one must recognize that there is still an inverse relationship (e.g., if yield to maturity increases, value decreases).

Volatility of interest rates has a significant effect on longer-term bonds. Therefore, in a more volatile environment, short-term bonds show only small changes in return performance while long-term bonds show larger changes in return performance. Intermediate-term bonds fall between the performance of the short-term and long-term bonds. It should be noted that the basis of the changes discussed here are based on the bond pricing theorems and duration concepts discussed previously in Chapter 3.

Changing Credit Quality
- Changing level of credit quality (default risk) offers both opportunity and risk
- Considerable changes occur from the initial rating over time (direct relationship)
    - longer the time to maturity the greater the number of possible changes
    - higher quality bonds tend to be downgraded
    - downgrading tends to be followed by a subsequent downgrading
    - BBB bonds tend to be upgraded
    - 'junk' or high yield bonds rated below Baa/BBB show no tendency
- Altman's Z score
    - relates to the probability of bankruptcy, total denigration of credit worthiness
    - based on discriminate analysis of fundamental valuation variables
    - provides a level of predictability of bankruptcy
    - various models exist, and one needs to match the model to the type of firm being analyzed

It is important to monitor the quality of bonds over time because research has shown that bond ratings do indeed change over time. For an investor who employs an active strategy of investing in bonds of lesser quality, this monitoring obviously becomes even more important. A process for monitoring bond quality begins with categorizing the bonds into standard rating classifications. Knowing the position of the bond with respect to these rating categories is an essential first step. While it is not possible to replicate the ratings using statistical techniques due to the "art" in the rating process, a reasonable next step is to incorporate the assessment of bond quality as it relates to bankruptcy. This involves using multiple discriminate analysis, such as an Altman Z score, to predict the probability of bankruptcy. The rationale behind using techniques such as the Z score is that changes in credit quality can effectively be assessed by analyzing trends in fundamental determinants. A Z score is just one piece of information that is used to evaluate a firm/bond rating. After exposure to credit risk is monitored in this fashion, the investor can then decide whether to anticipate individual rating changes in an effort to improve performance. This process should be repeated often as rating changes can occur frequently depending upon the position of the economy in its cycle.

- •. Ratings change and performance
  - investor should assess the impact of rating changes
  - use a framework to calculate return on portfolio and individual bonds
- • Monitoring bond quality
  - monitor bond quality by assessing trends in fundamental determinants (i.e., interest coverage, and debt/equity ratio)
  - use multiple discriminate analysis to classify bonds regarding credit risk, including bankruptcy

The major factors used in analyzing the credit quality are profitability, stability of earnings, debt service capability, liquidity, total size and market capitalization level. This analysis can help prevent buying bonds of companies which are near bankruptcy. Using discriminate analysis provides a systematic and objective way of monitoring these variables and thus the credit quality of bonds. All too often the market place has recognized the change in quality before the rating agency actual changes their rating of the bond, especially in the case when the quality has diminished.

If the credit assessment of a bond indicates a positive trend, and one estimates that the bond should be rated AA instead of its present A rating, a profitable opportunity could arise if the bond was purchased and subsequently it was upgraded by the rating agency as anticipated. This would be true because an increase in the quality of credit enhances the probability of meeting the terms of the bond indenture, and should result in an increase in the bond's price as its required risk premium declines.

Bond Swaps
- • A swap is the simultaneous purchase and sale of two or more bonds with similar characteristics in order to capture incremental capital gains and/or increased income and/or tax benefits
- • Swap strategies include:
  - substitutions swap
  - intermarket spread swap
  - tax motivated swap
  - credit quality swap
  - anticipation of interest change swap
- • Look for two factors: large yield differentials and short workout periods
- • Horizon analysis:

$$
\text{total return} = \underset{\text{(certain)}}{\underset{\text{component}}{\text{time}}} + \underset{\text{(certain)}}{\text{interest}} + \underset{\text{(uncertain)}}{\underset{\text{component}}{\text{yield}}} + \underset{\text{(uncertain)}}{\underset{\text{invested coupons}}{\text{interest on}}}
$$

- Risk of a swap is based on forecast being wrong or the change taking longer than expected

Horizon analysis is a logical framework which decomposes the various aspects of swap returns into four components with different levels of risk: two certain and two uncertain. For this analysis it is assumed that the coupon rate (stated interest rate) is fixed and not variable and that the maturity value is fixed in dollar terms. Certain components are time and coupon interest. Uncertain components surround gains/losses due to changes in yield to maturity and interest on invested coupons. The benefit of horizon analysis is that it provides a standardized mechanism for evaluating the returns generated by bonds, and with the different levels of risk identified the risk/return profile is more accurately assessed. It is important to recognize that horizon analysis is a future value concept and not present value. The reason for this is because of the fourth term of interest on invested coupons (or interest on interest). We now turn our attention to different types of swaps.

- Substitution swap
  - exchange of one bond for a perfect-substitute bond to earn several basis points due to transitory mispricing
  - increased return due to capital gain and/or income
  - risk is from a slower workout, adverse interim yield differentials, adverse changes in overall interest rates, and the possibility that bond is not a perfect substitute
- Intermarket spread swap
  - switching of bonds from different sectors, given belief that yield spreads between sectors are out of their proper alignment
  - anticipate yield spread to narrow or widen and capture resulting capital gains and/or yields
  - risk is from a market move in adverse direction, slower workout, and adverse interim price movements, or swap may be swamped by other differences between the bonds
- Credit quality swap
  - when bonds have their rating changed
  - when investor's risk tolerance changes
  - rebalance the bond portfolio to the desired credit quality
- Anticipation of interest rate change swap
  - forecast of future interest rates
  - swap into a bond that matches the forecast and objective of the portfolio
  - risk is from a market move in adverse direction, slower workout, and adverse interim price movements, or swap may be swamped by other differences between the bonds

A substitution swap and an intermarket spread swap are both initiated when an investor feels the marketplace has mispriced one security versus another. These swaps look at the relative value of one type of bond versus another based on historical pricing relationships. One would not undertake the swap unless the expected benefits exceeded the cost of the transaction.

For example, if the current spread is above the historical spread a possible swap would be to buy the bond at the higher yield and sell the bond at the lower yield. The expectation is that the spread will narrow with the yield of the higher yield bond decreasing and its price rising, and the yield of the lower yield bond increasing and its price falling. The risks associated with such an action include: market moves in an adverse direction, the workout period is slower than anticipated, adverse interim price movements, and the risk that the swap may be swapped by other differences between the bonds. Also, if the coupon rates differ, future variability of bond prices will be greater or smaller depending on how the duration changed (direct relationship).

Credit quality swap occurs when the rating of a bond changes, either up or down, and the bond portfolio needs to be adjusted to reflect this change. Alternatively the investor's risk averseness changes and the portfolio needs to be rebalanced to meet the new risk tolerance. For example, if a AAA bond is downgraded to A due to increased risk the investor switches into a higher quality bond. This could also be the case for an investor whose risk tolerance has decreased due to a life changing event and they need to move into safer bonds.

The interest rate change swap is similar to a substitution or intermarket swap. The investor is betting on a correct forecast and considers the objective of the investment. For example, if the forecast is for lower interest rates and the objective is income the investor may want to switch from a short term bond into a longer term bond to lock into the higher interest income stream. On the other hand, an investor may undertake the same action to capture a capital gain because a decrease in interest leads to higher bond prices and the longer to maturity the greater the price change. In the first scenario the investor would hold onto the bond and in the second the bond would be sold to capture the gain.

- Tax motivated swap
  - taxes influence the type of investments investors make:
    - taxability of the interest payments: municipal versus corporate bonds versus Treasuries
    - form of the investment cash flows: capital gain or loss versus income
    - timing of flow; generally, paying taxes later is preferred
  - many advantages can occur, especially in times of increasing interest rates
    - increasing interest rates mean bond prices decrease
    - sell the bond and simultaneous purchase an "identical" bond
    - recognize the loss on the bond sold to reduce the current tax obligation
    - when the replacement bond matures or sold most likely there will be a capital gain, which is taxable at that point in time
    - from a tax perspective it is better for an investor to take a tax loss today and recognize a tax gain in the future (time value of money concept)

A tax swap is the most common form of bond swapping because the outcome is known and one is not forecasting interest rate events. Overall the process is rather straightforward – replacing one set of bonds for another set of very similar bonds to generate a tax loss today that can be used to offset capital gains in other investments.

One of the challenges with this strategy is finding available replacement bonds. An actual case history of a tax motivated swap done by a former student, Apollo Visko, is presented on the next page. While dated it still shows the power of a tax motivated swap in an environment of increasing interest rates. The notes/results section on the example details

Tax Motivated Swap: done by Apollo Visko*, May 12, 1981

Rating	Yearly Income	Amount (m)	Description of bond	Coupon	Maturity	Market Price	Proceeds	Accrued Interest	Book Cost	Realized Loss
BBB	$ 3,200.00	50	Boston, MA	6.40%	6/1/1986	73	$ 36,500.00	$1,448.89	$ 50,000.00	$13,500.00
AA	$ 2,750.00	50	Florida State Board of Higher Education	5.50%	1/1/1989	73.125	$ 36,562.50	$1,015.97	$ 50,000.00	$13,437.50
AA	$ 2,625.00	50	Ohio State Public Facility	5.25%	5/1/1988	70.087	$ 35,043.50	$ 94.79	$ 50,000.00	$14,956.50
AAA	$ 3,100.00	50	State of Maryland	6.20%	5/1/1993	70.5	$ 35,250.00	$ 766.39	$ 50,000.00	$14,750.00
AAA	$ 3,200.00	50	State of Maryland Dept of Transportation	6.40%	7/15/1987	94.355	$ 47,177.50	$1,057.78	$ 50,000.00	$ 2,822.50
Totals	$ 14,875.00	250					$190,533.50	$4,383.82	$250,000.00	$59,466.50

Rating	Yearly Income	Amount (m)	Description of bond	Coupon	Maturity	Market Price	Net cost	Accrued Interest	Total Cost
AA	$ 3,125.00	50	State of Connecticut	6.25%	3/1/1996	70.72	$ 35,360.00	$ 633.68	$ 35,993.68
AA	$ 3,300.00	50	State of West Virginia	6.60%	11/1/1993	78	$ 39,000.00	$ 119.17	$ 39,119.17
AA	$ 3,100.00	50	State of Massachusetts	6.20%	8/1/1993	69.89	$ 34,945.00	$ 886.94	$ 35,831.94
AA	$ 6,500.00	100	State of Oregan	6.50%	11/1/1995	73.83	$ 73,830.00	$ 234.72	$ 74,064.72
Totals	$ 16,025.00	250					$183,135.00	$1,874.51	$185,009.51

Notes/Results of swap:
1. recognize tax loss of $59,466.50
2. increase annual income by $1,150.00
3. overall risk is about the same, fewer bonds and no BBB rating
4. face value of bonds is the same - $250,000
5. additional cash to invest or consume as needed - $7,398.50 pus tax savings

*Apollo, a friend and former student from Florida State University, joined God in his mid 40s... .

the benefits of the swap. In times of decreasing interest rates tax, motivated swaps are more difficult to find

Foreign Bonds

- Investment quality bonds offer the potential for diversification of interest-rate risk not available when investing only in domestic bonds
- Diversification into foreign bonds reduces interest-rate risk, but incurs exchange-rate risk
- In many cases non-investment grade foreign bonds have relatively greater risk than non-investment grade domestic bonds

Non-dollar bonds fit into a bond program by offering the potential for diversification of interest rate risk not available when investing only in domestic bonds. As long as foreign and domestic interest rates are not perfectly correlated, diversification benefits will accrue to the international bond investor. While this diversification benefit can be substantial, the investor must carefully consider the increased risk brought on by accepting exchange rate risk. This risk is greater for bond investors than for equity investors because bond markets are less volatile than stock markets and bonds typically have higher intermediate cash flows [i.e., interest payments are normally higher than dividends]. Therefore, when deciding whether to invest in non-dollar bonds, the investor must carefully weigh the benefits of reduced risk due to diversification to the prospect of increased risk due to currency fluctuations. Fortunately, the diversification benefits often outweigh the currency risk because investors are able to hedge against currency risk using derivatives. See Chapter 9 for a more complete discussion of global considerations.

- Market size and characteristics
    - non-dollar bonds constitute more than a quarter of the world's wealth
    - non-dollar bonds have higher returns and higher risk
    - relative returns and risk can vary significantly
    - correlation between domestic and foreign bonds varies over time, average is usually low and therefore provides diversification benefits
    - is a changing environment, from relative size to risk characteristics

Foreign bonds carry interest rate risk that is separate from U.S. debt instruments: therefore, diversification benefits are possible. However, diversifying into foreign bonds introduces exchange rate risk. The bond manager can deal with these risks by diversifying and attempting to hedge the interest rate or currency risk. For example, looking at the historical performance, non-dollar bonds in dollar terms had greater volatility than non-dollar bonds in local currency terms: 11.7% versus 3.9% standard deviation for the period of 1975-1990. In Chapter 9 the risk of global investments is discussed in greater detail.

- Diversification
    - risk-return for bond portfolios

- combining international bonds with domestic bonds offers possibility of portfolios with higher return and less risk than domestic only portfolios
- Currency Risk
  - currency risk is a significant component of total risk of a foreign bond
  - total risk can be broken down into volatility in local-currency terms and its currency-risk component
  - currency risk has a stronger effect on foreign bonds than on foreign stocks because bond markets are normally less volatile than stock markets
  - without exchange-rate fluctuations diversification benefits decrease (correlations between foreign and domestic increase)
- Currency Hedging
  - for bond portfolios where the proportion of foreign bonds is 25 percent or less, currency risk is normally considered a negligible incremental part
  - if greater than 25 percent, recommended course of action is hedging
  - lock in a dollar exchange rate for a specified amount of foreign currency for a specified period of time (sell a foreign currency futures contract)
  - hedging entails three types of direct costs:
    1) execution costs associated with buying and selling futures to establish hedge
    2) execution and opportunity costs associated with settling hedging transactions
    3) management fees

An advantage of hedging currency risk is the reduction of exchange rate risk. This risk can be a significant component of total risk in a foreign bond. Two characteristics of hedged bonds are (1) non-U.S. bonds hedged have 40% less risk and about the same return as unhedged non-U.S. bonds and (2) hedged-bond portfolios dominate the unhedged-bond portfolios. While benefits exist for hedging bonds, one needs to recognize the costs involved. Therefore, as in all decisions one must weigh the benefits and costs of undertaking an action.

Summary
- Bond investors use the yield curve to position bond investments and develop investment strategies (active and passive) to benefit overall returns
- Potential return and/or value can be added by accepting credit risk, undertaking swaps, and investing in global bond markets
- Potential return needs to be balanced against additional risks and costs

A disciplined investment approach combining fundamental research and appropriate risk analysis can produce enhanced long-term results. Risk analysis includes credit analysis, sector rotation, yield curve, and duration management. The construction of a bond portfolio should be driven by investment strategy recommendations, aligned with the objective of the investor, and follow consistent application of buy and sell disciplines. Paying attention to tax efficiency and keeping costs low help produce favorable long-term results. Except for the tax swaps, which are based on events that already occurred the other swaps require forecasting ability.

CHAPTER 10
THOUGHT QUESTIONS

1. Briefly discuss basic strategies for managing bond portfolios in both a domestic market and international market. Indicate why an investor would include foreign bonds in their portfolio, and whether or not they would hedge against currency risk.

2. Define the term structure of interest rate and discuss how it can be used to help manage bond portfolios.

Questions and Problems:

1. Go to the Internet and download a recent yield curve. Identify the type of curve appears to be (e.g., descending), and what it implies regarding future short-term interest rates.
2. Discuss the role of the yield curve in active bond management.
3. What is the expectations hypothesis of term structure, and how is it related to market efficiency?
4. Discuss why the realized return on a bond may differ from the anticipated return, as indicated by the yield to maturity.
5. Identify three theories to explain the shape of the yield curve, and their implications regarding the shape of the curve.
6. Explain the basis of the "subprime mortgage liquidity crisis," the impact it had on interest rates, and how behavioral aspects played a roll.
7. The price change of a bond is based on what two factors, and which is more important.
8. Explain "riding" the yield curve.
9. Discuss how embedded "options" impact the yield on a bond, and how can they be valued.
10. Identify different bond swap strategies and how they can be used to enhance return, and be sure to identify any risk factors.
11. A new 20 year bond with an 8% nominal yield is priced to yield 10%. An investor purchasing the bond expects that two years from now, yields on comparable bonds will have declined to 9%. Calculate the realized yield if the investor expects to sell the bond in two years.
12. What is horizon analysis, and why is it useful?
13. How are the substitution and intermarket spread swap similar?
14. How do nondollar (global) bonds fit into an investment program? What risk do global bonds reduce and what risk is increased?
15. Describe the advantage of hedging currency risk and identify the costs of hedging.
16. What are the key elements needed for implementing a tax motivated swap?

Section IV: Derivatives

In this section we move away from the basic asset classes (bonds and stocks) and valuation considerations and introduce derivative securities of options and futures, respectively, in Chapters 11 and 12. Derivative securities are riskier by nature, but they also allow the investor to reduce the risk of investments when used judiciously. Of course, because they are riskier they also afford the opportunity to "gamble" to enhance returns. The value of a derivative is based on some underlying asset, security, service or commodity. An option, simply stated, is the right to buy, or sell a security at some future date for a set price. The seller of the option is obligated while the buyer maintains the option to act or not. On the other hand a future is a contract to buy or sell a specific amount of a commodity or financial instrument at a particular price on a stipulated future date, both buyer and seller are obligated. Two roles of derivatives in the market place are to 1) provide liquidity and 2) transfer risk to those willing to bear it. In many cases derivatives are difficult to understand and/or require a high level of mathematical/statistical knowledge. The Internet/web is changing the financial landscape for all financial instruments, and as more people become involved in the investment process options are becoming an investment alternative for many individual investors. Commodities, or futures, are generally not in the purview of the smaller investor.

The focus of the discussions in the next two chapters is from an investor perspective of using derivatives to manage or hedge risk. Derivatives when used to enhance return is more akin to some the behavioral considerations first presented in Chapter 2, and include such factors as overconfidence and greed. While we recognize these behavioral aspects it is important to keep in mind the basics of systematic investing presented in Chapter 1. The operative word for derivatives is risk!

The larger players in the market place have been using "program trading" or "quantitative strategies" including derivatives for years. Now automated trading programs, similar to some of the complex trading algorithms used by the larger players, are being rolled out for the average investor by brokerage firms. As more and more brokerage firms roll out these programs that examine everything from stocks and options to currency and global aspects without human interaction the risk of the market will change. In theory we would like to say it will make the markets more efficient; however, will investors really understand the risk they are undertaking and what happens if it is poorly designed software. Some scary prognosis can come forth when one recalls Long Term Capital Management (1998) – the situation where the best from Wall Street and the brightest from academia misjudged the market and the FED stepped into the brewing crisis to avoid a potential global market 'meltdown' as the firm went bankrupt. A major lesson that should be learned from the sub-prime 'crisis' is that it is important to understand what you are investing in and the risks involved. Let us now turn our attention to derivatives before we move onto an brief introduction of modern portfolio theory in the last section of the book.

Chapter 11: Options: Valuation and Strategies

CHAPTER OVERVIEW

In this chapter, we describe option valuation models as well as the way these derivatives can be used to generate differing patterns of returns in investments. The chapter also presents some commonly used strategies to control investment risk or to enhance returns. Option terminology is presented and defined. The binomial and Black-Scholes models are presented and briefly compared. A variety of illustrations are presented to show the impact of using various option strategies, and the pattern of prices and returns. The chapter further discusses that the investor needs to recognize the limitations of the models and the need for suitable inputs. Strategies using options also need to recognize the objective, or the risk tolerance, of the investor.

Introduction
- Options offer an opportunity to generate different patterns of return
- Investors, not corporations, are generally the maker and buyer of options
- Some commonly used option-related strategies are 1) spreads, 2) straddles, 3) covered call writing, and 4) the protective put
- Options can be used to control risk or enhance returns
- Options can help avoid the excessive cost of implementing strategies and can present opportunities for return enhancement
- Any use of options should keep in mind the objectives of the investor and the risk tolerance embedded in the objectives

Options on listed exchanges are not "issued" by corporations. Instead an investor is the writer (seller or maker) of an option, and the typical buyer is another investor. Options for officers of corporations are not traded in the market place, and have nothing to do with the derivative markets. Additionally, it is important to recognize the risk inherent in options and keep the overall risk level in line with the objective of the investor. Definitions and strategies are covered as they are presented and discussed below. The key to remember is that options by themselves are riskier then stocks or bonds; however, they can be used to help reduce risk.

Security Options
- Definition: an agreement conveying the right to buy (call) or sell (put) common stock during a stated time period for a specified price (exercise or strike price)
- The buyer pays the seller a premium for the right but not the obligations to buy or sell the stock at a specified price during the stated time period
  - premium = purchase price of the option
  - the premium does not count towards the purchase or sales price, rather it is compensation to the seller for putting themselves in the disadvantage position of not having a future choice

- Call option: gives the buyer the right (but not the obligation) to buy from the writer (or seller or maker) a specified number of shares of a certain stock at any time on or before the expiration date
  - buyer profits if market price rises above strike price by an amount exceeding the premium
  - writer/seller profits if market price is not above the strike price
- Put option: gives the buyer the right (but not the obligation) to sell to the writer (or seller or maker) a specified number of shares of a certain stock at any time on or before the expiration date
  - buyer profits if market price falls below strike price by an amount exceeding the premium
  - writer/seller profits if market price does not fall below the strike price
- Round trip: buying and selling of an option
  - usually done to create a net-zero position to avoid higher transaction costs of the option being exercised
  - the vast majority of option trading in the market place are round trips, or the options expire worthless
  - very few options are exercised, the actual purchase of the stock from the writer or the actual sale to the maker of the option
  - buyers and sellers are not matched up, instead the Options Clearing Corporation [OCC] serves as the counter party and guarantor for all options sold on any exchange in the U.S.
  - if a buyer decides to exercise an option a seller of the option is then randomly chosen from those sellers that have not completed a round trip
- Need to account for premium (purchase price of option) and transaction costs to determine breakeven point
- European options differ from American options in that they can only be exercised at expiration

A call buyer has a very similar position to the stockholder who purchases the stock long; both want the price to rise (see diagrams below: c and e). However, the call buyer is in a leveraged position, which is a two-edge sword. If the stock purchase price of the stockholder is the same or lower then the exercise price, then both the stockowner and the call owner profit from an increase in the price of the stock beyond the strike price. However, the option holder also has to recoup the premium before moving into a positive position. While the call owner's profit is less due to the premium paid the percentage gain can be significantly higher. However, if the stock declines in price, then the call buyer could lose the full value of the investment while the stockowner loses only a portion of their investment [assuming no bankruptcy]. The call owner stands to lose the value of the premium paid if the stock never reaches the strike price before the option expires. While the loss is limited in dollar amount, as compared to the stockowner's possible dollar loss, the percentage loss is 100 if the stock price is equal to or less than the strike price.

The put buyer has a very similar position to the short seller, both want the price to fall (see diagrams below: d and g). If the short sale price is the same as the exercise price, then both profit from a decrease in the stock below the strike price. The difference is that the put owner's profit is less due to the cost of the call (the premium paid). However, if the stock rises in price then the short seller faces increasing losses until the sale is covered. The put owner only stands to lose the value of the premium paid. Losses for the put buyer are limited; however, there is no predetermined limit for the short seller (especially when one considers the short seller needs to pay any dividends paid by the company).

It should be noted that many options expire worthless – hence, the name of "wasting asset." Research studies have shown that the expected outcome for the buyer of a call is negative. Recent studies have shown that about 80% of call options expire valueless. With an expected negative return an obvious question is: Why purchase a call option? The answer lies in behavioral considerations unless you are using the call to implement a strategy (e.g., you are expecting an inflow of cash in the future and you know for sure that you want to purchase a security for the portfolio but want to avoid the risk of higher prices). Have you ever purchased a lottery ticket? What is the expected outcome? Correct, zero. Even if they know the expected outcome, which many do not, the buyer of a call knows the loss is limited to the premium, which is generally a 'small' amount, and they are overconfident that they will end up on the positive side of the distribution and receive an attractive percentage return on the small investment.

The Listed Options Market
- Options are traded on organized exchanges (e.g., Chicago Board of Options Exchange [CBOE])
    - the exchanges have certain specifications which range from maturity dates to fixed strike prices
    - maturity dates are typically nine months or less
    - LEAPS are options that have expiration dates greater than one year
    - the reader is referred to the website of the exchanges (e.g., www.cboe.com) or the website of the OCC (www.optionsclearing.com)
- Expiration date: Saturday following the third Friday of the month in which the option expires (at times other expiration dates exist)
- Organized options exchanges offer advantages to investors
    - standardized and simple
    - exchange acts as an intermediary, so trade is not between specific buyers and sellers
    - more efficient market
    - liquidity
- Patterns of returns (see diagrams below)
    - options allow for pattern of returns unattainable from the more conventional sort of securities
    - factors such as taxes, dividends, commission costs, interest, and opportunity costs have been ignored to avoid complicating the analysis
    - these ignored factors can have importance in the actual execution of an option strategy, and the investor needs to understand the consequences

- differing patterns associated with option strategies can be combined with conventional strategies to obtain more desirable risk-return combinations (e.g., protective put)

Profit and loss patterns from various financial instruments at termination:

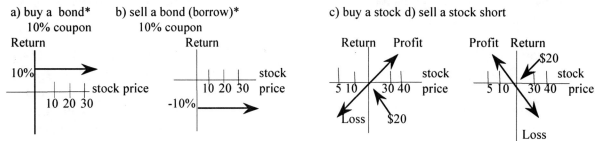

a) buy a bond*
   10% coupon

b) sell a bond (borrow)*
   10% coupon

c) buy a stock d) sell a stock short

* for a bond position stock price has no effect on return pattern

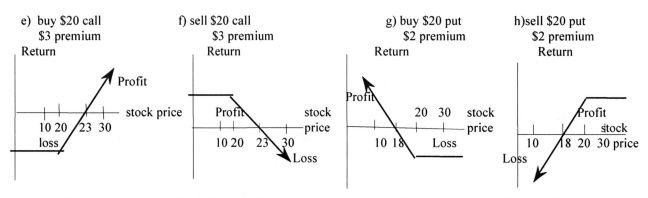

e) buy $20 call
   $3 premium

f) sell $20 call
   $3 premium

g) buy $20 put
   $2 premium

h) sell $20 put
   $2 premium

If one owns the underlying stock, a protective put position can be taken by purchasing a put option on the stock in order to guarantee a selling price for the stock. While preserving the upside potential of the stock (less the option premium), the downside risk can be essentially eliminated since the maximum loss is the premium paid. See the patterns of return in the diagram below.

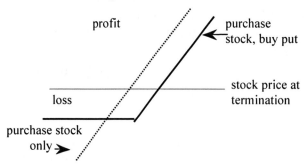

- Index options – options on an index (e.g., S&P 500) instead of a single stock
  - advantages include the following
    - o lower premium than a package of options on individual components
    - o includes all securities in the index
    - o lower transaction costs
    - o speed of implementation

164

- not stated in number of shares, rather multiply the level of the index by a stated multiplier (e.g., S&P 100 Index multiplier is 100)
- same techniques are used to evaluate and price index options as individual stock options
- more applicable to portfolio management activities

Index options can be used as a form of portfolio insurance. If your benchmark for comparison is the S&P 500 and you believe the overall market is going down and you do not want to sell your stock positions the portfolio can be protected by either selling a call option or purchasing a put option on the index. Selling the call would reduce the amount of loss by the premium received in the event of an actual downturn. Buying a put would allow the loss to be limited, similar to the loss for an individual stock. There is not a perfect match like there is for an individual security unless your portfolio has a beta equal to one, and the actual movement of the portfolio equals the market movement.

Option Valuation
- Option value = premium = economic or intrinsic value plus time value
- Typical point of view for options is from the investor buying a call
    - value of call option, buyer's perspective, before and at expiration
    - stock price versus exercise price:
      1) out-of-the-money: stock price is below exercise price
      2) at-the-money: stock price is equal to exercise price
      3) in-the-money: stock price is above exercise price
- Prior to expiration, total value is greater than baseline economic value due to time value (call buyer, chance of stock price moving higher)
    - time value at maximum when stock price is at exercise price
    - time value decreases when price of stock moves away from exercise price in either direction
    - at expiration time value goes to zero and option value equals economic value
- Factors affecting time value of option include: variance, time to expiration and level of interest rates (see figures below, where E = exercise price)
    - higher variance higher time value
    - longer time higher time value
    - higher interest rates higher time value

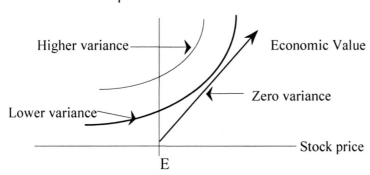

165

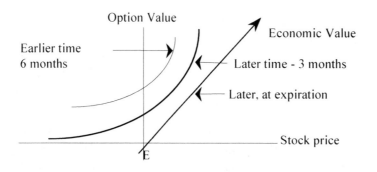

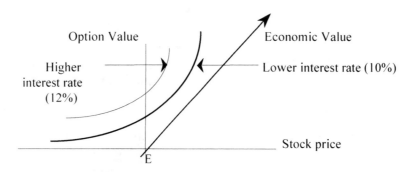

The time value is maximum when the option is first issued, especially if the option is just at-the-money. The time value increases as the option goes from being out-of-the-money to being at-the-money. If the option then goes into-the-money the time value declines and the economic value increases with increases in the price of the stock. Economic value is also known as intrinsic value.

An option can still have value even if the stock is selling way below the exercise price because options have both an economic value and a time value. If the stock was selling well below the exercise price, then the option would be out-of-the-money and thus have no economic value. However, depending on the time to expiration and the volatility of the underlying stock, the option will have time value. This time value is greatest with more time to expiration and expected high volatility in the stock price.

As a stock price decreases further below the exercise price (E), there is less likelihood that the option will go into the money, and consequently, the time value decreases. As the stock price increases past the exercise price, the economic value increases, and the time value decreases, as there is less likelihood that the stock price will decline below the exercise price, or that a large price increase will occur.

Factors Affecting Value of Options (see diagrams above)
- Primary factors:
    1) expected variance in price or return of underlying stock (direct relationship)
    2) time remaining to expiration (direct relationship)
    3) level of interest rates: i.e., risk free rate that matches time to expiration (direct relationship)

- Other factors
  - relationship between market price and exercise price
  - dividends on underlying stock (generally, only secondary importance)

The longer the time to expiration the greater the possibility of a price movement; hence, the value of the option is increased. Interest rates are another one of the determining factors in the price/value of an option. Higher interest rates imply a higher price for the option, whereas lower interest rates imply a lower price for the option. The rationale for this is evident when comparing the purchase of a call option to the purchase of the stock on margin. Both transactions are ways of leveraging the purchase of the security, and thus are inherently competitive. When interest rates rise, margin accounts become more expensive to maintain resulting in the investors' tendency to purchase the call options. This increased demand for the options increases the option price until another equilibrium occurs between the margin account purchase of equity and the call options.

Valuation of an option at expiration differs from valuation prior to expiration because the maturing of the option automatically reduces the time value of the option to zero because there is no longer time for the stock price to change. At expiration only economic value remains. If the strike price is greater than the market price the economic value is also zero and the options expires worthless – hence, options are known as wasting assets. A template for valuing options is presented at the end of the chapter.

Option Valuation Models
- Two complementary approaches to value an option
  (1) binomial model
  (2) Black-Scholes option-valuation model
- Binomial model:
  - simpler in derivation
  - more suitable for illustrating underlying concepts
  - requires considerable computer power and programming to generate a value
- Black-Scholes
  - more complex to derive, but 'easy' to use
  - provides a compact expression that can be manipulated to derive values
  - has widespread use in valuing listed options
  - used to determine the implied variance and if current premium is fairly priced
- Forces of arbitrage ensure that option is properly priced (theory)

Each model has its pros and cons and are discussed below. The Black-Scholes model is the more popular model in pragmatic settings and used extensively. Because it does have such wide spread use it is difficult to use it and capture excess returns. Additionally, one should recognize that research studies have shown that the expected return on the purchase of a call option is negative. However, behavioral characteristics such as over confidence allow the investor to 'know' that they will be the one to achieve a very high percentage return.

Binomial Option Pricing

- Basic assumption: over any time interval security prices can move in two directions, either up or down
- To determine value of an option over a single period
    1) determine the portfolio action that matches the option with a security that replicates the price action of the option but moves in a contrary direction
    2) determine the number of options needed to establish an appropriate hedge (returns from the portfolio are the same (riskless) no matter what the subsequent outcome)
    3) derive the price of the call based on the risk-free hedge and the composition of the replicating portfolio
- Hedge ratio between stock and call option can be established
- Arbitrage possibilities exist
- With hedging and riskless cash flows equilibrium price follows
- Inputs needed are the current stock price, the exercise price, the volatility of the stock price, and the interest rate
- Pricing Over Multiple Periods
    - repeat the same steps of the single period process in an iterative fashion over time.
    - as periods increase the process becomes more complex (volume of data and calculations multiply enormously)
    - start with period prior to expiration and move back to present
    - as number of periods is extended the valuation provided by the binomial model approaches the valuation derived by the Black Scholes model

The one-period binomial model is similar to the Black-Scholes option valuation model in that the operation of hedging and the hedge ratio are critical notions in both. However, only when the intervals used to evaluate the option are extended to a great number (with time interval becoming very small) does the valuation provided by the binomial model approach that derived by the Black-Scholes model. Generally the Black-Scholes model is used in pragmatic settings.

The Black-Scholes Option Valuation Model

- Possible to set up perfectly hedged position consisting of long position in underlying stock and short position in options on that stock (or vice versa)
- Position is theoretically riskless, so the hedge earns the risk-free rate
- It is assumed there are no transaction costs
- Option premium at which hedge yields a return equal to risk-free short-term interest rates is the fair value of the option; if premium differs, return differs and arbitrage forces would move the price of the option toward fair value
- Black-Scholes formula (see example below):

$$C = S[N(d_1)] - E[e^{-rt}][N(d_2)]$$

where C = market value of option; S = market price of stock, E = exercise price of call option, r = risk-free rate corresponding to time remaining (t), and $N(d_1)$ and $N(d_2)$ are cumulative density functions:

$$d_1 = \left[\frac{\ln(S/E) + (r + 0.5\sigma^2)t}{\sigma\sqrt{t}} \right]$$

$$d_2 = \left[\frac{\ln(S/E) - (r + 0.5\sigma^2)t}{\sigma\sqrt{t}} \right]$$

where σ = standard deviation of annual return of stock, and $\ln(S/E)$ = natural logarithm of (S/E)

- Comparison to binomial model:
  - allow time interval to approach zero and continuously rebalance the hedge
  - first term, $S[N(d_1)]$, is the amount of money invested in stock
  - second term, $-E[e^{-rt}][N(d_2)]$, is the amount invested in risk-free asset and negative sign indicates it is borrowed
- Inputs needed are the current stock price, the exercise price, time to maturity, the market interest rate, and standard deviation of annual price changes (volatility)
- The standard deviation is the input that is difficult to generate
  - use historical stock prices
  - use the implied value by using Black-Scholes model to solve for standard deviation when option premium is known
  - use a forecast for future; however, one may need to adjust standard deviation based on basic determinants of risk (e.g., interest rate risk, purchasing power risk, business risk, and financial risk)

An underlying theory behind the Black-Scholes option-valuation model is that options can completely eliminate market risk from a stock portfolio. The idea postulates that the ratio of options to stocks in a hedged position can be constantly modified to have gains and losses exactly off-setting. Theoretically the position is riskless and the return should be R_f. If the return differs it implies the option premium is mispriced and arbitrage forces should move the premium towards fair value.

Techniques an investor can use to estimate the price volatility of a particular stock include computing the standard deviation of historical returns for the stock over a specified period of time. Another technique, and perhaps the preferred method in pragmatic settings, is to compute implied volatility by taking the option premium (C), inputting into the Black-Scholes valuation model the other variables (S, E, r, t, and $\ln(S/E)$) and solve for volatility (σ). Both of these methods produce estimates that may need to be adjusted for changes in the risk profile of the stock (e.g., financial risk, purchasing power risk, et cetera). Observed values may differ from the calculated values due to pragmatic considerations such as transaction costs, sizeable price changes, and differing estimates of the inputs needed for the model (e.g., differing estimates of variability).

A major assumption of the Black-Sholes model is that one can instantly and continuously rebalance the hedge. This is generally not possible in pragmatic settings. The model also assumes no transactions costs; again, this is not pragmatic since it does cost to buy and sell. The model also assumes perfect input data which is most likely not always attainable in the pragmatic world, especially for the estimate of variability. The model also implies homogeneous expectations, which is not realistic. However, despite these limitations it is used extensively in the pragmatic world, and provides very useful information to investors and portfolio managers.

Valuation of Options
- Call option valuation
    - use of Black-Scholes option valuation
    - appropriate hedge ratio is given by $N(d_1)$, per call option purchased the number of shares of stock to be sold short
    - elegant model with limitations that include the pragmatics of transaction costs, possible large price changes in a short time frame, and the need for accurate inputs into the model

The hedge ratio describes how many options are necessary to create a riskless return when short-selling stock or how many shares of stock are needed when selling options short. With respect to option valuation, the hedge sets a fair price (premium) for the option. If the premium differs, arbitrage forces will move the price to equilibrium.

The hedge ratio approximates the shape of the curvilinear relationship between stock price and option price at a particular stock price. For small changes the relationship is approximately linear, for large changes or many changes over time the relationship is curved and gains and losses will not be perfectly offsetting. This is analogous to the convexity situation in bond duration.

- Put option valuation
    - derived by relating value of call [C] to that of put [P], based on put call parity relationship:
        $$C - P = S - PV(E)$$
    - put value estimated by first using Black-Scholes to estimate value of matching call, then adding amount equal to present value of exercise price [E], then subtracting amount equal to market price of underlying security:
        $$P = C + PV(E) - S$$
    - valid only for European puts on non-dividend paying stocks; provides only lower boundary for value of American put
- Hedge ratio
    - based on a probability $[N(d_1)]$, therefore must be between 0 and 1, or the number of shares owned for each call written is between 0 and 1
    - change in call price is never greater, and is usually less, than the change in stock price
    - number of calls must exceed number of shares of stock for hedge to work
    - represents the slope of option curve at a particular price level
    - used to ensure that gains/losses on long positions are offset exactly by losses/gains on short positions

- valid only for small changes in price and for short intervals of time

For example: price = S = 30
exercise price = E = 40
t = 3 months = .25 year
standard deviation = σ = .5
and r = 15%

$C = S(N(d_1)] - E\,[e^{-rt}][N(d_2)]$

$$d_1 = \left[\frac{\ln(S/E) + \left(r + 0.5\sigma^2\right)t}{\sigma\sqrt{t}}\right]$$

$$d_2 = \left[\frac{\ln(S/E) - \left(r + 0.5\sigma^2\right)t}{\sigma\sqrt{t}}\right]$$

$$d_1 = \frac{\ln(30/40) + [.15/4 + 0.5(.5)^2\,.25]}{.5\sqrt{.25}}$$

$d_1 = 0.876$

$$d_2 = \frac{\ln(30/40) - [.15/4 + 0.5(.5)^2\,.25]}{.5\sqrt{.25}}$$

$d_2 = -1.126$

$N(d_1) = 0.191$
$N(d_2) - 0.130$
$C = 30\,(.191) - 40\,[e^{-0.15\,(.25)}]\,(.130)$
$C = \$0.72$

The appropriate hedge ratio is given by $N(d_i)$, or 0.191

- Changing option values
  - many factors can change prices over time, so maintaining a riskiness hedge becomes a dynamic process
  - transaction costs impede the keeping of a riskless hedge as prices change
  - option traders and portfolio managers need to adjust for frictions and be alert to idiosyncratic price moves

The example presented above provides an indication of the pricing of a call option using the Black-Scholes model and developing an appropriate hedge ratio. Obviously the model output is highly dependent on the inputs and one must be aware of how the inputs change over time, sometimes quite rapidly, in the dynamic financial markets. Moreover, pragmatic obstacles like transaction costs impede the implementation of riskless hedges; however, excellent guidance is provided and the models are used extensively in pragmatic settings.

Options-Related Strategies
- Options offer opportunity to effectively tailor strategies
- Enhancing return strategies include
  1) spreads
  2) straddles
- Controlling risk strategies include
  1) covered-call writing
  2) protective puts
- Spreads
  - simultaneous sale and purchase of one or more options on an underlying security
  - two major types of spreads are
    1) money spread – different strike prices
    2) time spread – different expiration dates
  - examples:
    1) a bull spread: the purchase a lower exercise price and the sale of a higher exercise price money spread
    2) a horizontal spread where exercise prices are the same and maturities differ
    3) a diagonal spread where exercise and maturities differ
- Straddle
  - a particular type of spread where purchase of a call and a put that have the same exercise price and expiration date (a long straddle)
  - designed to capitalize on high stock price volatility (price must move enough to cover both premiums)
  - breakeven position: exercise price plus or minus the combined premiums
  - selling a straddle provides the following profit and loss pattern:

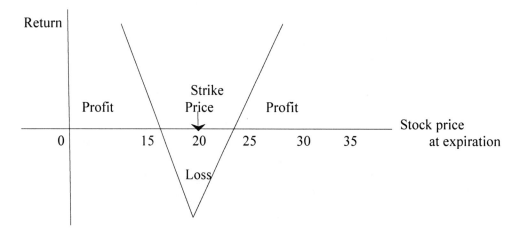

  - a short straddle, the opposite or a long straddle, is the sale of a call and a put that have the same expiration and exercise price, the bet is that the stock price will have little variability over the life of the options

172

- unless specified, when one refers to a straddle it should be considered a long straddle

A spread position in options consists of two or more options on a given underlying security or index. Spreads typically include both buys and sells, which implies lower cost and lower potential profit than a singe option. Investors use spreads to reduce risk from volatility in the security or to profit from changing prices. While many different names exist for spreads they are readily grouped into two major classifications: (1) money spread and (2) time spread. At times an investor my combine a money and time spread. Several examples are noted above.

A straddle is a special case of a spread strategy: an equal number of calls and puts on the same security or index, with the same exercise rice and maturity date. After the establishment of a straddle, based on market movements, each option can be exercised separately. See diagram above for a pictorial representation of possible outcomes for a long straddle. A short straddle would invert the diagram above based on the expectations of little price movement in either direction from the exercise price. A short straddle is generally more risky then a long straddle; however, the risk is based on expected price volatility.

- Trading volatility
  - expected volatility impacts value of options more that other model inputs
  - if able to forecast changes in volatility, identify patterns of volatility, or rate of changes in volatility, trading is possible

Option traders can take advantage of changes in volatility iff (if and only if) they are able to forecast changes in volatility, identify patterns of volatility, or identify rate of changes in volatility. For example, researchers at Salomon Brothers have applied advanced statistical techniques to develop a model that has some power for forecasting changes in underlying volatility. As volatility increases, the team buys a straddle where the purchased options should increase above the purchased price, leading to a gain.

- Writing covered calls
  - call option written against stock already owned by the writer
  - writing covered calls is considered a conservative strategy
  - if the stock is not owned by the writer it is known as a naked call, a higher risk strategy
  - need to consider benefit of premium received versus the possible cost of having the stock called away (especially in bull markets)
  - provides some protection in bear markets
  - a trendless trading pattern is ideal environment for the seller of the option

The advantages of writing covered calls are that the return distribution is truncated and you do not expose yourself to the potential unlimited risk associated with selling a naked call. Additionally, the premium received helps offset any loss from downside movements of stock price and can be used to help cover costs of investing. The disadvantage of writing covered calls is that you generally put a ceiling on any upside potential. The types of market environments that would be most favorable to a covered call strategy are markets that show little direction up or down and trading is in a limited range. In essence following a covered call strategy is a way to extract the time and interest rate value of the asset while waiting for the opportunity of capital gains to present itself. If one follows a disciplined program of writing covered calls it is possible to generate additional income which enhances the return of the investment. As noted previously, around 80% of covered calls expire worthless; hence, it would seem that writing covered calls is a solid strategy. This is especially true if the call price is above the purchase price of the security. The benefit of writing a call above the purchase price is that if the stock is called you still have some capital gain, plus the call premium.

- Overwriting opportunities
  - enhance returns by opportunistically timing the sale of options with desirable characteristics
  - a speculative practice by makers of options who believe security is mispriced
  - options with the potential for the highest rate of premium erosion (maximum decay over a given time period)
  - premium decay reflects a time effect and a volatility effect

The characteristics of stock options most favorable for option overwriting are ones with the potential for the highest rate of premium erosion. Having the maximum decay over a given time period provides the over-writer the opportunity to lock in profits on the transaction. A maker would write call options on an overpriced security with the expectations that they would expire worthless. If a security is underpriced puts would be written with the assumption that they would not be exercised.

- Protective puts
  - buy stock and buy a put to provide a guaranteed selling price for the stock
  - similar to an insurance policy in its workings
  - truncates the downside distribution and reduces upside potential by the amount of the premium
  - limits the loss, and at times can be used as part of a sell discipline

Inventors having a diversified portfolio, with a long-term investment horizon would most likely find the protective put inappropriate. Investors with short-term horizons or a defined need for investment funds facing adverse market movement would find the protective put an appropriate strategy. Also, investors who need to avoid losses because of policy or regulatory requirements could use a protective put strategy.

A strategy, normally referred to as a collar, to mitigate risk is to sell a covered call and purchase a protective put at the same time. It is even possible to create a zero cost collar by selling the call and using the funds to purchase the put. A collar strategy is useful if the portfolio manager is not sure of future movement price movements. Another use is to lock in a capital gain that you want to recognize in the next tax year.

A reverse-dispersion strategy, which is similar in nature to the collar strategy, is to sell calls on the stocks in the portfolio and then use the proceeds to purchase puts on an index that is closely aligned to the portfolio's benchmark. This strategy would be implemented when the investor wants to participate in the capital gains potential in the equity market but is worried about market downside risk. The concept behind this strategy is that generally the premium of individual options is greater than the prices of the options on indexes, or the sum of the parts is greater than the whole.

- Portfolio insurance
  - utilize protective put with index options to insure the total portfolio from adverse market moves
  - for long-term investors the loss of upside gain due to the cost of the premium is likely to preclude the persistent use of protective puts
  - for investors with short-term horizons or a defined need for investment funds, use of a put to protect against adverse market movements might well be warranted
  - also useful for investors or portfolio managers who need to avoid losses because of policy or regulatory requirements

To maintain a riskless hedge over time requires constant monitoring and adjusting the hedge to reflect price changes in the stock and/or option. The hedge ratio is a linear approximation (slope at a particular stock price) of a curvilinear relationship. Thus, as stock price changes, the hedge will also change. The value of the call option changes as the standard deviation (volatility) changes, a direct relationship. Interest rates and time also have a direct relationship with option values. As option values change the hedge ratio will change. Additionally, since values such as volatility and interest rates are estimates the hedge ratio would have to be adjusted if the estimates are not perfectly forecasted.

A protective put (discussed previously) limits the downside risk to the premium cost while allowing the owner to realize the entire upside potential less the premium cost. Like insurance, the put owner is paying a premium to manage risk.

The choice of exercise price on a protective put is like the decision on which deductible to take on an insurance policy. This is because a higher deductible means that the insured bears more risk and thus pays a lower premium. With a protective put, a lower exercise price means that you bear more of the risk, but the premium you pay will be less for the "insurance" that you do have (under the exercise price). Similarly, a higher exercise price will be like a low deductible, and you will pay a higher premium for the increased "insurance."

Summary
- Options are linked to other investment decisions or positions because of their ability to alter the return distribution
- Different strategies may be used to reduce risk or boost returns
- Options provide the investor with the capability to insure the portfolio

- Models have limitations that the investor needs to be aware of, and inputs need to be valid
- As with any derivative, options can reduce risk when used in a hedging strategy or increase risk when used in return seeking strategies
- The buyers of options exhibit behavioral characteristics of overconfidence if the purchase of the option is not part of a hedging strategy

Options are a valuable security class for investors; from diversification benefits to the generation of differing return patterns than those found using only stocks and bonds. The wise use of options is a prudent decision for investors, which can provide additional opportunities for return while reducing risk. However, in general, investors often underutilize options because they are not understood or even misunderstood. Security firms require additional information from an investor before they allow the investor to use options. Underutilization is probably the better alternative to the use of options by investors who use them to gamble with the expectation of earning excess returns. Gambling exhibits behavioral characteristics of overconfidence, optimism and at times herding.

CHAPTER 11
THOUGHT QUESTIONS

1. Briefly discuss the concept and status of using options in investing and/or portfolio management. In your discussion indicate why options are attractive, types of options, and major uses of options.

2. Briefly discuss the binomial and Black-Scholes models. In your discussion include the call-put relationship and how the models rely on the concept of efficient markets. Indicate how the relationships can be used in investing/portfolio management?

Questions and Problems:

1. Identify and define some commonly used option-related strategies.
2. Define a call option and a put option. Which one carries more risk for the buyer? For the seller (maker or writer of the option)?
3. What is meant by an option being
   a. in-the-money?
   b. out-of-the-money?
   c. at-the-money?
4. What is meant by the economic value of an option? Compare that to the time value of the option.
5. Why does an option have value even when the stock is selling well below the exercise price?

6. Explain why the value (premium) of an option can decreases when the stock price declines below the exercise price, as well as when it increases above the exercise price.

7. How does the time value of an option change as the price of the stock varies, and when is time value at a maximum?

8. Discuss how interest rates impact the value of an option.

9. Discuss the notion underlying the Black-Scholes option valuation model.

10. Identify several options-related strategies, and how they can be used to protect the investment or enhance the return of an investment.

11. How does risk relate to option strategies? When is it increased? Decreased?

12. Assume a bond yields 5%, a stock sells at $33, and a call and put on the stock each sell for $3 and have an exercise price of $33. Graph the profit and loss for each of the following categories:

    a. buy the bond
    b. sell the bond
    c. buy the stock
    d. sell the stock short
    e. buy the put
    f. buy the call
    g. sell the call
    h. sell the put

OPTION ANALYSIS

Option _____   Exchange _____   Current Position _____

Option Type:	CALL	PUT
Option Position:	BUY (LONG)	WRITE (SHORT)
Option Strategy:	SPECULATION	HEDGE STRADDLE

Option Characteristics:

Price of Underlying Security = _____   Premium = _____

Striking Price = _____   Intrinsic Value = _____

Expiration Date = _____   Time Value = _____

Gain/Loss Diagram for Option Position

Gain or
Loss (-)

Price of Underlying
Security at Expiration

Analysis of Investment Potential:
(include sensitivity analysis)

Investment Action: BUY   WRITE   NO ACTION

Rationale for Investment Action:

Chapter 12: Financial Futures: Theory and Applications

CHAPTER OVERVIEW

Financial futures allow investors to hedge risk effectively as well as rapidly change the underlying risk-return characteristics of a portfolio, with minimal cost. While there are many types of futures/commodities this chapter describes the valuation and application of three major types of financial futures: (1) stock market indexes, (2) interest rates, and (3) foreign currencies. We also discuss how investors/plan sponsors find futures to be useful in that they allow changes in asset allocation with minimal disruptions. While there are notable applications of futures to equities, the greatest volume of activity takes place with regard to interest rates. The futures on Treasuries and Eurodollars are the most actively traded. The chapter also discusses the fact that using futures, unless used wisely to hedge risk, adds lots of risk to the investment. Futures, especially when used to enhance returns, are more risky than options. Futures should only be used when they compliment the objectives of the investment and provide expected benefits greater than costs.

Introduction
- Financial futures can offer significant benefits in the investment process
- Futures not discussed in this chapter include commodities (e.g., agricultural products such as wheat, corn and rice; various grades of oil; precious metals like gold and silver; copper; and many other items)
- Futures are generally not for an individual investor, unless they have significant wealth
- Major type of financial futures include:
    - (1) futures on stock market indexes
    - (2) futures on interest rates
    - (3) foreign currency futures
- Uses of futures include: hedging, facilitating the application of strategies, price discovery, and speculation on price moves

Using futures requires an understanding of the futures market place and the risk inherent thereof. Speculating on price moves is highly risky, and if undertaken needs to be in line with the risk tolerance of the investor and the objective of the portfolio. As with options, discussed in the prior chapter, the focus in this chapter is hedging risk. Additionally, it is from the point of view of a portfolio manager or an investment manager and not an individual investor due to the high level of risk involved. This in turn is based on the belief that for an individual investor to invest in futures they need to be in a situation where losing fifty to an hundred thousand dollars would not impact their life style.

Spot and Forward Transactions
- Spot transactions are the same as cash transactions
- Forward transactions are those that take place at a later date in the same fashion as spot or cash transactions
- Major purpose of a forward contract is to assure a set price/rate for a transaction desired or contemplated at a future date
- Forward prices or forward rates are negotiated and agreed upon by the parties who enter into a contract where both buyer and seller are obligated to fill (as opposed to options where only the seller is obligated)
- Prices and rates
  - spot prices/rates: those prevailing currently
  - expected spot prices/rates: those that investors expect to prevail at the end of an investment time horizon
  - forward prices/rates: those established currently to be used in transactions at an agreed time in the future
  - realized spot prices/rates: those actually prevailing at the end of the investment time horizon
  - basis: the difference between spot prices and the future price

Expected spot prices are those rates that investors expect to prevail at the end of the investment horizon. Forward rates can be used as unbiased predictors for the future spot prices. If the portfolio manager is concerned with future rates and has an idea as to what the future rate will be, futures can be used to hedge this risk exposure. For example, a firm expects to receive a large cash inflow that needs to be invested in debt instruments and the investment manager believes that interest rates may be heading lower. The investment manager can lock in current rates by using a future. The relationship between the spot and future price is detailed below when we discuss futures valuation.

The basis is the difference in the spot or cash price and the price of the future. This basis is expected to narrow over the life of a futures contract until expiration, at which time it will be zero. A strengthening basis produces gains for the short hedge because the long spot position either increases more or decreases less than the short futures position. A long hedge is hurt by a strengthening basis because the short position either increases more or decreases less than the long futures position.

Forward Contracts and Futures
- Forward contracts are a special-purpose financial instrument where buyer and seller set terms to meet their requirements, generally there is no secondary market, and the buyer and seller assume all risk until delivery date (e.g., when you order a car for a future delivery date, or when you purchase a dress or a suit and it will be delivered in the future after the tailoring is completed)
- Futures overcome some of the limiting characteristics of forwards
  - they provide a "standardized contract" that is identical in all aspects
  - since they are a standardized contract a secondary market exists where investors can trade the future to either hedge risk or enhance return
  - contract price is negotiated, normally in an open outcry auction market with multiple buyers and sellers

180

- Advantages of futures over forward contracts
  - standardized features include: (1) amount and type of asset to be delivered, (2) the delivery date or maturity date, and (3) the exact place and process of delivery
  - traded in auction markets organized by futures exchanges
  - active secondary market
  - clearinghouse guarantees the performance of each party to fulfill the contract
- Two distinct types of investors
  1) actual supplier or user who has a 'covered' position
     - reducing risk or hedging their 'investment' position
     - seller reduces downside risk, but foregoes upside potential
     - buyer reduces upside risk, but foregoes downside benefit
  2) speculators
     - do not have, or need, underlying instrument
     - rather they bet on future price movements
     - akin to "gambling," more so then other investments
- Primary uses of financial futures in portfolio management include:
  1) facilitate application of strategies
  2) hedge (reduce) risk exposure
  3) speculation, the purchase or sale of a future without an underlying asset position or in conjunction with a broader strategy
     - highly risky activity
     - highly leveraged position which compounds returns (both positive and negative)
     - in essence placing a bet on future price with the expectation of enhancing returns
- Requirements for trading futures on the exchange
  - both buyer and seller deposit initial margin (performance guarantee)
  - daily mark-to-market
    o daily transfer of dollars between accounts to recognize any changes in market value of the contract!
    o this is not paper gains and losses, but real dollar transfers that change the investors cash account (margin account)
    o both buyer and seller need to have adequate liquid reserves to meet their obligations, especially for market-to-market obligations
  - maintenance margin, need to keep minimum amount in margin account
    o when the price of the commodity, financial instrument or service moves in an adverse direction and the margin account is lower due to mark-to-market the investor receives a margin call requiring the <u>immediate</u> deposit of cash
    o when the price of the commodity, financial instrument or service moves in an favorable direction and the margin account becomes higher due to mark-to-market the investor can take money out of the margin account
- Due to high likelihood of a margin call investors are typically required to keep $20,000 or more in liquid assets in their brokerage accounts
- Futures represent a contract, both buyer and seller are obligated

Forward contracts can be viewed as special purpose financial instruments that have terms set to meet specific (unique) needs of the two parties to the agreement. The forward market is a dealer market where transactions are negotiated. Buyers of a forward contract need to find a trader or seller willing to sell a contract suitable to the buyer's needs. With forward contracts buyer and sell are matched. Generally, there is no secondary market for forward contracts: both parties are locked into the contract and subject to the risk of failure to perform on the contract and the uncertainty of price fluctuations. For example, when you order a new BMW and expected delivery is in four months you have entered into a forward contract. Price fluctuations or exchange rate changes will not affect the agreed upon purchase price.

Futures contracts, on the other hand, overcome a lot of the problems associated with forward contracts. Futures contracts are standardized with the amount and type of asset to be delivered, the delivery date or maturity date, and the exact place and process of delivery. Also futures are traded in auction markets by organized exchanges and are liquid since there is a secondary market. Contract prices are negotiated in the auction market, and typically prices can only move so much on a given day. The amount of movement is set by the exchange and is dependent on the underlying security, product, good or service. With future contracts, like options, buyer and seller and not matched.

Both forwards and futures contracts are similar in that they allow investors the opportunity to lock in a price today for a future date in which the asset must be delivered. They enable investors to hedge against price fluctuations and interest rates. Since they are contracts both the buyer and seller are required to fulfill the obligation. This differs from the options discussed in the previous chapter where the buyer was not obligated; and hence, paid a premium (option price) to the seller. In futures both parties have a margin account which, in essence, represents a performance guarantee. With both options and futures the vast majority of the participants do a round trip so there is no remaining obligation or option. Futures are not wasting assets like options since they always have value at maturity. Consequently, investors either undertake a round trip (very low transaction costs encourage round trips), or fulfill their part of the contract.

- Cash flows and futures settlement
  - profits credited and losses debited daily to the margin account as prices of future varies – known as mark-to-market (with forwards, except for perhaps an initial deposit which counts toward the purchase price generally no funds flow until maturity)
  - with futures, real cash flows occur on a daily basis between buyer and seller margin accounts depending on the price movement of the future (see graph below)
    - o when price increases buyer has a gain and seller has a loss
    - o when price decreases buyer has a loss and seller has a gain
  - at end of contract profit and loss picture is the same for futures or forwards
  - interest earnings on daily settlements have only small effect on determination of futures and forward prices – assume interest earnings are offset by interest expense

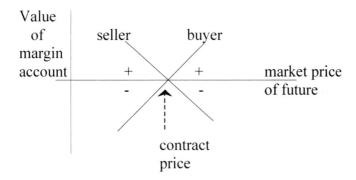

- Liquidity reserve
  - basic liquidity reserve is the initial margin, or deposit that both buyer and seller provide to the futures exchange
  - the initial deposit represents a performance guarantee
  - the initial deposit is <u>not</u> a down payment
  - due to daily fluctuations and possibility of large losses, need liquid reserve above and beyond the margin to meet obligations
  - variables to consider include: length of time, number of contracts, volatility, and acceptable probability of a zero balance
  - rule of thumb: initial margin requirement is around 5% to 10% of the value of the contracts, amount is predetermined by the exchange and is not dependent on the current price in the market place
  - when the value of the margin account decreases enough there is a margin call to increase the cash
  - when the value of the margin account increases the investor could take out the "excess" cash
- Futures settlement
  - based on the terms of the contract, futures can be fulfilled in several ways: delivery of the underlying instrument, cash that is equivalent in value to instrument, or an equivalent security identified in the contract
  - if equivalent security, cheapest-to-deliver is expected
  - the vast majority, high ninety percent, of contracts involve a round trip (both buy and sell position); hence, there is no ending settlement
- Futures markets
  - futures offer flexibility in providing liquidity and efficiency of implementation
  - growing proliferation of financial futures in portfolio management strategies
  - growing proliferation of different types of future contracts, especially those applicable to debt instruments, stock indexes, and foreign currencies
  - financial futures are the most actively traded instruments, especially the ones based on Treasury instruments

The total number of futures contracts outstanding at any one time is called the open interest. Each contract has both a long and a short position and counts as one contract of open interest. Futures that generally show the most open interest are ones that are more likely to be used in investment strategies. For example, interest rate futures (the T-

Bond, Eurodollar, and T-bill) commonly have the most open interest and are used extensively by knowledgeable portfolio managers. Stock index futures which show the greatest amount of open interest are the S&P 500 Index and NYSE Index. Currency futures with high open interest include the Yen, Pound, U.S. dollar, and Euro futures.

The futures exchange provides a secure means for portfolio managers to participate in the futures market. The clearinghouse acts as the second party to an agreement and therefore reduces the risk of non-completion. The exchange also provides a means for daily pricing of the futures contracts. Because the exchange provides for standardization of contract, assurance of the transaction and a central location for trading, there is greater flexibility in providing liquidity and efficiency for the futures trading process.

An investor employing a speculative strategy would be assuming additional risk in anticipation of future gain. A speculation position in futures is considered a high risk strategy and should not be undertaken unless the investor can suffer significant financial losses (say, $50,000 to $100,000) without impacting the objectives of the portfolio. Hedging strategies, on the other hand, attempt to reduce investment risk. A perfect hedge is one that eliminates the possibility of future gain or loss and in essence locks in a future price. Speculation is undertaken with the purpose of earning profits whereas the primary object of hedging is to reduce exposure to risk. The seller wants to reduce or eliminate downside risk (lower prices), while the buyer wants to reduce of eliminate upside risk (higher prices). As the risk is reduced or eliminated the benefit side of the relationship is foregone. Speculators, whether burying or selling, are betting on future price movements in the expectation of earning a profit.

Futures Valuation

- Three-way relationship between spot prices, forwards/futures prices, and expected spot prices
- Generalized process based on interest rates, and arbitrage ensures equilibrium pricing between futures and current prices
- Relationship between spot prices and futures/forwards provides basis for establishing fair value for futures/forwards:

    current security price = forward price/$(1 + r)^t$
    forward price = current security price*$(1 + r)^t$
       where r is equal to the risk rate for period t

    - arbitrage forces keep prices in line
    - this generalized process is called the spot-futures parity theorem
- Relationship between futures/forwards and expected spot prices has potential use in price discovery, and setting standards of comparison
    - spot price = expected spot price/$(1 + r)$, where the discount rate r is based on risk and is greater than r_f
    - with r_f as the link between spot price and futures price and r as the link between spot and expected spot prices, $(1 + r)/(1 + r_f)$ is the connection between futures price and expected spot price

- Futures prices are generally greater than spot price, which in turn are less than expected spot prices to the extent that the security bears a risk premium
- A basic template for valuing futures is presented at the end of the chapter.

The spot price is the current price of a security in the market. The forward price is the expected price today of the security at a specified time in the future. The general relationship is:

$$\text{spot price} = \text{forward price}/(1 + r_f)^t$$
where: r_f = risk-free rate
t = term of the forward contract

The risk-free rate is the link between the spot price and the futures price. The discount rate serves as a link between the spot rate and the expected spot rate. One plus the discount rate divided by one plus the risk-free interest rate is the link between the futures price and the expected spot price.

Financial Futures: Types and Strategies
- Interest rate futures
  - useful in environment where interest rate changes are expected
  - overall very successful and becoming more popular, Treasuries and Eurodollars
  - LIBOR (London Interbank Offer Rate) is one of the best indicators of the cost of short-term borrowing
  - contract specifications differ between financial instruments, for details of the various contracts the reader is referred to the website of the exchanges (e.g., http://www.cmegroup.com/,)
  - for interim interest payments it is necessary to adjust the price:
    o [PV(C)] = present value of cash distribution (C)
    o $F/(1 + r)$ = P - PV(C), where r = discount rate, F = future value, and P = present price
  - not an exact relationship since it ignores flows attributable to mark-to-market, and equivalent security delivery options
- Stock index futures
  - useful for hedging and applying stock market strategies
  - success depends on the degree to which the underlying index is representative of the investor's portfolio
  - representative stock index futures include the S&P 500, S&P 100, Nikkei 225, Russell 2000, et cetera (again the reader is referred to the futures exchange website)
  - it is necessary to adjust price for dividends similar to interest payments presented above
    [PV(D)] = present value of dividends (D)
    $F/(1 + r)$ = P - PV(D)
    where r = discount rate
    F = future value
    P = present price
  - settlement is in cash

- not an exact relationship since it ignores mark-to-market, and the necessity to forecast dividends

A spread strategy using futures would be appropriate for a portfolio manager who assesses that smaller capitalization stocks are overpriced relative to large capitalization stocks. She/he could sell a small capitalization index (i.e.; Russell 2000) and buy a future based on a large capitalization index (i.e.; S&P100). The compound futures position would allow the investor to capture the expected differential performance of large versus small capitalization stocks through the differential exhibited by the futures. The portfolio manager could balance the trade by equating the dollar values of the two positions and have a "net zero" position and still earn returns.

- Index arbitrage
  - program traders, index fund managers, and others monitor the relationships between the futures [F] and the underlying indexes [I] to detect any price discrepancies
  - at any point in time, say t = 0, a hedged portfolio should return the risk free rate
  - Return to the Hedged Portfolio (RHP) [need to convert to percentage]

    $RHP = (F_0 - I_0) / I_0 + D/ I_0$

    $RHP = $ basis + yield

    where F = future price

    I = index price

    D = dividend
  - fair value comparison
  - may have mispricing during periods of market stress

Example:
    S&P500 is trading at 1343.80
    S&P500 dividend yield is 1.91%
    Current risk-free rate is 3.19%
The implied risk-free rate when the future is selling at 1360 is:

$$RHP = \frac{F_0 - I_0}{I_0} + Yield = (1360 - 1343.80)/1346.80 + 1.91\%$$

$RHP = 1.20\% + 1.91\% = 3.11\%$

RHP < Rf, futures are undervalued, they should be selling at 1360.94 to equate risk-free rates. While the difference may not be substantial enough (8 basis points, 3.11% versus 3.19%) to arbitrage, the appropriate action would be to purchase the undervalued futures and a money market instrument in order to outperform the S&P500.

- Foreign currency futures
  - useful for transactions that involve more than one currency or portfolios invested globally
  - there is an active forwards market among large traders

- International Monetary Market [IMM], part of the Chicago Mercantile Exchange [CME], is a primary futures market, and offers currency futures and interest rate futures
- hedging currency is helpful when investing in international bonds

Tactical hedging strategies attempt to assess the direction of the relevant markets and change the risk exposure of the portfolio according to the assessed market condition. Full hedging strategies implement a constant minimal risk exposure without attempting to predict market movements. Consider a multinational firm with a German subsidiary that will need to convert Euros to dollars at a future date. It currently holds a long position in Euros and is exposed to the risk of the Euro weakening. A tactical hedger would therefore reduce the effective hedge when the Euro is forecast to appreciate and increase it when the Euro is expected to depreciate. A full hedger would maintain the same hedge regardless of forecast currency fluctuations.

- Interest rate parity
  - explicit relationship between spot and future currency rates that is defined by interest rates
    - for foreign currency, interest rates are relative to one another
    - domestic interest rate is related to foreign interest rate as a comparative ratio
    - resulting spot-futures currency exchange rate is known as interest-rate parity relationship
  - foreign currency should be priced in the futures market according to:
    $$F = S[(1 + I_f)/(1 + I_d)]$$
    where F = forward rate, S = spot rate, I_f = foreign r_f, and I_d = domestic r_f
  - return opportunities are available in the short term if equilibrium does not exist
  - empirical evidence generally supports interest rate parity
  - circumstances that can create divergences include: risk of governmental control, taxes, and rapidly changing inflation or an unexpected change in inflation

Example:
  Short-Term interest rate = 6% in U.S.
  Short-Term interest rate = 4% in Japan
  Spot rate of exchange = 100 ¥ / $

  $$F = S \frac{(1 + I_f)}{(1 + I_d)}$$

  $$F = 100 \frac{(1 + .04)}{(1 + .06)}$$

  $$F = 98.11 ¥ / \$$$

- Uncovered interest rate parity
  - a second version of how interest rates and exchange rates are related

- uncovered interest rate parity states that the expected change in the exchange rate over time will equal the domestic-foreign interest rate differential
- interest rate differential will be equal to the expected change in spot prices, when inflation adjusted (real) rates are equalized across countries (the International Fisher Effect)
- if International Fisher Effect and interest rate parity hold, there is a three-way relationship where the expected rate of the exchange rate equals the forward premium or discount
- empirical evidence shows that this theory does not hold up well in the pragmatic world; with varying degrees of inflation risk the ability to earn equivalent ghs becomes less attainable

Interest rate parity is an explicit relationship between spot and future currency rates. In Chapter 9, Global Investing, the fundamental determinants of exchange rates were presented and discussed. Futures allow portfolio managers to implement strategies based on these determinants of exchange rates. With regard to foreign currency, the interest rate connects the spot and the forward rates, where the domestic interest rate is related to the foreign rate as a comparative ratio. The spot and future currency rates represent rates of exchange between domestic and foreign currency with the spot rate representing the current exchange rate and the future rate representing the future rate.

The strategies presented above focused on more macro concepts from interest rates and indexes to foreign markets and exchange rates. We now turn our attention to more specific strategies that range from tactical asset allocation to bond and stock applications to alpha capture. By using futures a portfolio manager can typically implement strategies at lower costs and have less disruption to the portfolio.

Tactical Asset Allocation
- Tactically molding shifts in the weighting of the major asset classes to take advantage of valuation discrepancies
- Preference is to use futures in making tactical reallocations since it is not disruptive to management of underlying assets
- If active asset managers are outperforming the index, the use of futures permits the portfolio manager to fully capture the value added with the asset classes
- Tactical asset allocation may be able to take advantage of occasional mispricing of futures that occurs around cyclical peaks and troughs in the market
- Using futures instead of selling and buying underlying assets is beneficial

The advantage of implementing a tactical asset allocation program with futures involves two benefits. The tactical asset allocation strategy will (1) increase the speed of implementation and (2) lower the transaction costs. These advantages are the result of the greater liquidity that the futures market makes available to investors. Furthermore, futures can be used to implement a tactical asset allocation strategy without changing the underlying composition or make-up of the portfolio.

Bond Applications
- Futures can be a highly effective means of hedging interest rate risk as well as changing duration of a portfolio
- Important that durations of portfolio and futures underlying assets match
- Interest rate hedging
  - short-hedge: sell futures against the bond position as the bond portfolio manager disposes a relatively illiquid position over time
  - long-hedge: purchase of interest rate futures to offset adverse price movements related to the future purchase of bonds (desire to lock in current yields)
  - hedging should create situation of no net loss or gain (ignoring transaction costs)
- Changing the duration of a bond portfolio
  - futures facilitate the implementation of active investment strategies due to lower transaction costs, greater liquidity and speed of implementation
  - changing the duration of a portfolio using futures is straightforward, and do not interfere with the underlying portfolio
  - futures allow a target duration to be achieved/maintained

The underlying instrument for a bond future is the par value of a coupon bond. At the settlement date, the seller of a futures contract is required to deliver to the buyer the par value of the bond. Since such a bond may not exist, the seller must choose from other acceptable deliverable bonds that have been specified by the exchange. This can result in an inequity for the buyer, because the seller wants to deliver the cheapest instrument. To make delivery equitable for both parties and to tie cash to the futures price, the exchange (CBOT – CME) uses conversion factors to determine the invoice price of each acceptable and deliverable debt instrument. However, the buyer should expect to receive the cheapest instrument allowed.

Once the anticipated deliverable is determined the portfolio manager can determine an appropriate hedge. A short hedge would be one involving the sale of futures contracts. This hedge would be used by a bond portfolio manager during a period of rising interest rates. If the manager does not want to sell or otherwise alter the underlying portfolio of bonds, the manager could sell interest rate futures, which would gain in value as interest rates rise, to help offset the loss that would occur on the underlying bond assets.

A long hedge would require the purchase of interest rate futures. An example of this strategy would be if a manager wanted to lock in today's yields for bonds to be purchased with funds coming in at a later date. If the manager thought yields would decline between now and the date that the cash was received, the manager would buy interest rate futures, which would increase in value if indeed interest rates fell. This would help to offset the lower yield he/she will have to accept at the future date.

Stock Applications
- Futures can be useful for hedging or changing the exposure of an equity portfolio with respect to its three major risk-return components:
  1) market
  2) sector/group

3) specific stock
- Futures can be used to change the beta of a portfolio with active management strategies
- Futures allow the manager to strip out the stock selection or alpha component of a portfolio (see IX below)
- Important to correlate the portfolio with the underlying assets of the future
- Changing portfolio beta
    - market timing strategies can change the beta in three ways:
        1) change level of cash
        2) change securities within portfolio
        3) use futures
    - futures offer speed of implementation and lower transaction costs and they do not interfere with the underlying portfolio
    - to achieve a beta target different from neutral position (portfolio beta without use of futures) buy or sell index future (e.g., S&P 500)
- Sector allocation
    - altering the exposure of the portfolio to major sectors within the equity market
    - spreading: buying and selling futures on broad-based index and an index that is more structured on sector (e.g., Russell small cap stock index)

Buying and selling futures is a method used to change the beta of a portfolio that can be easier to implement than changing securities or the cash level in the portfolio. Futures can also be employed to change the sector allocation of a portfolio. Moreover, using futures is generally cost effective. However, one must also keep in mind that the mark-to-market risk is automatically incorporated into the decision and process.

Alpha Capture
- Hedging strategies are employed when investor wishes to retain an existing position but offset risk created by this position
- Alpha capture: returns of hedging strategy will reflect a risk free rate plus stock selection capabilities
- Hedging will most likely be imperfect due to improbability of exact match of future index and portfolio, which implies increased risk
- Alpha capture applied
    - invest in positive alpha securities, short negative alpha securities
    - can be effective in short-term, but may lose advantage in long-term
- Transporting Alpha
    - once alpha has been captured, it can then be "transported" and combined with other strategies such as passive strategies, or another active strategy
    - potential to enhance the return, but risk increases (risk of expected alpha not realized)
    - opportunities to use futures to strip out the alpha components from other market segments (e.g., foreign market alphas)
    - captured alphas could be used as part of a basic underlying strategy

Alpha is based on the CAPM and identifying positive alpha securities, ones that lie above the CAPM line. In theory the returns in alpha capture should be greater than the normal expected return of the security and is considered an active strategy, especially if one shorts negative alpha securities to purchase the positive alphas. The security can either be individual stocks, indexes or portfolios. Hedging strategies using futures can be implemented to offset the risk created by the actual position to capture alpha.

Summary
- Finance futures offer investors increased latitude to hedge risk in three major areas: 1) stock market indexes, 2) fixed income securities, and 3) foreign currencies
- Futures provide opportunity to create new strategies or variations on existing strategies
- Futures increase the flexibility in applying strategies and the opportunity for adding value
- Futures add risk if speculating or reduce risk if hedging, especially with a perfect hedge

Futures offer the portfolio manager another way besides options to alter return patterns and enhance performance. In this chapter, the focus was on finance futures, but the strategies and cautions noted apply to all futures. Additionally, commodities could be used instead of interest rate futures. For example wheat futures could be used to offset inflation in times of rising food prices. Technical analysis is used extensively in trading of commodities. The challenge is that futures inherently have greater risk than most other asset classes and are difficult to understand. Therefore we recommend that before undertaking futures in an investment strategy the investor/portfolio manager has to fully understand the risks involved and until such a stage is reached we suggest not using them because the risks can quickly outweigh expected benefits if you do not know what you are doing. Moreover, even if you think you know what you are doing the risks can change quickly and the result is a significant loss – e.g., Long Term Capital Management, which had the brightest from academia and the best from Wall Street, misjudged the market and had to be bailed out so the world financial markets would not collapse. If using futures/commodities to enhance return think twice before leaving an exposed position overnight, and especially over a weekend. Markets are twenty-four hours per day and from the close in the USA to the next opening many global influences can influence the markets.

CHAPTER 12
THOUGHT QUESTIONS

1. Briefly discuss the concept and status of using futures in portfolio management. In your discussion indicate why futures are attractive, types of futures, and major uses of futures.

2. Briefly discuss the spot futures, expected spot relationships and how they help keep markets efficient. Define terms and indicate how the relationships can be used in portfolio management.

Questions and Problems:

1. What factors distinguish a forward contract from a futures contract? What do forward and futures contracts have in common?
2. Identify the major types of financial futures and how they can be used to hedge risk.
3. Why does the book present futures from an investment managers perspective and not an individual investor?
4. Identify the two distinct types of investors in the futures market place, and describe their risk profiles.
5. What is mark-to-market, and what are the implications for investing in futures?
6. Assume that an investment manager assesses that smaller capitalization stocks are overpriced relative to large capitalization stocks. Describe a course of action she could take to take advantage of this pricing divergence.
7. Identify the advantages of implementing a tactical asset allocation [TAA] strategy using futures.
8. Identify two strategies for modifying a bond portfolios characteristics by using futures.
9. Assume that the short-term interest rate is 2% in the USA and 4% in Japan. With the spot rate of exchange for dollars and yen at 100 yen per dollar, what should be the three-month futures rate of exchange?
10. For stock portfolios how can futures be used to change the beta of a portfolio? To capture alpha? What are the implications for risk?

FUTURES/COMMODITY ANALYSIS

Characteristics:

    Type of Future:

    Exchange:

    Strategy: Speculation _____   Hedge _____

    Contract Size:

    Spot Price:

    Future/contract Price:

    Contract Date:

Analysis of Investment Potential

Investment Action: BUY   SELL   NO ACTION

Rationale for Investment Action:

Section V: Modern Portfolio Theory and Evaluation

In the first twelve chapters of the book financial markets, behavioral considerations, valuation techniques, investment concepts, the importance of good information and forecasting which relate to applications and strategies aligned with investing were presented and discussed. There is no doubt that financial markets coupled with behavioral factors make it a challenge to invest successfully. Throughout the book portfolios have been reference, for example the segment in Chapter 6 titled "Portfolio Construction, Optimization and Performance." Additionally, in Chapter 8 there was a brief segment titled "Portfolio Construction: Passive and Active Strategies." However the basics of modern portfolio were not discussed, nor were the foundations developed. In this section of the book the basic concepts and foundation behind modern portfolio theory are presented.

Objectives, which are based on the investor's risk tolerance, determine appropriate assets for investment. However, one question that has not been introduced is: Which assets should we invest in to maximize returns while reducing risk? Moreover, while we have a solid framework developed within the book there is one critical piece of information missing – namely, evaluation of investment performance. Therefore, in this section we briefly explore modern portfolio theory [MPT] and the evaluation of investment performance.

MPT relies heavily on theory and the fact that pragmatic world situations including behavioral aspects are assumed "away" does not invalidate the resulting models that provide a base on which to invest and create portfolios in the pragmatic world. In fact many of the techniques, process and methods for creating portfolios and management thereof, especially by the professionals, is based on the concepts introduced in this section of the book. Diversification is the underlying concept in constructing portfolios and the Markowitz model using the efficient frontier provides a sound and logical way to construct portfolios while maximizing return for a given level of risk. As noted in Section I risk is the key element in investing: one manages risk not return. Risk drives returns! When using individual securities the Markowitz model requires a massive amount of work and is relatively cumbersome. However, by using only major assets classes the workload becomes manageable, and the results provide excellent information in pragmatic settings. Financial managers typically use some form of the Markowitz model to determine asset allocation for their clients. Additionally, capital market theory and the CAPM are based on MPT.

An important element in investing is performance evaluation. Obviously the goal of investing is to do well, to beat a relevant benchmark of comparison – whether it is an index, fellow investor, another analyst or your friend. Investing is at a minimum a two dimensional event; hence, the evaluation needs to consider both risk and return. Furthermore, one needs to attribute the performance to the major tasks of investing, initially introduced in the first chapter: asset allocation, sector or group rotation and individual security selection. This section provides a brief overview of how to evaluate the performance of the three major tasks.

194

Besides examining the three tasks we also indicate how to evaluate the investment performance from a risk return perspective.

As you read the material in Section V remember that it is not antipodal to behavioral finance. Instead they should be viewed as going hand-in-hand. MPT provides a basis to construct portfolios and behavioral aspects help us appreciate the challenges involved in building efficient portfolios. A working knowledge and understanding of both is necessary to be a successful investor or portfolio manager.

By now you have an appreciation for how difficult it is to successfully invest, ice fishing is also difficult. While the models, from DDM to the CAPM to the efficient frontier, have their detractors and challenges they provide excellent information for an investor/portfolio manager to build a portfolio. The challenge of investing is to establish buy and sell disciplines and develop strategies that work overtime. Reducing downside risk is important! Reflecting on lessons learned to modify the disciplines and strategies is also essential. Of course, one should understand and appreciate the 'luck' factor in investment performance. With this in mind let us turn our attention to modern portfolio theory and evaluating performance.

for success you need	*investing*	*ice fishing*
Capital	*dollars*	*equipment including clothes*
Knowledge	*from models & strategies to applications*	*from equipment & bait to applications*
Time	*yes, little doubt*	*yes, plus patience*

Chapter 13: Portfolios and Evaluation

CHAPTER OVERVIEW

Diversification is the underlying concept in constructing a portfolio and diversification should be across asset classes and individual securities. This chapter describes the Markowitz model that provides the conceptual framework for constructing *efficient portfolios* – ones with the highest expected return for a given level of risk. Basic inputs required, and how variation in these inputs impacts the resulting risk-return characteristics of the portfolio are also discussed. Risk is defined and related to portfolio concepts in order to operationalize the Markowitz model of modern portfolio theory. Applications are then discussed, along with expanding asset classes to include international securities. The chapter concludes with a brief introduction into evaluation of investment performance.

Introduction
- Selecting asset classes and securities, determine appropriate weighting to construct portfolios
- Markowitz model: based on several underlying assumptions and the use of fundamental mathematics and statistics
  - *efficient portfolios:* using math derive the highest return for a given level of risk or lowest level of risk for a given level of return
  - *optimization:* disciplined process for constructing portfolios
  - *asset allocation:* best mix of major asset classes
  - *risk*: variance, as measured by the standard deviation [σ], of expected returns
- Understanding the basic concepts of risk allow us to make the model operational

For thousands of years people knew that you should not put all your eggs in one basket; however, there was no efficient way of deciding where to place the eggs. In 1952 Harry Markowitz developed a logical and mathematical model to systematically determine an appropriate asset mix to optimize performance for the risk undertaken. His concept of dominance was to maximize return for the level of risk, or alternatively minimize risk for a given level of return. Professor Markowitz is considered the founder of modern portfolio theory [MPT].

Markowitz Model
- Five basic underlying fundamental assumptions
  1. single time period
  2. investors, all of them, maximize one-period expected utility and exhibit diminishing marginal utility of wealth (or act as though they do)
  3. investors risk estimates are proportional to the variability of expected returns
  4. investors are willing to base their decisions solely on expected return and risk (mean, variance)
  5. dominance – for a given level of risk investors prefer higher returns, or for a given return investors prefer less risk

- Model inputs and characteristics
  - the three major inputs of the model are:
    1. expected return
    2. standard deviation
    3. how the securities correlate with each other
  - relevant characteristics of a portfolio are expected return and some measure of dispersion of returns around expected return (usually standard deviation or variance which is the square of the standard deviation)
  - rational investors choose to hold efficient portfolios
  - possible to identify efficient portfolios by proper analysis of information
  - computer programs using fundamental mathematics and statistics "easily" calculate the set of efficient portfolios

The five assumptions listed above allow the development of a model that allows an investor to determine how to select securities/assets to maximize return for a given level of risk. Computer programs make the calculations relatively "easy." The difficult part is getting the necessary data; which, with the advent of the Internet, is becoming less challenging. Risk is defined as the possibility of loss, or in financial terms the likelihood of receiving less than expected. Hence, the assumption of using variability as a measure of risk is straightforward. Assuming that investors base their decisions on risk and return is also reasonable. The assumption of single period implies that all investors have the same investment horizon. Utility is a function of satisfaction, which in turn is based on consumption, which in turn is based on initial wealth and the growth of wealth and variability thereof. Investors maximize expected utility when making investment decisions. As shown in the diagram below, the utility of additional wealth increases at a decreasing rate. For a typical student to receive $50,000 a large increase in utility would be generated. For a $50,000 increase in Warren Buffet's wealth additional utility would be generated but the amount would not be as large as the student ($\Delta_S > \Delta_B$, see relative Δs in diagram below). The delta for the student is relatively large as compared to the delta for Buffet which appears to be a single line).

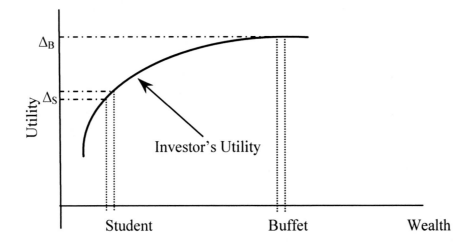

The key assumption to the Markowitz model is dominance, and it has a logical intuitive appeal. By recognizing the dominance concept and the math underlying the application thereof, investors are provided an understanding of what assets should be combined together to achieve the highest return for a given level of risk. This, of course is based on the belief that risk is 'measured' by the variance/standard deviation of expected returns. The dominance principle is detailed below as we discuss portfolio construction.

As in many economic models that attempt to configure the pragmatic world simplifying assumptions are required in order to develop the model. One obvious question is: do the assumptions invalidate the model? The answer is **NO!** – remember, finance models provide information not answers. The Markowitz model, along with the other models presented in this book, provides a base to judge from, which allows the portfolio manager to make better, more informed decisions.

Portfolio Construction Process and Dominance
- Markowitz model, basic assumptions and inputs are presented above, provides a conceptual framework and analytical tools
- Define the universe of eligible asset classes and securities
- Risk is measured by the variance (standard deviation) of expected returns
- Develop expectations with regard to risk exposure and return potential for each asset class and/or individual securities
- Efficient set: portfolios offering the highest return for a given level of risk or less risk for same return level (see diagram below)
- Investors will choose portfolios on the efficient frontier [EF] based on risk aversion
- Risk aversion/risk tolerance
  - risk matters and is disliked
  - all investors are risk averse or behave as though they are
  - risk tolerance should **not** be based on the ability to bear risk
- Actual optimization entails selection and weighting of securities

Dominance refers to the process where one maximizes an expected return for a given degree of risk or minimizes risk for a given expected return. Risk is based on the variance of expected returns and is 'measured' by the standard variation (the square root of variance) of expected returns. From a portfolio management point of view, a certain level of expected return and risk is associated with each possible portfolio. Graphically, this is the efficient frontier – EF [see diagram below]. Only portfolios with maximum return for any given level of risk lie on this efficient market frontier and they dominate all portfolios and individual securities for the same level of risk. Rational investors seek portfolios that lie on the EF at an appropriate level of risk, which depends on an investor's level of risk aversion. The amount of risk undertaken should not be increased just because an investor is wealthy, instead the risk should relate to their tolerance of risk and not their ability to bear risk.

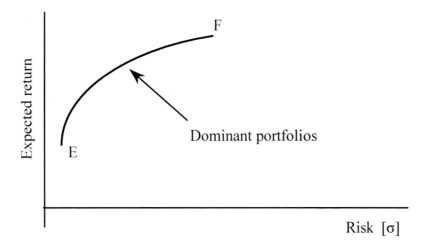

Security and Portfolio Risk and Return
- Securities derive value from expected cash flows
- Such flows are discounted to the present period based on expected risk
- Discount rate (or required return) is composed of two elements
  1. risk-free return, R_f
     - o is composed of
       - real return and
       - inflation premium
     - o risk-free does not mean no risk (still have inflation risk), instead it means a certain outcome or $\sigma_{R_f} = 0$
  2. risk premium – composed of
     - o interest rate risk
     - o purchasing power risk
     - o business risk
     - o financial risk

The nominal return is comprised of two elements: (1) a risk-free return R_f and (2) a risk premium. A hierarchy of risk and return exists among asset classes and we should compare the return earned on these assets with inflation to determine real return. Treasury bills are the least risky. Long-term government bonds have greater risk because of liquidity and time considerations. Corporate bonds generally carry credit risk higher then that incurred by governments. Treasuries are normally tax exempt at the State level, and municipal bonds are tax-exempt at the Federal level and the State in which they are issued. Stocks have the highest return because of the higher risk associated with them. International securities carry additional risk and are discussed in greater detail in Chapter 9. Derivatives have even higher risk unless they are used in hedging strategies.

- defining and measuring risk
  - risk is defined as loss or, in financial terms, receiving less than expected
  - standard deviation $[\sigma]$ or variance $[\sigma^2]$ of return provides a measure of risk
  - normal distribution, based on the Central Limit Theorem, allows for decisions to be based on expected return and standard deviation of returns

There is uncertainty associated with returns from risky assets. Assume we can assign probabilities to the returns expected, given an assumed set of circumstances. The average expected return is:

$$\hat{r} = \sum_{j=1}^{n} \rho_j r_j$$

where : ρ_j is the probability of event, j

r_j is the return for event, j

n is the number of events

The standard deviation [σ] measures how much a particular return deviates from the expected return [r]. It is measured with the same units as the expected return. To find σ, calculate the variance [Var] first:

$$Va\left(\hat{r}\right) = \sum \rho_i \left(r_i - \hat{r}\right)^2$$

The square root of the variance is the standard deviation (σ), so variance is often represented in Finance as σ^2. However, percent squared is difficult, at best, to understand. Therefore, typically, the standard deviation is used because the unit of measurement is percent.

- Diversification: risk in a portfolio context
    - covariance measures the riskiness of a security relative to other securities in the portfolio
    - negative correlation and covariance are desirable characteristics because they reduce the risk in the portfolio
    - higher correlation among securities leads to higher covariance and higher risk for the portfolio
    - calculation of portfolio variance: weighted sum of individual security variances plus twice the covariance between two securities
    - adding securities reduces overall risk (unless perfectly positively correlated)
    - combining securities or asset classes with lower correlations helps to reduce the risk of the portfolio (achieve the efficient frontier)

Diversification involves adding additional securities to a portfolio to reduce risk. The benefit is that the return can be maximized for the given level of risk undertaken. Consider a two security portfolio, the portfolio risk is given by:

$$\sigma_p = [w_1^2 Var(R_1) + w_2^2 Var(R_2) + 2w_1 w_2 Cov(R_1 R_2)]^{1/2}$$

where $Cov(R_1 R_2)$ can be written as $\rho_{12}\sigma_1\sigma_2$

ρ_{12} = correlation between security 1 and security 2

$\sigma_1\sigma_2$ = standard deviation of security 1 and 2, respectively

w = proportion of security, and $\sum w = 1.0$

R_1 = return on security 1

R_2 = return on security 2

Covariance, as described in the equation above, is equal to the correlation coefficient between two securities times the standard deviation of each security. Holding standard deviation constant the higher the correlation between two securities, the higher the covariance and thus the higher the risk of the portfolio. Conversely, the lower the correlation, the lower the covariance; hence, the lower overall risk of the portfolio. By adding securities, especially those with a lower correlation (covariance), a reduction in the portfolio risk occurs. This illustrates the power of diversification.

The variance of return and standard deviation of return are alternative statistical measures that are proxies for the total risk of return. These statistics in effect measure the amount to which returns are expected to vary around the mean over time. Covariance is a statistic that measures the riskiness of a security relative to others in a portfolio of securities. Correlation is a statistical measure of the degree of relationship between two variables. It varies from +1.0 (perfect positive correlation) to 0.0 (independent) to -1.0 (perfect negative correlation). The sign indicates the direction of the relationship and the size of the correlation coefficient indicates the degree or closeness of the direction of the co-movement between the two variables. Correlation coefficients do not include the magnitude of the movements, they only denote the direction thereof. From a portfolio management perspective, the smaller the correlation the greater the diversification benefit and negative correlation is desirable. However, negatively correlated securities are difficult to find in pragmatic settings.

- Security correlation and portfolio risk
  - diversification provides no risk reduction when securities are perfectly positively correlated [only have risk averaging]
  - diversification can eliminate risk when securities are perfectly negatively correlated or uncorrelated (at least in theory)
  - gains from diversification is due to the role of correlation in portfolio risk
  - risk reduction only occurs when the assets are less than perfectly correlated
  - risk-return character changes as weights of securities vary
  - degree of correlation [+1.0, 0.0, and -1.0] impacts results
  - lower the correlation the greater the diversification benefit
  - see graph below for a pictorial representation of how correlation leads to risk diversification: combining securities 'a' and 'b' with different levels of correlation

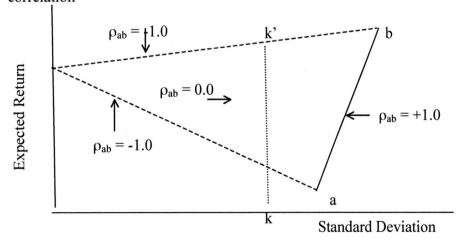

201

When securities 'a' and 'b' have correlation equal to zero combining them together creates a straight line between them. This line is just a weighted average of risk and return (ρ_{ab} = +1.0). Securities with a correlation of 0.0 add diversification benefits, and securities with a correlation of -1.0 add the most diversification benefit. This can be seen on the above graph: for a given level of risk, say k, you want to maximize return; hence, as you go straight up from the x-axis the dominate position, k', is on the top ρ_{ab} = -1.0 line. In pragmatic settings, correlations of zero or less than zero are not readily available (not counting a risk free security that would have a correlation of zero with risky assets or risky securities). Moreover, in pragmatic settings most securities are correlated between zero and plus one, with many having correlations of 0.7 or higher. While any correlation less than +1.0 adds diversification benefits having correlations of less than 0.8 is desirable.

- Systematic and diversifiable risk
    - adding securities to eliminate risk – see graph below
    - market-related risk (systematic risk) increases as a proportion of portfolio risk as the size of portfolio increases
    - risk unexplained by market is diversifiable or unsystematic risk
    - a relevant index of risk is systematic risk, assuming one can diversity away unsystematic risk

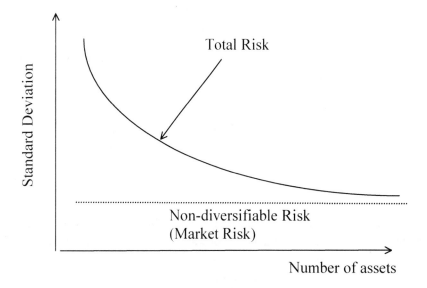

The difference between total risk and non-diversifiable/market risk is the unsystematic risk. Adding securities decreases total risk (assuming correlation less than +1) and it generally takes relatively few (i.e., 12 to 20) securities to reduce the unsystematic risk in a portfolio so the total risk approaches the non-diversifiable risk level. Some researchers have indicated that with the increasing correlation among many securities and assets the number needed to decrease the diversifiable risk has increased (e.g., 30 t0 50). However, to date the majority, generally, say that 20 securities are enough to achieve diversification assuming that do not have high correlation among each other. The risk return characteristic of the portfolio is also related to the weights of each security or asset class.

Short Selling
- Selling something not owned
- Should allow investor to develop better risk-return combination
- Strategy would be to short stocks with lower expected returns and invest proceeds of the sale in stocks with higher expected returns (theoretical concept)
- Potential to increase portfolio returns, but also increases risk
- Short selling more beneficial the higher the correlation between securities

In pragmatic settings while one is able to short sell they cannot use the proceeds to purchase another security. However, in theory the principal does work, is logically appealing and it allows for the development of models in capital market theory. In the pragmatic world short selling increases risk because it is possible to lose more than 100% - e.g., sell a security short for $2, and then cover the short sale when the stock has increased in value to, say, $5.23.

With the removal of the up-tick rule in 2007 the ability to short sale a security is no longer restricted. Clayton, Reinhart and Schmidt show that the volatility of securities and the market place increased once Rule 10a-1 of the Securities and Exchange Act of 1934 and the National Association of Securities Dealers (NASD) up-tick rule were eliminated. It is also speculated that the unrestricted ability to short sell has driven some firms into bankruptcy, mergers or bailouts.

Required Model Inputs
- Markowitz model is the most comprehensive, but the burden of estimating inputs (return, variance and covariance) can be overwhelming
- Index models circumvent difficulty of covariance and are discussed in the next two chapters
  - single index or single factor model is the simplest, with fewest estimates for inputs
  - multi-index or multi-factor model is intermediate in complexity and in number of required estimates

Input for the Markowitz model can be cumbersome due to the covariance measurements. For a sample size of J you need estimates of J returns, J variances, and J(J-1)/2 covariance calculations: or

$$inputs = 2J + J(J-1)/2$$

If J = 100 the number of inputs is 5,150. For a sample size of 500 the inputs required increases to 125,750. While the Markowitz model is the most comprehensive it is generally not used for a large number of securities. However, the Markowitz model is used for asset allocation strategies when the sample size is relatively small (e.g., a stock index, a bond index, and a money market fund; or several equity sector indexes, a bond index, an international index, and a money market index). Using five or six indexes provides an efficient frontier that is useful for allocation decisions once a risk level is specified.

Asset Allocation
- Markowitz process to determine asset classes to meet investment goals/objectives
- Three major classes
  - (1) common stocks
  - (2) long-term bonds
  - (3) money market instruments
- Data available, and good perspective on behavior of these three asset classes
- Possible to expand and include other asset classes
  - international securities, from equities to debt instruments
  - derivatives
  - real estate
  - real assets
  - sectors of the economy, or any group/industry or style index
- Asset allocation is based on the desired risk level
- Asset allocation relates strongly to the performance of the portfolio and is the key determinant of long-term rates of return

Asset allocation refers to the process where investors develop the most appropriate mix of assets to meet their investment goals. The objective of this process is to obtain a blend of asset classes that provide the highest return at an acceptable level of risk to the investors. The level of risk should be based on the investor's risk tolerance, and not the portfolio manager or financial advisor. When an investor invests in a mutual fund they should be sure the objective of the fund is in line with their risk tolerance and objectives.

The mean-variance portfolio approach for asset allocation is operationally feasible as the problem of developing inputs is manageable. This is due to the fact that the number of asset classes that are included in the analysis is small. When determining an asset allocation, many organizations deal only with three classes of assets 1) common stock, 2) bonds, and 3) money market instruments. For this purpose there is a need for three return and variance estimates, as well as three estimates of the correlation between asset classes, all a manageable task. In addition, there is relatively good historic data on returns, variance, and correlations for such asset classes as common stocks, bonds and money market instruments. This data has provided good perspective on the historic risk-return behavior of these asset classes. This in turn has helped researchers develop a way of modeling and projecting return and asset risk characteristics into the future. Current practice also has the same information available for many other indexes that can be based on sectors of the economy, industry classification, styles of investing, and so on. Even if one wants to include seven asset classes they only need to come up with thirty five estimates ($7 + 7 + 7(6)/2 = 35$).

Mutual funds and exchange traded funds [ETF] are typically classified as stock, debt, or perhaps a combination of stock and bonds. The holdings of the funds determine how they will be classified. Mutual fund prices are generally based on the end of the day while ETFs are traded throughout the day (similar to the way stocks are traded). Funds have the advantage of providing a portfolio of securities and not just one security. As noted previously when investing in either mutual funds or ETFs one should recognize the impact of the turnover and costs associated with the management of the fund.

Generally real assets such as collectibles have a low correlation to the standard asset classes of stocks and bonds. In fact the art market has a low, even negative correlation with equities. During the downturn of the equity markets in the early 2000s art outperformed the S&P 500. During inflationary times collectibles do well. During the 1970s comic books earned a 20 percent compounded annual return, far superior to the equities and debt instruments during that time frame. Additional risks with collectibles, as compared to stocks and bonds, include lack of transparency, high transaction costs, faxes, forgeries, and inefficient markets. In many ways gold and other precious metals are similar to collectibles. However, gold and precious metals have greater transparency and organized markets. In the early 21st century gold and silver outperformed stock and debt securities. Conversely, if the time frame is from 1980 to today the precious metals do not look so well.

Fine wine, a member of the real asset class, is becoming an investment item. A *Wall Street Journal* article by Jeff Opdyke in February 2007 reported that wine investing among alternative investment strategies is gaining favor with many investors. In 2003 the Wine Investment Fund was started and was converted into cash in August 2008, with annualized returns approaching 20%. Their strategy is to buy good quality wine, cellar it for 5 years and then sell it, hopefully for a tidy profit. Since 2003 they have started several other funds based on the same strategy. A recently launched fund, Fine Wine Fund is more like a hedge fund than a standard mutual fund. The Fine Wine Fund charges a 2% annual fee plus a performance fee of 15%. These investment pools are lightly regulated at this point in time and are catering to wealthier investors with a minimum required investment ranging from $20,000 to $100,000. There is also the futures market for French Bordeaux. Many wine merchants across the U.S. are offering wine futures online. The market is far from efficient; so, if one wants to get involved there may be potential profits due to arbitrage opportunities. However, risks are high because the wine market lacks transparency. If you need an index to benchmark against try the Liv-Ex 100 for top Bordeaux, or go to the London International Vintage Exchange for a more general benchmark. In 2007 the Vintage Exchange was up 42%.

- Efficient frontier and risk-return characteristics of asset classes
  - generating the efficient frontier
    - o risk-return data for asset classes
    - o quadratic optimization program (i.e., Excel)
    - o target returns
    - o certainty equivalent rate of return
    - o programs to generate an efficient frontier are available on the Internet
  - benefits:
    - o helps evaluate behavior of asset classes over different economic cycles
    - o returns measured over sufficiently long periods may represent benchmarks for investors
    - o availability of various measures enables comparisons across asset classes

- risk premiums to consider
  o   liquidity premium
  o   default premium
  o   risk (market) premium

In evaluating the desirability of portfolios along the efficient frontier, many investors prefer to think in terms of the probability of loss or failure to meet a target return rather than the mean-variance characteristic of the portfolio. This is a more intuitive way for many investors to view risk. Typically, target returns for investors might be to either avoid an excessive loss or for that matter any negative return, and would be expressed as the probability of the return being below zero over the period. Alternatively, some investors are concerned about earning a real rate of return: for example, matching or exceeding the rate of inflation over the investment time horizon. Other investors may set their goals as beating the rate of inflation by five percent. Obviously, the higher the desired return the higher the risk that must be undertaken. All too often investors say they want a return of, say, 15% along with the safety of a Treasury since they are risk averse.

The certainty equivalent rate of a portfolio is the rate that "risk portfolios" need to offer with certainty to be considered equally attractive to the risk-free instrument. The certainty equivalent approach relates a person's risk preferences to the idea of utility. Moreover, it relates to an investor's concept of expected return and lower risk. When utility values are compared to rates for risk-free investments, a portfolio value in terms of rate of return can be determined for the investor. Or what rate of return is needed to induce the investor to move from a risk free portfolio to a defined risky portfolio. The certainty equivalent approach can be used to deduce the risk aversion of an investor when one knows his or her existing portfolio holdings. Once this risk-return trade-off is known, we can determine any portfolio changes to be made in the context of maintaining this trade-off, or what needs to be done to change the trade-off relationship as the risk profile of the investor changes over time.

- The capital market line
  - introduce a risk-free asset into the Markowitz model
  - risk-free (R_f) means certain outcome, or the standard deviation equals zero
  - with the standard deviation being zero combining R_f with any other asset results in a correlation and covariance of zero
  - R_f = y intercept in a mean variance space like the efficient frontier
  - including R_f means a linear combination of the risk-free security and a portfolio on the efficient frontier
  - the most efficient would be where a ray from R_f is just tangent to EF at point 'm' (see graph below)
    o   the resulting line is known as the capital market line |CML|
    o   only efficient portfolios lie on the CML
    o   m = market portfolio, all risky assets in the proportion that they exist in the marketplace

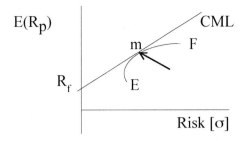

Introducing a risk-free asset produces a new set of optional portfolios known as the capital market line [CML]. The CML dominates the old efficient frontier (EF). Because the correlation and covariance of any asset with the R_f is zero the CML is the straight line from R_f that is just tangent to EF. The portion of the CML above the market portfolio (m) implies the ability to borrow at R_f and invest the borrowed funds in the market portfolio (see below for more details on this concept). All investors should want to be on the CML.

- Lending and Borrowing
  - investors can mix risk-free and risky assets to obtain a desired risk-return combination for the portfolio (combinations of R_f and m)
  - assume that the risk of lending is equal to the risk of borrowing; hence, the rate is the same (R_f)
  - borrowing to buy additional risky assets increases the total risk of the portfolio: financial leverage
  - variance of portfolio depends exclusively on the proportion invested in the risky asset and the proportion invested in the risk-free asset
- Tobin's separation theorem
  - all investors hold the market portfolio [m], remaining decision is how to finance the investment in m
  - the form of financing, the amount of R_f, is based on the investors aversion of risk
  - for portfolios on CML, expected rate of return in excess of R_f is proportional to standard deviation of the market portfolio
  - between R_f and m on the CML an investor would be lending, and between m and D an investor would be borrowing (see graph below)
  - CML slope is additional expected return for an additional unit of risk for efficient portfolios

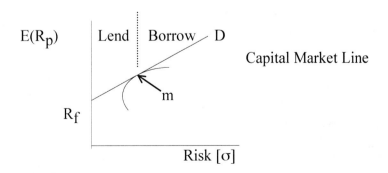

Capital Market Line

The possibility for lending and borrowing changes the original efficient frontier to a straight line (R_f D). This is because when investors combine risky assets with the risk-free asset, the expected return increases proportionally to risk. The shape of the line changes from a straight/curve to a completely straight line known as the capital market line. The CML provides a risk-return relationship for efficient portfolios as shown in the following equation:

$$ \hat{r}_p = \hat{r}_f + \left[\frac{\left(\hat{r}_m - r_f \right)}{\sigma_m} \right] \sigma_i $$

In essence the CML is an efficient set of portfolios obtained by leveraging or de-leveraging an investment in the market portfolio 'm.'

Operationalize the Model
- The CML (and the EF) provide a selection of optimal portfolios, the question then becomes how to know where an investor is on the CML
- Risk aversion – risk matters and is disliked
  - portfolio selection and level of risk aversion
  - all investors are risk averse, or act as though they are
  - risk is measured by standard deviation
  - indifference curves [IC] (see graph below)
  - investors are indifferent along a particular IC
  - investors prefer to be on a higher IC, maximize utility (IC_1 is preferred to IC_2)
  - utility as a function of expected returns and investor's aversion to risk

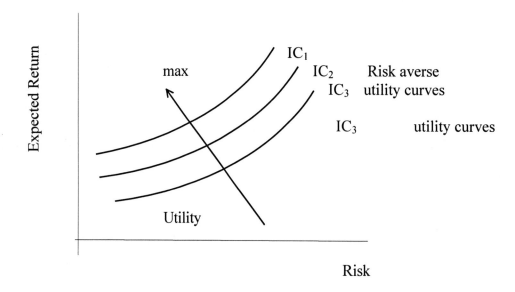

- Optimum portfolio [OP] for a risk averse investor (see graph below)
  - combine the CML with ICs
  - an IC tangent to the CML represents the highest level of IC attainable
  - OP is the optimum combination of R_f and m (say 70% m and 30% R_f)

208

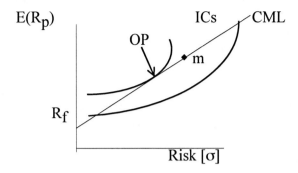

Investors want to maximize their expected utility and hence want to obtain the highest level of indifference curve possible. The limiting factor on this concept is the CML since investment opportunities do not exist above the CML. ICs will intersect the CML, as shown above, but these intersections are not optimal. An optimal portfolio [OP], as shown in the graph above, is based on each individual investor's tolerance for risk and is the tangent point of an IC to the CML. If an investor was risk neutral (risk does not matter) their indifferent curves would be parallel to the x-axis and no solution would exist since there is no tangent point. Likewise, if an investor is risk seeking the indifferent curves would be convex and no optimal tangent point occurs. This does not imply that each and every individual investment is "risk averse," rather overall the portfolio has risk averse characteristics. At times a risk averse investor will be risk seeking such as when they invest in the lottery – the expected outcome is zero, yet they still invest. The lottery investment is based more on psychological reasons then "dollar denominated" logic. Behavioral aspects of investing were introduced in Chapter 2.

- Expanding asset classes [see figure below]
    - favorable covariance characteristics
    - less than +1 correlation
    - international equities (global investing)
        o strong trend to include in portfolios
        o diversifying potential and higher returns
    - "world market" portfolio
        o asset allocation
        o performance benchmark

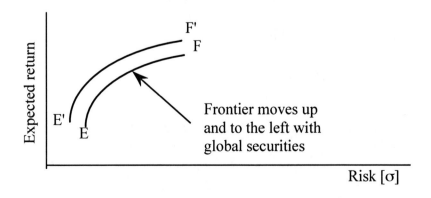

Expanding the universe of securities under consideration allows the investor to have a greater potential of finding diversification benefits. The Internet has helped to expand the universe of assets and securities. Information about other asset classes is becoming more available as time passes. Of course, one should always consider the reliability (source), timeliness and accuracy of the information – especially when using Internet sources. With the expansion the probability of finding securities with lower correlation increases. Adding asset classes, especially those that have favorable covariance characteristics, results in reduction in portfolio risk without sacrificing expected return. This process also provides a higher certainty equivalent return than the domestic only portfolio, which in turn lends to gains in investor utility.

By expanding the selection universe to include foreign and U.S. securities, a world portfolio is created. The availability of foreign securities has created a new asset class to include during asset allocation and moves the efficient frontier up and to the left (EF to E'F') as shown in the diagram above. Pension plans and other major money managers are using the world portfolio. In these cases, the world market portfolio should be considered as a benchmark for performance measurement. Global investing is presented in Chapter 9.

Evaluation – A Brief Overview

- Investment performance should be evaluated from the major aspects of the investment process (referred to as a process of attribution):
  - asset allocation
  - weighting shifts across major asset classes
  - individual security selection with asset classes
- Investment/portfolio performance can also be evaluated by focusing on the overall investment strategy
- Benchmarks need to be established *ex ante* not *ex post facto* 1

Performance attribution analysis allows one to examine various decision points within the investment process to determine the relative areas of success or failures within the portfolio. Three areas that attribution addresses are asset allocation, sector or group selection and lastly individual security selection. These three areas represent the philosophic level of asset selection based on the objective of the portfolio, the strategic decisions regarding sectors and shifting thereof, and the tactical decisions regarding the selection of individual securities. Performance attribution is becoming widely used in pragmatic settings because it allows one to gauge effectiveness more accurately and can separate out market performance from skill.

- Evaluating investment strategies
  - compare relative performance
  - use a composite measure that also considers risk
- Analyze the productivity of generating above-average performance: market timing and stock selection

- Studies have shown that for well-constructed, diversified portfolios performance is mostly attributed to asset allocation (over 90%), approximately 5% for stock selection, less than 2% for market timing, and the remainder for other factors
- Calculate rate of return earned over relevant comparison period, include changes of value and any income earned over the period

Without knowing the objectives of the portfolio it would be very difficult to evaluate the investor/portfolio manager. As noted throughout the book the investments/portfolio should match the risk tolerance of the investor. In the case of mutual funds the objective needs to be written in plain English so investors know the risk characteristics of the fund. Returns follow risk undertaken, and objectives determine the amount of risk. In addition to the overall performance an evaluation should recognize the different levels of strategies and disciplines and judge each one separately.

Return is defined to include changes in the value of the investment over the performance period plus any income earned over that period less costs. Returns can be distorted by fund cash flows (in or out) during the interim between valuations. Thus adjustments need to be made for contributions and withdrawals of cash. Adjustments that need to be undertaken are "time-weighted" return (when did the flows occur). The time-weighted return is a method to adjust the return by accounting for interim cash flows that are not part of the performance of the investments. The technique is to calculate a return at the time of each cash flow and then link (compound) these returns to derive the time-weighted return over the period of interest.

- Adjust returns for differences in risk exposure
- Return per unit of risk
  - relate absolute level of return achieved to the level of risk incurred to develop a relative risk adjusted measure for ranking fund performance
  - Sharpe ratio [SR]: reward-to-variability or total risk
    - $$SR = \frac{(r_P - r_f)}{(\sigma_P)}$$
    - SR = portfolio return less the risk free rate all divided by the standard deviation of the portfolio
    - appropriate when evaluating risk-return relationship for well-diversified portfolios
  - Treynor ratio [TR]: reward-to-volatility or systematic risk
    - $$TR = \frac{(r_P - r_f)}{(\beta_P)}$$
    - TR = portfolio return less the risk free rate all divided by the beta of the portfolio
    - appropriate when evaluating less than fully diversified portfolios or individual stocks
  - SR and TR rank the same when portfolios are well-diversified; if the portfolios are not well-diversified, ranks may differ

Risk must be considered in evaluating performance because a portfolio manager needs to recognize risk-return relationships when they invest. A higher return with lots of risk may not be as favorable as a lower risk investment. Return is but one axis on a two-axis graph, or as the saying goes 'risk and return represent the two sides of a coin.'

Two return-per-unit of risk performance measures are the Sharpe Ratio [SR] and the Treynor Ratio [TR]. Both of the ratios look at the 'excess return' above the risk free rate. The Sharpe Ratio, reward to variability, is based on total risk (σ): $SR=[r_p - r_f]/\sigma_p$. The Treynor Ratio, reward to volatility, is based on systematic risk (β): $TR=[r_p - r_f]/\beta_p$. Sharpe is appropriate when evaluating risk-return relationship for well-diversified portfolios. Treynor is more appropriate when evaluating less than fully diversified portfolios, or individual stocks. Higher numbers imply better performance. However, for either ratio to have meaning it needs to be compared against an appropriate index or standard. Comparing the ratio over time adds value to the evaluation of performance.

Portfolio/Investment Choices & Behavioral Aspects

While the math concept behind diversification is relatively straightforward individual investors are challenged with not knowing about the correlation of assets/securities and they typically make decisions that require the least amount of effort -- or they fall prey to behavioral factors such as short cuts and herding. Moreover, behavioral aspects of overconfidence, mental accounting and mistaken beliefs have investors overlook correlation as they seek return without fully considering risk aspects. Instead, all too often, investors, if they have heard of diversification, simply diversify by putting various securities, in their portfolio and figure that solves the problem and that makes their portfolios OK. Others who have not heard about the need for diversification, or get swayed by physical factors or deadly sins, concentrate their investments: for example, employees of Enron who put their retirement contributions into Enron stock. Studies have shown that employees typically put their retirement contributions into one or two funds even when they are offered multiple choices.

In order to overcome behavioral considerations in establishing portfolios investors should seek advice from unbiased financial advisors. Additionally, generally, target date funds or the 110 minus age for equity and debt allocation approaches are viable strategies with lower risk profiles for individual investors to follow.

Summary
- Markowitz model provides conceptual framework
- Diversification – combine securities/assets with less than +1 correlation
  - only "free lunch"
  - foundation for equilibrium models
  - it works in pragmatic settings
- Practical applications are numerous and readily observable
- Evaluation is a critical component in investing

212

The Markowitz model provides the foundation for modern portfolio theory [MPT] and is used extensively in pragmatic settings. The key concepts are: (1) the covariance, or how asset classes and/or securities are correlated, and (2) asset allocation is the driving force behind performance. In turn asset allocation should be based on the risk tolerance of the investor because one manages risk and not returns. As MPT is implemented the overall satisfaction of investors is increased because a lot of the 'guess work' that used to go into investment decisions is eliminated. One challenge with the Internet and the increased use of MPT is that securities are having higher correlations.

Modern portfolio theory is not antipodal to behavioral finance. Rather the two, as indicated in Chapter 2, are tied closely together. Behavioral finance uses MPT as a benchmark so different/irrational behavior can be identified and analyzed.

The objective of evaluation is to assess how well the investment plan is meeting its goals and asses how well the investor/portfolio manager is doing. The important evaluation aspects of the investment process relate to asset allocation, weighting shifts, security and return per unit of risk undertaken.

Keep in mind that this chapter is just an introduction to portfolio management and investment evaluation.

CHAPTER 13
THOUGHT QUESTIONS

1. Explain how the Markowitz model provides an explicit and disciplined process for constructing portfolios that attain the goal of being efficient. How is this optimization process used by portfolio managers in pragmatic settings?

2. Describe the basic inputs needed to implement the Markowitz portfolio construction process and the impact that variations in these inputs have on the resulting risk-return characteristics of the portfolio.

3. In Chapter 1 you learned that the two critical features of financial markets are (1) risk-return trade-off and (2) market efficiency. Relate these two features to portfolio evaluation analysis and the implications they have for evaluation of investors or portfolio managers in today's investing environment.

Questions and Problems:

1. Identify the five basic assumptions underlying modern portfolio theory and which one is the key to developing efficient portfolios.
2. Determine the number of inputs needed to analyze a 250-stock universe and a 70-stock universe using the Markowitz model.

3. Describe the concept of efficiency.
4. Describe the process of diversification and its benefits. Be sure to include the roll of variance or standard deviation, covariance and correlation coefficient of securities.
5. What is asset allocation, and how is the Markowitz model appropriate for this activity.
6. Why is it reasonable to use only the three major asset classes to develop the efficient frontier?
7. What is the relationship between the covariance and the correlation coefficient? Why is the correlation coefficient considered more useful?
8. What happens when the risk free (R_f) is introduced into the Markowitz model? What are the investment implications?
9. What role does an investors utility and risk aversion play in investment strategies?
10. Explain how expanding the universe of securities (e.g., international securities) under consideration can be helpful in improving the risk-return tradeoff.
11. What elements are necessary for evaluation of investment results? Be sure to include the relevance of benchmarks and the need for differences in risk exposure. Identify two risk performance measures and how they are used in the evaluation process.
12. Use the following data to calculate the variance and standard deviation for a two asset portfolio:

$$\rho_{1.2} = 0.75 \qquad \sigma_1 = 10 \qquad \sigma_2 = 20$$
$$w_1 = 2/3 \qquad w_2 = 1/3$$

13. How does behavioral finance relate to modern portfolio theory and how can an investor "use" behavioral factors to enhance return?
14. In theory short selling can increase the return of a portfolio by investing in securities with higher expected returns. Can short selling in the pragmatic world also potentially increase portfolio returns? If so, how? If not, why not?
15. Explain why risk must be considered in evaluating performance.
16. Compare and contrast the two return-per-unit-of-risk performance measures. In what context is each best applied?
17. Consider the three portfolios below, and decide which you would prefer to invest in and indicate why you would invest:
    a. excess return of 7% and standard deviation of 18%
    b. excess return of 9% and standard deviation of 28%
    c. excess return of 5% and standard deviation of 11%
18. After you responded to the above question, using risk and return characteristics determine the superior and inferior portfolios. Which would you consider investing in after the risk-return analysis, and does it agree with your initial preference? What behavioral aspects played a role in your initial and follow up decisions?

Ice Fishing

See page iv , ix and other pages in book.

Ice fishing is similar to investing in numerous ways. First of all it is difficult, you cannot "see" what you are doing, and a touch of luck is always helpful. Cutting a hole in the ice is like drilling down in the financial data of a potential investment. Will the time and effort be worthwhile or will it draw a blank. Where you drill a hole is like forecasting – each contains a lot of uncertainly about what the future will hold, do you strike out or do get a hit? If a hit, is it good enough to keep? Both should be done with a margin of safety, and for sure emotions play a role in both activities.

Fishing is akin to investing, from lots of uncertainly to high expectation of success. Fishing in not catching, investing in not always positive returns, and both are associated with risk. Ice fishing is like investing in recessionary times, while summer fishing is like investing in boom times.

Give a person a fish you feed them for a day. Teach a person how to fish you provide a way for them to be self-sufficient. Give a person a hot tip they may be able to buy a fish. Teach a person good investment techniques you provide a way for them to purchase the necessary equipment to fish.

Selected References

The following references represent some of the more recent references. Many of the original articles relating to portfolio management and capital market theory are not included in this listing.

Abate, James, James Grant and G. Bennett Steward III. "The EVA Style of Investing." *Journal of Portfolio Management.* Summer 2004, Vol. 30, Issue 4, pp 61-72.

Anderson, Jeff and Gary Smith. "A Great Company Can Be a Great Investment." *Financial Analyst Journal*, Jul/Aug 2006, 62.4, pp 86-93.

Ang, James, Jess Chua and Walter J. Reinhart. "Monetary Appreciation and Inflation-Hedging Characteristics of Comic Books." *Financial Review*, May 1983.

Anson, Mark. "Strategic versus Tactical Asset Allocation." *Journal of Portfolio Management.* Winter 2004, Vol. 31, Issue 1, pp 8-22.

Baltussen, Buido and Gerrit T. Post. "Irrational Diversification: An Examination of Individual Portfolio Choice." *Journal of Financial and Quantitative Analysis*, 2011, 46(5), pp. 1463–1491.

Bhandari, Golul and Richard Deaves. "The Demographics of Overconfidence." *Journal of Behavioral Finance.* 2006, Vol 7 No 1, pp 5-11.

Board of Governors of the Federal Reserve System. *Flow of Funds Accounts of the United States.* March 8, 2007 release.

Boardman, Calvin, Steven Celec, and Walter J. Reinhart. "The Role of the Payback Period in the Theory and Application of Duration to Capital Budgeting." *Journal of Business Finance and Accounting*, Winter 1982, pp 511-522.

Braswell, Ronald C., Barry R. Marks, Walter J. Reinhart and Dewit Sumners. "The Effect of Term Structure and Taxes on the Issuance of Discount Bonds." *Financial Management*, Winter 1988, pp 92-103.

_____, Walter J. Reinhart and James R. Hasselback. "The Tax Treatment of Municipal Discount Bonds: Correction of a Fallacy." *Financial Management*, Spring 1982, pp77-81.

_____, DeWitt Sumners and Walter J. Reinhart. "The Effect of the Tax Act of 1982 on the Appropriate Coupon Rate Strategy for Issuing Corporate Bonds." *National Tax Journal,* June 1983, pp 255-256.

Brown, Stephen. "Behavioral Considerations in Risk Analysis." *CFA Magazine*, Sept – Oct 2003, pp 50-51.

Chen, Long, David A. Lesmond, and Jason Wei. "Corporate Yield Spreads and Bond Liquidity." *Journal of Finance.* Vol. LXII, No. 1, February 2007, pp 119-149.

Chincarini, Ludwig B. and Daehwan Kim. *Quantitative Equity Portfolio Management.* New York, McGraw-Hill, 2006.

Clayton, Ronnie J., Walter Reinhart and Bill Schmidt. "Bears and Bulls: Greater Volatility without Ticks?" Banking and Finance Review. December 2010, Vol. 2, Issue 2.

Cohn, Michael D. "Using Options as a Risk Management Tool, Protecting Assets, and Increasing Investment Income." *Journal of Wealth Management.* Fall 2005, Vol. 8 Issue 2, pp 36-41.

Costa, Bruce A., and Gary E. Porter. "Mutual Fund Managers: Does Longevity Imply Expertise?" *Journal of Economics and Finance.* Vol. 27, No. 2, pp 224-235.

Covel, Michael W. *Trend Following How Great Traders Make Millions in Up or Down Markets.* New expanded edition, New Jersey, FT Press, 2007.

Cunningham, Lawrence A. *How to Think Like Benjamin Graham and Invest Like Warren Buffet.* New York, McGraw-Hill, 2001.

Deaves, Church, and Lucy F. Ackert. "Emotion and Financial Markets." *Economic Review.* June 2003, pp 33-40.

Dimson, Elroy; Paul Marsh and Mike Staunton. "Irrational Optimism." *Financial Analysts Journal.* Jan/Feb2004, Vol. 60, Issue 1, p 15-25.

Downes, John and John Elliot Goodman. *Dictionary of Finance and Investment Terms.* Hauppauge, N.Y., Barron's Educational Services, Inc. Seventh Edition, 2006.

Dubofsky, David A. and Thomas W. Miller, Jr. *Derivatives Valuation and Risk Management.* New York, Oxford University Press, 2003.

Elton, Edwin J., Martin J. Gruber, and Jeffrey A. Busse. "Are Investors Rational? Choices among Index Funds." *Journal of Finance.* Feb. 2004, Vol. 59 Issue 1, pp 261-288.

Fabozzi, Frank *Bond Markets, Analysis, and Strategies.* Fifth edition, New Jersey, Pearson/Prentice Hall, 2004.

_____, Lionel Martellini, and Philippe Priaulet. "Predictability in the Shape of the Term Structure of Interest Rates." *Journal of Fixed Income,* June 2005, Vol. 15, Issue 1, pp 40-52.

Fama, Eugene and Kenneth French. "Value versus Growth: The international evidence." *Journal of Finance.* Vol. 53. No. 6.

Forster, Graham. *The Power of Positive Profit.* John Wiley and Sons, November 2006.

Faugere, C., H. A. Shawky and D. M. Smith. "Sell Discipline and Institutional Money Management." Working Paper Series, Center for Institutional Investment Management, University at Albany, State University of New York, June 2003.

Garvey, Ryan, Anthony Murphy, and Fei Wu. "Do Losses Linger?" *Journal of Portfolio Management.* Vol. 33, Summer 2007. pp 75-83.

Graham, Benjamin. *The Intelligent Investor A Book of Practical Consel.* Revised edition/updated with new commentary by Jason Zweig. New York, Harper Collins, 2003.

_____ and David L. Dodd. *Security Analysis Principals and Technique.* New York, McGraw-Hill Book Company, Inc., 1940.

Gringold, Richard C. and Ronald N. Kahn. *Active Portfolio Management : A Quantitative Approach for Providing Superior Returns and Controlling Risk.* New York McGraw-Hill, 2000, 2nd edition.

Grotheer, Christina. "John Nofsinger Frames the Behavioral Finance Counter Revolution." *CFA Magazine.* Sept-Oct 2003, pp36-39.

Gupta, Francis, Rogertus Prajogi, and Eric Stubbs. "The Information Ratio and Performance." *Journal of Portfolio Management.* Fall 1999, pp 33-39.

Gwilym, O., J. Seaton, K. Suddason and S. Thomas. "Does the Fed Model Travel Well?" *Journal of Portfolio Management.* Vol.33, Issue 1, Fall 2006, pp 76-85.

Hailey, Arthur. *The Moneychangers.* New York Doubleday & Company, Inc., 1975.

Han Seung, Hun, Yoon S. Shin, William T. Moore and Walter J. Reinhart. "Market Segmentation Effects in Corporate Credit Rating Changes: The Case of Emerging Markets." *Journal of Financial Services Research.* Vol. 35, No. 2, April, 2009.

Haugen, Robert A. *The Inefficient Stock Market What Pays Off and Why.* Second edition, New Jersey, Prentice Hall, 2002.

Hood, Mathew; and John R. Nofsinger. "Hedge Funds in Portfolio of Risk-Averse Investors." *Journal of Economics and Finance.* Vol. 31, No. 2, Summer 2007, pp 219-233.

Hong, Harrison, and Jeffrey D. Kubik. "Analyzing the Analysts: Career Concerns and Biased earnings Forecasts." *Journal of Finance.* Vol. LVIII, No. 1, February 2003, pp 313-349.

-------, Jeremy C. Stein, and Jialin Yu. "Simple Forecasts and Paradigm Shifts." *Journal of Finance.* Vol. LXII, No. 3.

Jagric, Timotej; Boris Podobnik, and Marko Kolanovic. "Does the efficient Market Hypothesis Hold?" *Eastern European Economics*, Vol. 43, No. 4, July-August 2005, pp 79-103.

Jegadeesh, Narasimhan, and Joshua Livnat. "Revenue surprises and stock returns." *Journal of Accounting and Economics.* April 2006, Vol 41. Issue 1/2, pp147-171.

Jensen, Gerald, and Jeffrey Mercer. "New Evidence on Optimal Asset Allcoation." *Financial Review.* August 2003, Vol. 38, Issue 3, pp 435-454.

Jiankoplos, Nancy Ammon; and Alexandra Bemasek. "Financial Risk Taking by Age and Birth Cohort." *Southern Economic Journal.* Vol. 72, Issue 4, 2006, pp 981.1001.

Johnson, Sarah. "Goodbye GAPP." *CFO Magazine.* April 2008, pp 49-54.

Kecskes, Ambrus; Scattar A. Mansi and Andrew (Jianzhong) Zhang. "Are Short Sellers Informed? Evidence from the Bond Market" *The Accounting Review*, Vol. 88, No. 2, 2013, pp 611–639.

Kritzman, Mark, and Donald Rich. "The Mismeasurement of Risk." *Financial Analysts Journal.* May/June 2002, Vol. 58, Issue 3, PP 91-100.

MacKay, Charles. *Extraordinary Popular Delusions and the Madness of Crowds*, (1841); with a foreword by Andrew Tobias New York: Harmony Books, 1980.

Malkiel, Burton G. "Reflections on the Efficient Market Hypothesis: 30 Years Later" *The Financial Review.* 40, 2005, pp 1-9.

_____. *A Random Walk Down Wall Street.* New York, W. W. Norton & Company, 1996.

Mauboussin, Michael J. *More Than You Know Finding Financial Wisdom in Unconventional Places.* New York, Columbia University Press, 2006.

Merriken, Harry and Walter J. Reinhart. "The Implications of Tax Reforms on Firm Valuation and Management Decisions." *Akron Business and Economic Review*, Summer 1990, 94-104.

Nofsinger, John R. *The Psychology of Investing.* New Jersey, Prentice Hall, 2002.

Odders-White, Elizabeth and Kenneth Kavajecz. "Technical Analysis and Liquidity Provision." *Review of Financial Studies.* Winter 2004; 17,4.

Opdyke, Jeff D. "Investors Buy Wine To Drink In Profits." *The Wall Street Journal.* February 24 - 25, 2007.

"Out of the Doghouse?" *CFO Magazine*, February 2007.

Pettengill, Glenn N., Susan M. Edwards, and Dennis E. Schmitt. "Is Momentum Investing a Viable Strategy for Individual Investors?" *"Financial Services Review."* Issue 15, 2006, pp 181-197.

Plender, John. "Restoring Trust After the Bubble." *Business Economics.* July 2003, pp 21-24.

Poteshman, Allen M., and Vitaly Serbins. "Clearly Irrational Financial Market Behavior: Evidence from the Early Exercise of Exchange Traded Stock Options." *Journal of Finance.* Vol. LVIII, No. 1, February 2003, pp 37-70.

Pozen, Robert C. and Brett A. Fleishman. "An Alternative Approach to International Growth Investing." *Journal of Portfolio Management,* Spring 2005, Vol. 31 Issue 3, pp 19-26.

Puchkov, Anton V., Dan Stefel, and Mark Davis. "Sources of Return in Global Investing." *Journal of Portfolio Management,* Winter 2005, pp12-21.

Reinhart, Walter J. "Municipal Deep Discount Bonds: Tax Regulations and Implications." *Registered Representative*, October 1983, pp 41-45.

_____. *Multiple Discriminate Analysis of Industrial Bond Ratings.* MBA Thesis, Oklahoma State University, 1971.

_____. *Portfolio Management: Theory, Behavioral Aspects and Applications.* Forth edition, McGraw-Hill, 2009.

_____. "Zero Coupon Bonds." *Registered Representative*, November 1984, pp 67-73.

_____. Kermit O. Keeling. "Treasury Inflation-indexed Securities Provide Protection Against Inflation." *Journal of Taxation and Investments.* Summer 2004, pp 350-358.

Rogers, Jim. *Adventure Capitalist.* New York, Random House, 2003.

Roll, Richard. "A Critique of the Asset Pricing Theory as Tests. Part I: On Past and Potential testing of the Theory." *Journal of Financial Economic.* March 1977, pp 129-176.

Rubinstein, Mark. "Markowitz's 'Portfolio Selection:' A Fifty-Year Retrospective." *Journal of Finance*, June 2002, vol.57, no.3, pp.1041-1045.

Schefrin, Hersh. *Beyond Greed and Fear.* New York, Oxford University Press, 2002.

_____, and Meir Statman. "Behavioral Portfolio Theory." *Journal of Financial and Quantitative Analysis.* June 2000, pp 127-151.

_____, "The Disposition to Sell Winners Too Early and Ride Losers Too Long: Theory and Evidence." *Journal of Finance.* July 1985, pp. 777-790.

Schilit, Howard. *Financial Shenanigans.* Second edition, New York, McGraw-Hill, 2002.

Schiller, Robert J. *Irrational Exuberance.* New York, Broadway Books, 2001.

_____. "Tools for Financial Innovation: Neoclassical versus Behavioral Finance." *Financial Review,* Vol. 41, No. 1, pp 1-8, February 2006.

Serwer, Andy. "The greatest money manager of our time." *Fortune.* November 27, 2006.

Siegel, Jeremy J., "Perspectives on the Equity Risk Premium." *Financial Analysts Journal.* Nov/Dec 2005, pp 61-73.

Sharpe, William F. "Expected Utility Asset Allocation." *Financial Analysts Journal.* Sep/Oct 2007, pp 63-68.

Shkliko, A; B. Van Ness and R Van Ness "Short Selling and Intraday Price Pressures." *Financial Management,* Summer 2012, pp 345–370.

Singh, Shashank; Shailendra J. Singh and Dylan Jadeja. "Venture Investing in India? Think Twice." *The Journal of Private Equity.* Fall 2005.

Tempelman, Jerry H. "An Engine, Not a Camera: How Financial Models Shape Markets." *Financial Analysts Journal.* Spet/Oct 2007. Vol. 63. Issue 5.

Trammell, Susan. "Nearly 40 years after the introduction of the Efficient Market Hypothesis academics and practitioners are still at odds." *CFA Magazine,* Nov – Dec 2003, pp 27-31.

Vardharaj, Raman, and Frank J. Fabozzi. "Sector, Style, Region: Explaining Stock Allocation Performance." *Financial Analysts Journal.* May/Jun2007, Vol. 63 Issue 3, pp 59-70.

Webb, Robert I. *Trading Catalysts How Events Move Markets and Create Trading Opportunities.* New Jersey, FT Press, 2007.

Westheimer, Julius. *Generation of Wealth.* Baltimore, MD, Bancroft Press, 1997.

Appendix A

Internet Sources

The Internet provides a wide range of information on many topics. The websites presented below represent sites that students have found of value when they researched investments, and the write-ups on the site are based on student input. However, a general word of CAUTION is still needed because the Internet is a dynamic place and web sites are constantly changing: when you are using the Internet avoid opportunists hawking puffed-up promises and/or using unauthorized (illegal) hyperlinks to respected brokers/firms.

The information is grouped according to topics: 1. Ethics and Standards, 2. Educational Tools, 3. Portfolio, 4. Technical Analysis, 5. General, 6. Bonds, 7. Equity, 8. International Equities, 9. Derivatives, 10. Investment Advice, 11. Forecasting, 12. Personal Finance, and 13. Websites that may/will get you email. Many of the sites could be listed under several of the topic headings, and in fact a few are listed more than once. Many more sources exist besides the ones listed below. Hence, the reader is encouraged to explore the web and see what else is available for them to use: e.g., on a search engine type in 'bonds.' Additionally, information that must be paid for is not listed below, i.e., Morning Star Library Edition, Argus Research, Compustat, CRISP, WRDS, Bloomberg Professional, et cetera.

1. Ethics and Standards

www.cfainstitute.org   The CFA Institute (Association for Investment Management and Research, Ethics and Professional Standards) plus CFA information.

2. Education Tools

www.investopedia.com   Provides many learning resources such as articles, tutorials, calculators, and a dictionary. It has pages for beginners, experience investors, active traders and retired persons. Is informative without being overwhelming and includes a free online investment simulator. Preparation tools for CFA (all three levels) and Series 7 exams.

www.teachmefinance.com Lots of subjects from time value of money, to stock valuation. User friendly.

www.zenwealth.com Online learning environment and quizzes to validate understanding of topics. Includes financial news articles. Link to Business Finance online, including a interactive tool for corporate finance. Also a link for a financial calculator use guide.

www.fool.com Explains how to value stocks, insight into investment strategies, and provides personal finance information.

www.moneychimp.com Provides a variety of material and educational tools, including: volatility, valuation, index funds, bond concepts, and modern portfolio theory.

www.exinfm.com/training Financial management training center with short courses on various finance topics.

http://www.duke.edu/~charvey/Classes/wpg/bfglosc.htm Finance glossary – over 8,000 definitions and 16,000 hyperlinks to other definitions.

www.finra.org Educational resources to help a wide range of uses, from beginners to more sophisticated investors. Information on both stocks and bonds, plus options.

3. Portfolio

http://www.effisols.com Portfolio optimization software (30 day trail), calculate s single period or multi-period MVO, and efficient frontier.

http://www.schaeffersrearch.com Specializes in research of equity and index options, investor sentiment and market timing – lots of detailed information along with extensive educational material. Free access to quantified sentiment indicators on stocks, ETFs, options. Rank aspects such as technical trends, institutional ownership, insider transactions, short interest, et cetera.

www.riskgrades.com A risk analyzer tool evaluates the potential risk of individual securities, the overall portfolio or watch-lists to help make educated investment decisions. Able to compare to various benchmarks, plus it allows you to compare your asset risk across all asset classes, regions, and currencies.

www.sec.gov Provides a calculator to find out how important the impact of expenses can be on mutual fund performance. Also it has 10K and 10Q filings.

www.kickassets.com Based on MPT. Allows investor to measure the risk and return of an investment profile.

4. Technical Analysis

www.stockcharts.com Point and figure and other types of charts, including ticker cloud data, plus educational content and explains the many different kinds and uses of technical analysis charting.

www.naviamarkets.com/dzine/techanal.htm Good summary of technical analysis terms and strategies.

www.Dorseywright.com Provides technical research services including charting, in-depth technical analysis and support, mutual funds and ETF's. Is not a free good.

www.fastquote.com Nice location for prices and charts.

www.barchart.com Technical analysis with explanations, extensive reporting of analysts' opinions.

www.bigcharts.com Excellent source of date, easy to navigate, direct links to other sites.

5. General

www.morningstar.com/ Provides great information on stocks, bonds, options, mutual funds, hedge funds, and other derivatives. Historical data, performance ratios plus tools for portfolio management.

www.conference-board.org/ Presents useful information regarding the global economy (e.g., http://www.conference-board.org/data/globaloutlook.cfm), and economic indicators for the USA and various countries under global indicators. Provides business insights.

http://www.tradingeconomics.com/ Provides basic economic information (i.e., GDP, inflation, jobless rate, et cetera), indicators, calendars, and forecasts for many countries.

www.thestreet.com Good for security evaluation and market data, lots of news articles and analyst opinions.

www.quote.com Financial information and trading tools for active traders and new investors. Lots of statistical data. Covers USA and global markets, including derivatives. Equipped with advanced caring capabilities and a stock simulator for practice investing.

http://www.ft.com/home/us A financial website that it is also a leading financial newspaper and global events are covered, rather than domestic news only. Overabundance of data relating to the capital markets around the world. Data on stocks, bonds, commodities, mutual funds, ETFs, and currencies. User has the ability to create a portfolio of investments and download to Excel. Information on ADRs as well as securities in local markets. FT Lex section has expert opinion and analysis. Numerous blogs to choose from, podcasts, educational tools, regional pages for different countries, arts & leisure section, currency converter, interactive charting, and Financial Times Lexicon which is a definitive glossary of economic, financial and business terms.

www.nasdr.com National Association of Securities Dealers [NASD] – brings you to http://www.finra.org/index.htm Learn about investing and how to build your financial knowledge. We offer articles, interactive tools, alerts and other resources that help you protect yourself. FINRA is the largest independent regulator for all securities firms doing business in the United States. We oversee nearly 4,380 brokerage firms, 163,150 branch offices and 633,000 registered securities representatives. Our chief role is to protect investors by maintaining the fairness of the U.S. capital markets.

www.seekingalpha.com Provides top news stories, event transcripts, company information and SEC filings. Written primarily by investment professionals and serious investors.

www.bloombergcom/markets/economic-calendar/ Overview of current economic indicators, a daily list of key economic events for the week – each event is defined and projected, and has historical data.

Woodrow.mpls.frb.fed.us [http://woodrow.mpls.frb.fed.us/economy/usindex.html] Great source for economic information, detailed forecast and statistical data, easy to use. Economic information, detailed forecast, and return rates dating back to the 1930's. The statistical data includes: Fed Funds, Discount Rate, Prime Rate, one-year and 30-year Treasuries, CPI, & Foreign Exchange Rates - data ranges from weekly to monthly and yearly. Also provides current and past Beige Book Economic Forecast on a quarterly basis. Another attractive feature of this site is information pertaining to recent Federal Reserve meetings as well as Department of Labor meetings.

http://finance.google.com/finance Provides an array of standard financial information for equities (like P/E ratios, dividend yields, and beta). Provides crisp clear graphics, calculates stock returns automatically, quick and easy links to news and information relevant to stock being researched. Clear and user friendly charts and graphs on overall market and sectors – plus details as to what stocks have moved the sector and comparison to the S&P500 (or other benchmark). Offers current and historical price data and key statistic for stocks on world markets.

www.martincapital.com Has a link for current economic data and leading economic indicators. The date is presented in simple and easy to understand format

www.financewise.com A search engine to focus on financial-only content, special reports on finance topics or related areas.

www.hoovers.com Good for mergers and acquisitions.

www.marketwatch.com Lots of good info, including latest news, historical charts, advice, and future info before market opens. Both domestic and international information. The economic data provided by this site includes international market stats, up to date quotes, quarterly and yearly forecasts, and historical data for the past 40 years. MarketWatch provides a wide range of financial information, technical analysis of stocks and bonds, currency movements, bond ratings, mortgage rates, interactive charts, option to create portfolios to track specific interests.

www.inflationdata.com Current and historical inflation information.

www.yahoo.finance.com Statistical information on each company with views by competitors and industry, good stock and bond screener to help identify investment candidates, very user friendly. General all around information, good market recap, the free financial data competes with high price data.

http://money.cnn.com/?cnn=yes Similar to http://finance.yahoo.com and provides financial statements, including cash flow, along with current events. New reports have a liberal bias to them.

www.sec.gov/edgarhp.htm S-4a registration statement for mergers and acquisitions which provide a "fairness opinion" which can provide excellent industry data.

www.sec.gov.edgar.searchedgar/ Company's filings and history.

www.TheStreet.com Good to perform research and review market news on a daily basis.

www.cnnfn.com Basic information, somewhat biased news.

www.Forbes.com Provides trend charts with news tags at each point, the tags provide news summary and there is a link to the complete news for more information

http://www.zerohedge.com/ A source for commentary on anything and everything dealing in the investment arena. Information may be, most likely is biased. The home page is comprised of blog style writings that detail topics that follow equities, derivatives, swaps, bonds, commodities, or just market news in general. However, it also has a news feed that brings current reports in on a consistent basis.

6. Bonds

www.bonds-online.com Provides good broad-based information relative to government, municipal, zero-coupon, and corporate bonds, can sort by type and rating.

www.bondpage.com Provides price and CUSIP of bonds, also rating information, first date and frequency of coupon payments, and callable status of the bond.

www.valuebond.com Need to register, but has lots of helpful information on all fixed income securities.

www.investinginbonds.com Provides a great deal of information about bonds (including yields) and the ability to look up individual bonds (government, corporate, municipal and mortgage backed). Plus it has commentary and educational content about and other fixed income instruments. Site is maintained by the securities Industry and financial Markets Association.

7. Equity

www.yahoo.finance.com Basic financial information; under the stock quote-profile section is good preliminary data to screen stocks, include market cap, beta, net income margin and return on stockholders equity; also has ability to chart stock prices, and provide access to company news. Offers the ability to download historical prices into Excel. For international investments, it offers a currency converter.

www.justquotes.com Provides research and technical information.

www.freeedgar.com Provides access, in easy to read and print format, of SEC filings for publicly traded companies; excellent source of raw data on company's financials.

http://online.wsj.com/mdc/age/marketsdata The *Wall Street Journal*, Markets Data Center. Provides excellent market summaries and in-depth analysis in different market sectors. Helpful in identifying undervalued or overvalued ETFs.

www.wsrn.com Offers links to lots of other information including Bloomsberg, SEC filings, earnings estimates, the economy, international and technical analysis, enter ticker symbol in "Get Research" box and wow.

www.tscn.com/AmexGuest/ Enter ticker symbols (only once since it remembers you) and receive summary of the daily activity for each of the stocks on a 15-20 minute quote delay.

www.cbs.marketwatch.com can overload the novice user with a plethora of market data; however, after a few visits to the site one should be able to sort through all the information to quickly retrieve the desired data.

www.zacks.com Research website that provides thorough, in-depth analysis of individual stocks, ETFs, and mutual funds. Also provides financial and economic news, outlooks, recommendations, and forecasts for valuation variables like the p/e ratio and growth.

www.stockfetcher.com Provides great information on historical returns by industry and sector; historical trends from a 2 year period to the last few days; able to drill into industry or sector and see the basket of stocks that make up the index

www.nakedcapitalism.com Insightful posts each day; provides links to other sites; and …

http://seekingalpha.com Excellent site for stock picking opinion and analysis. Investing articles and blog posts organized in the following categories; Macro View, Sectors, Global Markets, ETFs, and Investing Ideas. Particularly useful is the "Wall Street Breakfast," a daily briefing available on the website or via the mailing list. Also of note, the "Market Currents" blog provides frequent market updates throughout the day (4-5 per hour). Site offers conference call transcripts for over 1500 companies, as well as basic data on returns for areas such as bonds, commodities, currencies, real estate and more. Basic portfolio feature tracks daily price changes and aggregates related articles. All content is free.

8. International equities

www.adr.com   Very helpful and the most thorough international equity resource on the web – from news articles to company information, plus it provides extensive country information.   Provides users with financial news and information on international companies that have shares listed in the USA. The "Market Overview" page displays the top gainers and losers, top sectors and countries, and news and ownership information on American Depository Receipts (ADRs) from around the world. The "DR Search" area of the website allows the user to screen for companies by exchange, region, or sector. Once a company is located, there is a wealth of information related to valuation, financials, ownership, and industry comparisons.

http://beginnersinvest.about.com/od/globalinvesting/Global_Investing.htm   Provides of global investing resources (more of a commercial site).

www.adrbny.com   Vast amount of information regards ADR's, such as company financials, industry comparisons and company recommendations.

www.aon.com/politicalrisk Provides information and an assessment of political risk.

9. Derivatives

www.cboe.com   Provides information and tutorials regarding options.

www.cbt.com   Provides information and tutorials regarding futures.

www.optionsanalysis.com   Provides high- and low-volatility screens and useful links.

www.commodityfutures.com   Provides a listing of websites that pertain to the commodity or future in question and is a quick way to get derivative research information.

www.futuresource.com   Provides a wealth of information on the futures markets, from charts and price tables to articles and research. Everything from treasuries and equity indices to precious metals, livestock, energies and grains. Does a technical analysis for each market, discussing moving averages, swing points and levels of support and resistance.

www.alaron.com   Provides daily research and investment strategies for a variety of futures markets. Helps investors to understand the drivers of the different futures markets, forecasts movements and suggests strategies and positions for investing in futures/commodities.

www.wtrg.com and www.eis.doe.gov Both provide information regarding sweet crude oil futures.

www.bohlish.com Provides extensive information about futures, charts provide historical picture of the future in question.

www.optionmonster.com   Informative for novice option investor (strategy screener, option positions with interactive tools), educational (from online classes to portfolio builder), and impart of option on your portfolio.

http://seekingalpha.com Provides stock market opinion and analysis from various sources along with it own high-value, complementary financial content. Focus is on options.

www.dailyfutures.com   Provides daily summaries and aggregated news on commodity futures.

www.888options.com   Learn about options, trading and strategies, virtual trading system

10. Investment Advice

www.investools.com   Provides investment opinions.

www.fool.com   Provides good analysis on trading and holding strategies, especially for value investing.

www.tradejuice.com   Contains many articles about trading techniques and styles. Its focus is day trading and it provides links to many other helpful websites for day trading techniques and tactics.

www.footnote.org   Investigates information buried in footnotes of SEC filings; written for experienced investors, but novice can benefit; insights into accounting shenanigans; and has a good section that explains how to analyze SEC reports

11. Forecasting

www.intrade.com   A prediction market website, where a user can bid on outcomes of everything from political races to Oscars, and from global events to events that impact financial markets. Provides information about what the "market thinks will happen around specific situations (i.e., raising the debt ceiling, presidential elections, et cetera). Provides behavioral information or the wisdom of the crowds.

12. Personal Finance

www.futureadvisor.com   FutureAdvisor is an investment advisor web application that automatically gives you personalized recommendations to save on fees, maximize tax-efficiency, and have the right asset class mix for your situation. If you have one, you'll even get recommendations on your workplace plan account like a 401(k).

www.mint.com Get a handle on your finances the *free* and fast way. Mint does all the work of organizing and categorizing your spending for you. See where every dime goes and make money decisions you feel good about.

13. Websites that may/will get you email:

https://www.wikinvest.com/?_acn=portfolio&_acm=ad&_acs=wire&_acc=news
Keep track of all your investments/portfolio

www.Stockgumshoe.com
WELCOME TO STOCK GUMSHOE! **Travis Johnson** the Stock Gumshoe
Frustrated or intrigued by email teasers from investment newsletters and advisers? We solve them and track their performance here ... so stick around, participate and subscribe (it's free)!   Have a stock teaser for us to unravel? Email it to ILoveStockSpam [at] gmail.com or try the search (top right) to see if it's been covered

Appendix B
Class Information

The items included in this appendix deal with possible class assignments. These assignments have worked successfully for the author over multiple years. Most students will appreciate the benefit of the assignments because it prepares them for the pragmatic world. Also because the project is basically a comprehensive take home exam that students have all semester to work on there is no "final exam" on the last day of class, or during the exam period.

Some students have successfully used the final project as an example of the work they can do when interviewing for a job. Most employers are impressed with the comprehensiveness of the project and it does show the depth of knowledge that the student acquired while in the investments course.

Items included in this appendix include:
> Project Requirements
> Check and return reports — used to motivate the student to keep up with the work, and they are not 'graded," instead they are used to provide feedback to the student.
> Check & Return #1
> Check & Return #2
> Check & Return #3
> Summary -- a summary page that presents the major findings of the project
> Analysis Reports: provide a formal structure for analysis of a bond, stock and option. Templates for valuing a bond, a stock and an option are presented at the end of the chapters where the securities are discussed.
> Ethics – because ethics and profession standards are so important in finance a typical assignment is included.

If adopters of the book, or users for that matter, have suggestions for other class information or assignments that should be included in future editions of this book please do not hesitate to send them to the author. Thank you.

Project Requirements

The project, according to former students, **can be considered a take home comprehensive exam that takes a semester to complete!!** It requires you to conduct an appraisal of a company, and the financial instruments (debt and equity) of the company. Thus it strongly recommended that you select a firm that has publically traded debt and equity – you need access to financial statements and other information about the company. Selecting a firm that pays dividends will make your life easier. During the project you will address the sort of points that an analyst or informed investor would consider before making an investment decision. As you do your project you will also need to consider the general economy and the prospects for the industry that includes the firm you selected. Ultimately you will determine the expected risk, the expected rate of return, and the desirability (or lack thereof) of investing – an investment decision regarding financial instruments that represent the company with reasons thereof, including both the downside and upside potential. Your evidence, logic, justification, analysis and format of the recommendation are as important (if not more so) as the results and conclusion at which you arrive. *I strongly recommended that you select a firm that benefits you.*

Your final report must be typewritten, double-spaced, on one-sided pages. Any tables, equations, calculations, or graphs may be handwritten provided they are neat. Appendices may be used for analysis reports, graphs, diagrams, tables, and/or calculations if they are not appropriate for the body of the report. Footnotes (if applicable) and a reference section, including websites used, must be included.

The project is due by _____ PM on ____*day*____, __*month*_ ___*date*___. Late projects are not looked upon favorably (if accepted a heavy penalty will be assessed). If you have any questions, are having difficulty, or foresee any problems please be sure to discuss the situation with me so a successful result can be achieved. The goal of the course/project is for you to have a positive learning experience! The reports will NOT be returned to you. Therefore if you wish to have a copy please duplicate it before turning in the project. For your information, in the past, projects have been helpful for finding employment.

Sample projects are on _____. However, it should be noted the projects are from prior semesters, and more importantly requirements and the investment environment have changed. The samples are not necessarily complete projects and there are differences among the samples. The samples are to provide guidance and insight regarding expectations and 'work' involved. Also in an effort to assist you in completing the project in a timely fashion you are required to hand in "check & return" status reports. The check & return reports are to ensure that you have familiarized yourself with the material covered in the textbook and the class, and to make sure that no one in the course gets left behind in terms of keeping up. See the Tentative Weekly Schedule for due dates of the check & return status reports – yes, late check & return status reports are not viewed favorably; however, they will be accepted. Hence, if you miss class be sure an electronic copy is sent in a timely fashion and a hard copy handed in the following week, or mail the hard copy with an appropriate and timely postmark on it. The original check & return reports (the ones with the green ink on them) must be turned in with the final report.

232

The report will consist (at a minimum) of the following:

I. Title page, followed by the summary sheet (see Summary handout) – if this order is not followed and the summary sheet is not the "original" your grade will suffer!!

II. Executive Summary

III. Firm selection
   a. Initial reasons
   b. Internet sources

IV. Economic Environment & Industry Analysis
   a. Identify and forecast the broad forces that affect the performance of your firm
   b. Elements to consider include: inflation, government actions (including taxes), interest rates and money supply, GNP, politics/elections, growth, competitive conditions, earnings, dividends, consumer sentiment, et cetera

V. Company analysis
   a. The company and its relation to the economy and industry environments, significant internal and external developments, and forecasted performance
   b. Debt valuation/rating [include an analysis report]
      i. risk premium elements (duration)
      ii. show model and ratios
      iii. compare to benchmarks
      iv. risk-return relationship
   c. Equity valuation and growth prospects (avoid circular reasoning) [include analysis report, including an option report]
      i. risk elements, duration
      ii. dividend models (including H-model, 2-stage and 3-stage): the growth rates between the valuation models must be consistent, the time frame must also be logically consistent between the 2-stage, 3-stage and H models
      iii. cash flow model(s), residual income valuation
      iv. multiplier models
      v. value vs. price (if differ, why)
   d. Technical analysis

VI. Recommendation/conclusion
   a. Your opinion
   b. Investment recommendation(s)

VII. Appendix
   a. Original check & return reports [if not the originals with green ink on them your grade will suffer!]
   b. Other items you feel are important, but not worthy of being included in the main body of the report (e.g., analysis reports – bond, stock, …)

VIII. Selected References (including Internet sources)

As the semester progresses requirements will be refined and clarified. <u>DO NOT HESITATE to ask questions</u>. Remember this is a learning experience; hence, do not be afraid to explore and try different approaches to valuation. Bring in your prior education and work experiences.

This page is left blank intentionally.

Investments Project
Check & Return #1
Due date: _____ ___*month*___ __year___

This Check & Return [C&R] is due relatively early in the semester. Therefore it is highly possible that some of the items/terms are unknown to you at this point in time – they will be introduced during the semester. If something is unknown to you at this point in time feel free to place a "?" in the space for the information to be put. There are no negative consequences for doing this on a C&R report, but be sure you know the item/term by the time you turn in the project.

Firm Selection:

Name _____

Ticker _____

Fiscal Year: month _____ day _____

Stock: Current market price _____

P/E ratio   _____

EPS   _____

P/B ratio   _____

Growth of _____ is _____%

DPS _____ (*if zero, assumptions needed and <u>lots</u> of potential difficulties*)

Cash flow   _____

Residual income   _____

Preferred Stock: _____ yes _____no

Debt: Price/yield   _____

Maturity [>10 years] _____

Coupon [%]   _____

YTM   _____

Current yield   _____

YTC   _____

Duration   _____

Options available: _____ yes _____no

Industry:

Name _____

Future growth rate _____

Standards/Averages available _____ Yes _____ No

Three sentence overview and forecast

_____

_____

_____

_____

_____

_____

Economy:

Basic Direction _____

Future growth rate _____

Expected inflation: near term _____ % long term _____ %

Expected government regulation: _____

_____

_____

Three sentence overview and forecast

_____

_____

_____

_____

_____

_____

_____

Remember this is a check & return status report to provide motivation and guidance. The majority of the information can be gained from various sources on the Internet, or you can calculate ratios, et cetera. The final report will obviously be in greater depth and detail – see project requirements handout and sample projects. Also, the information in the final project can differ from what you have on the initial check & return reports. If information changes <u>you do not have to redo</u> the check & return report.

Investments Project
Check & Return #2
Due date: _____ ___*month*___ __year___

Name of firm _____

Debt valuation (per $1000 bond):

Market Price (in $)   _____

Maturity date (> 10 years)   _____

Coupon [%]   _____

Coupon dates [e.g., March and Sept 15th] _____

The bond is selling at a Premium _____ Discount _____ or Par _____

YTM[*]   _____

Current yield[*]   _____

Approximate yield[*]   _____

Call date and price   date _____ price _____

YTC if applicable   _____

Duration (today to maturity) _____ Date _____

Modified duration   _____

Bond rating   _____

Your value ($ amount)   _____

[*] Note relationship of yields – expected or ???

_____

_____

_____

_____

Remember this is a check & return status report to provide motivation and guidance. The majority of the information can be gained from various sources on the Internet, or you can calculate yields, et cetera. The final report will obviously be in greater depth and detail – see project requirements handout and sample projects. Also, the information in the final project can differ from what you have on the initial check & return reports. If information changes you do not have to redo the check & return report.

This page is left blank intentionally.

Investments Project
Check & Return #3
Due date: _____ ___*month*___ __year__

Name of firm & ticker _____ Industry _____

Stock (common equity) valuation (per share):

Market Price   _____

P/E ratio   _____

EPS   _____

DPS & most recent date of dividend   _____

Expected growth rate (g) of   _____ is _____%

Retention rate (b)   _____

Investors return (r)   _____

P/E of firm relative to S&P500 P/E   _____

Return on equity (ROE)   _____

Return on investments   _____

Cash flow   _____

Residual income   _____

P/S ratio   _____

P/B ratio   _____

Dividend model values* (be sure g_s, g_h, and times are consistent)

DDM   _____

2-stage   _____

3-stage   _____

H-model   _____

* If necessary make up 'fictitious' assumptions and identify as such. Also indicate which you think is the most representative of the future. _____

_____

_____

Cash flow value: _____

Residual income value: _____

Equity Duration   _____

S&P500 duration   _____

Your value of stock (per share)   _____

Implied growth rate(s) for:

    Current market price   _____

    Your valuation   _____

Which growth rate is in line with the industry?   _____

Which growth rate is in line with the economy?   _____

Option: Strike price _____ Expiration date _____ Premium _____

Other information/facts that are relevant for making a recommendation: _____

_____

_____

_____

_____

_____

_____

Technical analysis: _____

_____

_____

_____

_____

Remember this is a check & return status report to provide motivation and guidance. The majority of the information can be gained from various sources on the Internet, or you can calculate ratios, et cetera. The final report will obviously be in greater depth and detail – see project requirements handout and sample projects. Also, the information in the final project can differ from what you have on the initial check & return reports. If information changes you do not have to redo the check & return report.

Summary

Name of firm: _____

       Ticker: _____   Exchange: _____

Debt Information (fundamental factors):

    Maturity date: _____   Bond rating: _____
                                                  Note: be sure to discuss bond rating
                                                  factors in the report.

    Current market price: _____   Your value: _____

    Coupon rate [%]: _____   **Recommendation:**

    Yield to maturity (YTM): _____

    Duration: d = _____   Modified duration: $d^* =$ _____

    Anticipated yield change [must be + or -]_____% Change in price: _____

Stock/equity Information (fundamental factors):

    Current market price: _____   Your value: _____
           Date: _____

                                                Recommendation:
    Dividend $ amount & yield $____ ____%

    Growth (g): _____

    Earnings per share: _____   Price earnings ratio (P/E): _____

    Retention rate (b): _____   P/E relative to S&P500 P/E: _____

    Investors return (r): _____   Return on equity (ROE): _____

    Q ratio [P/B]: _____   Price sales ratios (P/S): _____

Model values: NOTE: in the body of the report be sure to note necessary assumptions used to derive
    model values (e.g., superior growth rate, time frame, et cetera).
                            Implied growth rates(s), must be consistent, between models
    DDM: _____ $g_s =$ _____

    2-stage: _____ $g_s =$ _____ $g_h =$ _____ t = _____

    3-stage: _____ $g_s =$ _____ $g_h =$ ____ t's _____

    H-model: _____ $g_s =$ _____ $g_h =$ _____ H = _____

    Cash flow: _____   Best model to use: _____

    Other valuation model: _____

    Duration: _____   S&P500 duration: _____

    Subgrouping/industry/class: _____

Option Information: Strike price _____ Expiration date _____ Premium _____

This page is left blank intentionally.

Ethics and Professional Standards
for the Finance Profession

Ethics and honorable conduct are the way of life in the field of finance. This is true whether we are discussing Corporate Finance, Banking/Financial Institutions/Capital Markets, Behavioral Finance, or Investments/Portfolio Management. In academics there is a set of literature and field of study that deals with ethical behavior known as Agency Theory. Succinctly put, Agency Theory deals with the potential conflict of interest in a principal-agent- relationship.

Of course, a major battle we fight in the field of finance is that the tiny minority of practitioners, who lack honor and behave in unethical ways, are the ones that make the headlines in the media. As we well know it only takes one rotten apple to spoil the barrel. Hence, in the field of finance, especially in the pragmatic world, it is a constant battle to overcome the negativism that the media, especially the "liberal media," projects about finance and business in general. This is further compounded by the fact that there is an opinion among many people that profits are "bad" – unless it is their own profit, then it is OK ☺.

The CFA Institute, formerly the Association for Investment Management and Research [AIMR], established a code for ethics and set of professional standards for its members, and others who are trying to become members. Simply put the Code of Ethics is a set of principles that defines the professional conduct AIMR expects from members and Chartered Financial Analyst (CFA) candidates. In turn the Code works in tandem with the Standards of Professional Conduct. The Standards of Professional Conduct sets "clear" guidelines for members as to what constitutes fair and ethical business practices.

To better understand what a code of ethics means it is worthwhile to review the definition of ethics and moral. From Oxford Advanced Learner's Dictionary:

Ethics –
1. a system of moral principles or rules of behavior;
    a. moral principles that govern a person's behavior
    b. the branch of philosophy that deals with moral principals

Moral –
1. Concerned with principles of right and wrong behavior; ethical;
2. Based on one's sense of what is right and just, not on legal rights and obligations;
3. Following right and accepted standards of behavior, good in character;
4. Able to understand the differences between right and wrong;
5. Teaching or illustrating right behavior.

   NOTE: who or what determines/sets 'sense' and 'accepted standards of behavior'?? (e.g., Western culture, Eastern culture, Mideast culture, ...)

Your assignment is to go to the web site cfainstitute.org and explore the Code of Ethics and the Standards of Professional Conduct. In a brief review of these items be sure to indicate your opinion of the Code and the Standards, how one can run into conflicts in your position, and how you would address such conflicts. Have you every faced an 'ethical challenge,' and if so how did you address the situation? After your review of the Code and Standards, respond to the questions listed below.

- What frame of reference are you using?
- Investing in self-described ethical investment funds means what?
- How does the Code of Ethics relate to these funds and to investing in general?
- In investing and in handling investors' money, what role, if any, should moral and/or social convictions, and/or political correctness play?
- What is your opinion of the governmental response (Congress and Executive branches) to "accounting scandals," corporate and investment banking behavior, "media pressure," and investor reactions/perceptions? Should Congress be held to the same standards?
- Why are Congress (House and Senate) and Executive branches not held to the same standards, or to many of the rules and regulations they pass and 'impose' on society?
- What is your opinion about the 'subprime/liquidity' crisis, how the government responded to it and the resulting recession?

You received, via Moodle, "Business 'ethics' wrong focus It's government, not the corporate world, that is inherently unethical" by Thomas DiLorenzo – what is your opinion of this article.

Additional questions may be added during the semester as we discuss investment analysis/management along with ethics and standards. See Preface for more information regarding the importance of ethics in finance.

Appendix C

Personal Finance – Investing

Within the main body of this textbook the fundamentals of investing are presented along with behavioral considerations and a brief overview of portfolio management. The investing information presented is based on "theory" and has assumptions about the pragmatic world so things can be "modeled." Do the assumptions hold when we look at human emotions, taxes, rules and regulations – unlikely!! However, they are close enough so the models developed can be used – to not use them would be foolhardy. At a minimum the models, process and strategies provide a base to judge from. Without a base of comparison investing becomes more challenging if not doomed for failure.

Many times students ask are they some basic guidelines one can follow regarding personal finance. First of all it is necessary to recognizing that investing is just part of personal finance, and financial planning is an important aspect in ones life. Everyone should develop a financial plan, and in essence we all do have a financial plan because **having no financial plan is a plan for failure.**

Some general guidelines:
- develop a budget and follow it
- do not spend money that you do not have
- avoid credit card debt
- avoid, if possible, student loans, and think about your major and expected salary (having a degree in history and having student loans of $137,000 is not a good idea and you have put yourself into a hole that you many never get out of) -- a university or college degree does not always translate to a good salary (one reason why you see people with Ph.D.s driving taxis in New York City)
- if you use a credit card pay it off at the end of each month
- be sure you get some 'benefit' from using a credit card (e.g., cash back, airline miles, or whatever), and avoid annual fees
- there are lots of credit cards that provide perks and have no annual fee
- know your credit score (FICO score), it impacts your ability to get credit and what you will pay for the credit (e.g., interest rate on home mortgage, car loan, et cetera)
- do not depend on social security (social security has no cash, despite what politicians tell you – the government is currently paying out more in social security then it is taken in from workers and it has no reserves to draw on, only IOUs to itself, yes social security is a "ponzi scheme")
- set up an emergency account – used only in the case of a "true" emergency, and not just because you lust after something
- invest in yourself first – put aside at least 5% of your salary each payday into a retirement account after you have set up an emergency fund

- Roth IRAs are an excellent portion of a retirement plan (they can be funded with cash gifts, say, from your parents as a Christmas present)
- know your partners spending habits, and how much debt they owe before committing to a "permanent" relationship
- talk to your partner about money, saving, and financial goals
- be aware of prices, and shop wisely
- watch out for skimming scams (when someone steals you credit/debit card number, including your pin number)
- identity theft is on the rise – many places keep your personal information on file (from your fitness center to your employer), plus all too often people put too much personal information on social media sites (a reliable credit monitoring company may be worthwhile considering)
- shred personal information, people do search trash for personal information (e.g., credit card numbers)
- when you use a credit card to pay a bill be sure you get back your credit card and not another one that looks similar to yours
- consider online banks for saving accounts – they usually pay better interest rates then brick-and-mortar banks (but be careful of fraud)
- you need to have adequate insurance – from health to auto, and from home to life (assuming someone is dependent on you)
- develop a sound and honest relationship with a financial advisor (see note below about advisors)
- if you have a home mortgage make at least one extra payment each year – it will have a major impact on the amount of money you pay over the life of the loan, and the length of the loan (one extra payment per year can reduce a 30 year mortgage down to about 22 years)
- having biweekly payments is the same as making one extra payment per year (52/2 = 26 half payments with when divided by 2 equals 13 monthly payments, or one extra per year)
- **develop a financial plan, stick to it, and modify as needed over time**
- **not having a financial plan is a plan to fail!!**

Financial planning should be a systematic process that considers important elements of an individual's financial affairs in order to fulfill financial goals and improve your standard of living. It is also about spending money "wisely," accumulating wealth, and learning how to be responsible/smart with money.

Personal financial planning typically has several steps, and all steps are important. One six step process is:

1. Define your financial goals – both near term and long term – formalize them by putting them in writing
2. Develop a plan of action – plans & strategies (based on your current status – keep track of all your income and expenditures over a short period of time and develop your own balance sheet), keep then reasonable and not pie in the sky, and be sure they have some flexibility
3. Implement your plan and strategies

4. Develop and implement budgets – important if you want to achieve your goals
5. Use financial statements to evaluate results – e.g., your own income statement, balance sheet and cash flow statement
6. Review your progress, reevaluate, and revise your plan as circumstances change

It is also important to recognize that individual investors are at the end of the food chain in the investing world. It has been said that "investors are like plankton in the ocean," and other players on Wall Street most likely have more knowledge and insight, from investment bankers to financial advisors. One rule of thumb to consider is to always ask your financial advisor what benefit is it to them regarding their advice for you to buy or sell some asset/investment.

After developing a financial plan and implementing it the key to success is following your plan and revising as it as needed (e.g., as life events occur such as a new job, marriage, kids, health challenges, et cetera). For the investment portion of your financial plan the keys to success are forecasting ability, buy and sell disciplines, and having a fortunate dose of luck is always helpful.

As many have said – work hard, play hard, but be sure to keep them in correct order!!

INDEX

CPSIA information can be obtained at www.ICGtesting.com
Printed in the USA
LVOW09s1504030913

350793LV00008B/80/P